Poetry Wars

PETER BARRY is Professor of English at the University of Wales, Aberystwyth. He is Reviews & Poetry Editor of *English* (the journal of the English Association). In the 1970s he was a member of 'Alembic Poets' (with Ken Edwards and Robert Hampson), and his previous work on contemporary poetry includes *New British Poetries: the Scope of the Possible* (co-edited with Robert Hampson, 1993, Manchester U. P.) and *Contemporary British Poetry and the City* (2000, Manchester U.P.).

Poetry Wars

British Poetry of the 1970s and the Battle of Earls Court

PETER BARRY

Foreword by ANDREW MOTION
Preface by ROBERT HAMPSON

SALT

CAMBRIDGE

PUBLISHED BY SALT PUBLISHING
PO Box 937, Great Wilbraham PDO, Cambridge CB1 5JX United Kingdom
PO Box 202, Applecross, Western Australia 6153

© Peter Barry, 2006

The right of Peter Barry to be identified as the
author of this work has been asserted by him in accordance
with Section 77 of the Copyright, Designs and Patents Act 1988.

First published 2006
Reprinted 2007

Printed and bound in the United Kingdom by Lightning Source

Typeset in Swift 10/12

ISBN-13 978 1 84471 248 9 hardback
ISBN-10 1 84471 248 6 hardback

ISBN-13 978 1 84471 247 2 paperback
ISBN-10 1 84471 247 8 paperback

TB

1 3 5 7 9 8 6 4 2

For Robert and Ken of 'Alembic Poets'
and the 'neo-rads' mentioned at the end of Robert's Preface

Contents

DOCUMENTS

Foreword

When I took over the Editorship of the *Poetry Review* from Roger Garfitt in 1981, I inherited a magazine which had a troubled past. According to others then working in the building, and in the poetry world in general, the story went like this. In the middle part of the century, the *Review* had published for a readership which generally regretted the Modernists, and wanted to turn British poetry back to the good old Georgian ways. Then in the 1970s, Eric Mottram had been appointed Editor and published poems, articles and opinions, which jerked the Society so fast and far towards the opposite camp, the membership suffered a collective heart attack. When Mottram eventually stood down in 1977, after an adventurous and rancorous term of office, Garfitt was brought in to restore a balance between the old guard and the radicals. My own job, taking over from him, was to stop 'balance' becoming boring, to give the magazine more flair, to build new kinds of bridges between diverse poetries, and to increase the subscription list.

Whether or not I succeeded is a side-issue in Peter Barry's book. His focus is on the adventurous/rancorous years—to explain how Mottram became editor, to analyse what he published, to describe the 'alternative' traditions he nurtured, and to make the whole episode seem an epitome (and in some ways the climax) of the poetic 'wars' between Modernism and conservatism which raged through a large part of last century. Barry does all these things very well, researching deeply into long-forgotten minutes and listings to provide an extraordinarily detailed account of the time. In this respect alone his book has a self-sufficient usefulness—as well as a value for posterity. But his greatest success is to present the larger picture of the 'wars' in a way which makes them seem slightly dotty in certain peripheral respects, but fundamentally very important. Mottram may have sometimes been impatient, cantankerous, blinkered, but he was fighting a necessary fight: to rescue sidelined traditions from obscurity, and to give them a more secure place in the sun.

One measure of Mottram's success lies around us today—in the comparatively well-tempered acceptance that we live in a culture of poetries, not in one world dominated by an Establishment. In this sense, Peter Barry's book has an optimistic mood, despite its feistiness and fascination with what is (or has been) embattled. And that's one reason why it makes such good reading. Some of the characters' names may have slipped from the record; some of the issues seem long-resolved; some of the intensities now sound excessive. But the fundamental truth remains. For most of last century, Britain marginalised the heirs of the great Modernists. We're more accommodating today—but that doesn't stop us finding Mottram's *Poetry Review* story intriguing, enlightening, and in its own way heroic. It still has a good deal to teach us.

ANDREW MOTION

Preface

When Redell Olsen and Susan Johanknecht invited me to take part in their installation, 'writing instructions/reading walls', at the Poetry Café, Covent Garden, their proposed intervention in a public space associated with the Poetry Society unavoidably raised for me memories of the brief period of my membership of the Society and the principled boycott of the Society with which it ended for the faction with which I identified.[1] I had vivid memories still of the brief period in the early 1970s when the Poetry Society was being run by poets for whom the tradition of modernist poetry in Britain was, as Peter Barry shows, something to be celebrated, extended and developed—or whose work tapped into other European and North American traditions of experimentation such as visual poetry and sound poetry. I had good memories of a regular series of evening lectures in the Poetry Society bar where poets presented and discussed earlier poetries which had been important for their own practice—Lee Harwood on surrealist poetry, for example, or Bill Griffiths talking about and performing Old English lyrics. I had memories, too, of exciting and challenging readings—Henri Chopin abusing microphones and tape-recorders; Bob Cobbing, booming and roaring, finding performance texts in over-printed xeroxes; Paul Buck's engagement with contemporary French poetry and theory; Allen

---

[1] The installation, 'writing instructions/ reading walls', extended over the period January-May 2003, and included work by nine artists/writers. See Redell Olsen and Susan Johanknecht (eds), *here are my instructions* (London: Gefn Press, 2004), which marks two further stages of the 'writing instructions' project.

Fisher's presentations of early sections of *Place*.[2] There was the excitement, too, of hearing poets read who had been only names: Basil
Bunting, whom I had first encountered in print as one of Ford Madox
Ford's 'young men' on *the transatlantic review*, giving one of his many
'final readings' in London; the similarly quasi-legendary Scottish
Nationalist, Marxist modernist, Hugh MacDiarmid; and Roy Fisher,
whose late-modernist long poem *City* had been a revelation about the
possibilities of an urban poetics.[3] But there were memories, too, of the
end of this period: AGMs in dusty West London church halls; what felt
like a campaign of misrepresentation in the press; and the sense of pressure from the Arts Council, ending in the imposition of Arts Council
nominees on the elected committee—after which it felt impossible to
remain a member of the Society. Like many others who had joined the
Society in this period, for whom Eric Mottram's editing of *Poetry Review*
produced issues that fulfilled William Carlos Williams's description of
poetry as 'news that stayed news', I resolved to join the boycott of the
Society—and what had briefly been a high-profiling of the submerged
traditions of British poetry, the mainstream from modernism, was
replaced by a dispersal and dissipation, the returning of those streams
to the underworld.

My installation, 'Crime Scene', was planned to engage with this
history–to return the silenced voices and exiled poets to the public spaces
subtended by the Poetry Society. The wall-space for the installation would
become the incident board, and I set about collecting evidence.
Fortunately, I thought, I had kept an archive, which could form the basis
of my investigation. However, when the file was opened, it was far
less substantial than I had remembered: a few cyclostyled documents
announcing Poetry Society elections, lists of candidates, a couple of news
items, a couple of manifestos—but not the full and detailed documenta-
tion that I had hoped for. When I made discrete inquiries among
survivors from this period, I was met with the advice that I shouldn't re-
open old wounds. As Peter Barry makes clear, the events that led up to the
disappearance of this group of poets from the Poetry Society—and from

---

² Allen Fisher, *Place I-XXXVII* (Carborro: Truck Press, 1976) was the first volume of this
  ten-year project in four books. The first complete, collected edition of the various
  separately published volumes was *Place* (Hastings: Reality Street Editions, 2005).

³ At that time recent publications by the three included Basil Bunting's *Briggflatts*
  (London: Fulcrum, 1966); Hugh MacDiarmid's *A Drunk Man Looks At The Thistle*
  (reprinted by University of Massachusetts Press, 1971); and Roy Fisher's *City*
  (Migrant, 1961).

public visibility—did not produce a clean break: different poets pursued different strategies in response to the imposition of nominees, and these different strategies produced friction and long-lasting estrangements. In addition, I was conscious that I did not have the inside story of events: I was simply an ordinary member of the Society, an avid reader of *Poetry Review*, a keen attender of readings and events, and a voter in elections. I read the newsletters and manifestos, I heard the rumours and gossip, but I had no access to the arguments in the Committee. 'Crime Scene', accordingly, did not so much offer a solution, as perform the problematics of the reconstruction of a past event.

In the volume that follows, Peter Barry has put in the legwork to investigate the events around the arrival and expulsion of late-modernist poetry into and from the faded gentility of Earls Court Square. He has investigated the events from both sides, mining the archives of the Arts Council and the Poetry Society, as well as the Eric Mottram Archive at King's College, London. Where Blake Morrison's early work, *The Movement*, usefully showed how a small group of poets took over key points in the post-war economy of poetry and imposed an anti-modernist model on British poetry for the next thirty years, Peter Barry's in-depth study of the official archives shows how that modernist tradition briefly emerged before disappearing from public view again.[4] Eric Mottram is one of the central figures in this story, and Peter Barry offers an affectionate appraisal of Mottram's role, importance and limitations, considering his work as editor, teacher, critic and poet. Among other things, the event narrative constructed here is concerned to assess the strategies followed by the different parties and their consequences. The modernist poets' decision to boycott the Poetry Society can, in retrospect, perhaps be seen as unwittingly colluding in their subsequent marginalisation—although perhaps no other strategy was possible at the time. We didn't know that 1975 would turn out to be a critical year in terms of little magazines: the surge of little magazine production between 1965 and 1975 was followed by a series of closures in the late 1970s.[5] Similarly, no-one could have foreseen the collapse of the

---

4 Blake Morrison, *The Movement: English Poetry and Fiction of the 1950s* (Oxford: Oxford University Press, 1980).

5 Wolfgang Gortschacher notes that more than 400 little magazines were founded between 1965 and 1975, although about half of these failed to survive the first year. By comparison, between 1976 and 1981 more than 110 little magazines ceased publication. See *Little Magazine profiles: The Little Magazine in Great Britain, 1939–1993* (Salzburg: University of Salzburg Press, 1993), 170, 184.

specialist bookseller, on which this area of activity had depended, as Compendium Books reduced its poetry stock and then eventually followed Turret Books into oblivion. No-one anticipated the political struggles that were to follow after 1979 with the closing down of the coal-industry, anti-union legislation, and the poll-tax. The dispersal of this area of poetic activity to community centres, colleges, and, most of all, rooms over public houses during the 1980s meant that, though the work continued and developed beyond the late-modernism of the 1970s, it could now be safely ignored. The 'Battle of Earls Court' left the alternative traditions of British poetry divided into factions and heavily wounded. However, to end there, would misrepresent the outcome. There was a diaspora after the events described in this book, but the continued existence of Writers Forum and its workshop, the longevity of Sub-Voicive and the Cambridge Conference on Contemporary Poetry, not to mention the success of publishers such as Reality Street and Salt, has seen the re-emergence of these traditions in the 1990s, refreshed by a new generation of poets taking them in radically new directions, involving performance, installation, visual and digital media as well as a variety of page-based and language-based practices. It seems appropriate to end this Preface with a Mottramesque list of some of this new 'post-post' generation: Sean Bonney, Andrea Brady, Miles Champion, Drew Milne, Jeff Hilson, Ira Lightman, Helen McDonald, Brigid McLeer, Peter Manson, Redell Olsen, Keston Sutherland, Scott Thurston, Catherine Walsh and many more.[6]

ROBERT HAMPSON

---

[6] See, for example, Nicholas Johnson (ed.), *foil: defining poetry 1985–2000* (Buckfastleigh: Etruscan Books, 2000) or the forthcoming anthology edited by Keston Sutherland. Johnson describes the poets his anthology brings together as the twentieth century's 'last invisible generation' (ix).

Acknowledgements

I was enabled to write this book by a period of a year's research leave from the University of Wales Aberystwyth in 2004-5, partly funded by the AHRC, and with additional support from the University's Senate Research Fund and from the British Academy. I am extremely grateful to professors Andrew Motion and Robert Hampson, both of Royal Holloway, University of London, for their Foreword and Preface (respectively), and for their pre-publication comments to Marjorie Perloff, Professor Emerita of Stanford University and President of the Modern Language Association, and to poet, novelist, writer and critic Iain Sinclair.

I am very grateful to King's College London for permission to quote from material in the Eric Mottram Collection; to the Arts Council England for permission to quote from material in the Arts Council of Great Britain records, 1928-1997, held at the Archive of Art and Design of the Victoria and Albert Museum; and to Newcastle University for permission to quote from material in the Barry MacSweeney Collection.

Finally, I am indebted to yet another professor, my friend, former colleague, and fellow coffee connoisseur Claire Jowitt (now of Nottingham Trent University) who supplied the title.

Introduction

The UK poetry scene is smaller than its US counterpart, so the 'poetry wars' there must be like a knife fight in a phone booth. ('A Reader', reviewing *New British Poetry*, ed. Don Paterson and Charles Simic, on *Amazon.com*)

An odd thing happened in British poetry in the 1970s, but the full story has never been told. A small group of 'radical' or 'experimental' poets took over the Poetry Society, one of the most conservative of British cultural institutions, and for a period of six years, from 1971 to 1977, its journal, *Poetry Review*, was the most startling poetry magazine in the country. Some revered it, others reviled it, but nobody in the 70s who was seriously interested in poetry could ignore it. Then, in the summer of 1977, it was over, almost as suddenly as it had begun. Of course, when looked at closely—which is the business of this book—these events neither began nor ended as suddenly as all that. But the conflict at the Poetry Society was a key moment in the history of contemporary British Poetry, polarizing the rift between the 'neo-modernists', who sought to continue the 1960s revival of the early twentieth-century's 'modernist revolution', and the neo-conservatives, who sought to further the 'anti-modernist counter-revolution' of the 1950s. Echoes of this conflict continue to reverberate today, and the deposed radicals of the 1970s were effectively written out of the record of contemporary British poetry, and have only recently been restored. They feature, for example, in the Oxford University Press *Anthology of Twentieth-Century British and Irish Poetry*, edited by Keith Tuma in 2001. Tuma remarks elsewhere that the 1970s Poetry Society episode 'remains one of the first object lessons British "alternative" poets refer to when speaking of negotiations with a mainstream.' So the present book is, among other things, a case study of the inevitable frictions and tactical struggles between an avant-garde and a 'mainstream'.

British poetry in the 1970s had been through a long post-war period in which there was a keenly-felt sense of inferiority to the poetry of the United States. Poetry from the States, epitomised by the work of Ezra Pound and the early T. S. Eliot, had been the predominant poetic influence in the period of high modernism, and American poetry was indisputably the major body of contemporary poetry in English in the 1950s and 60s. In the polemical introduction to his 1962 anthology *The New Poetry*, A. Alvarez famously accused British poets of turning away in genteel distaste from the full-frontal impact of the modern world, and he held up the model of the American 'confessional' poets—Robert Lowell, Sylvia Plath, Anne Sexton, and John Berryman—as poets who registered the trauma of modernity in their own addictions, obsessions, and breakdowns. The radical poets associated with the Poetry Society in London in the 1970s also looked across the Atlantic for models, but they regarded the 'confessionals' as the conservative 'Establishment', and instead felt strong affinities with the dissenting voices of American poetry (the poets assembled in 1960 in Donald Allen's definitive Grove Press anthology *The New American Poetry*, 1945–1960), such as the Black Mountain poets—Charles Olson, Robert Creeley, Ed Dorn—the New York Poets—Frank O'Hara, Jack Spicer, James Schuyler—and the 'Beats'—Allen Ginsberg, Gregory Corso, Lawrence Ferlinghetti. Elsewhere in Britain, poets loosely linked to the Cambridge lecturer and poet J. H. Prynne were interested in a different branch of the American poetic 'anti-establishment', namely, the 'Objectivists' of an earlier generation—Lorine Niedecker, Carl Rakosi, Louis Zukofsky. By the 1970s, a major resurgence of British poetry was taking place among poets who looked to these various 'dissenting' American poets for inspiration and example when the British scene seemed moribund. In 1974 Eric Mottram, a lecturer in American Literature at King's College, London, who had become the controversial new editor of *Poetry Review*, christened this movement the British Poetry Revival (which I abbreviate to the 'BPR' in this book), and sought to display its fruits—along with the work of the related American dissenters—in that journal. Since *Poetry Review* had declined in the 50s and 60s into settled mediocrity, the result was the outbreak of civil war at the Poetry Society, as related in what follows.

But the frictions of the 1970s were not completely without precedent at the Poetry Society. The novelist Muriel Spark was editor of *Poetry*

Review from 1947 to 1949, and in the Spark Archive at the National Library of Scotland is the notebook she kept at the time, containing 'the only surviving record of the increasingly tempestuous meetings of the Poetry Society, when [her] policy of encouraging new writers caused problems for some of the long-standing contributors to the journal.' Spark discusses the Poetry Society in her autobiography *Curriculum Vitae* (especially pages 165–180), and draws upon her experiences there in her novel *Loitering with Intent*. Indeed, the conflicts she experienced at the Poetry Society, and the period in the Society's history documented in the present book, are hardly aberrations. Rather, they are typical and necessary occurrences in the life-cycles of cultural institutions. On the day I began this introduction, in December 2004, I read in the paper that the Royal Academy of Arts has just been 'plunged into turmoil' by 'the resignation of its controversial Secretary', who says that 'frustration with the arcane structures of the RA has forced her out.' The report speaks of 'tensions between the members and the [paid] administration', with the former seeing the growth of the latter as a threat, and of 'wrangles over finances'. All these are familiar elements from the Poetry Society affair of the 1970s, in which differences of opinion between, on the one hand, officers elected by the membership, and, on the other, the organisation's paid officials and its grant-awarding body, were at the heart of the matter. Indeed, we could go further and say that these tensions are similar to those often seen, not just in cultural politics, but in politics at all levels, where distrust and conflict between elected representatives and professional administrators are endemic.

The two main figures in the Poetry Society struggle of the 1970s were Charles Osborne, Literature Director of the Arts Council, and, as already indicated, Eric Mottram. Both were poets with a parallel professional life as (respectively) a civil servant and an academic. Both were persuasive and charismatic figures, both temperamentally inclined to a certain intellectual arrogance and impatience. The fierceness and bitterness of the struggle in the 1970s was partly due to this head-on clash between two powerful and influential figures both accustomed to persuading others that they were right. Furthermore, both the 'radicals' and the 'conservatives' of the period were (for some of the time, at least) well organised, deeply committed, and capable of concerted collective action. It is partly this 'fearful symmetry' between the personalities and dispositions of the two camps that attracted me to the idea of telling this story, although I will not give these two key figures equal attention, since Charles Osborne has already put his own account of these events on record in his memoir *Giving it Away: Memoirs of an Uncivil Servant* (1986).

As well as claiming to tell the full story of these events for the first time, I should also state clearly what this book does not do. It has not been my aim to write a comprehensive history of the Poetry Society in the 1970s. Rather, I have concentrated on one major aspect of it, which is the editing and publication of *Poetry Review*, and on the struggles and conflicts which took place in committees, campaigning, and correspondence between the radicals and the conservatives. This means that Eric Mottram is a central figure, even though (as a full-time academic) he was only a marginal presence in the day-to-day running of the Poetry Society. In terms of what happened on a daily basis at the Poetry Society's headquarters at 21 Earls Court Square, the key figure was Bob Cobbing, a poet who was at the centre of the international movement in 'sound texts' and 'visual poetries' (also known as Concrete Poetry), and a major figure generally in the London 'counter-culture' of the 1960s and 70s as a performer and small-press publisher. He was the driving force behind the most radical aspects of the Poetry Society in these years, such as the Society's basement print-shop, and its involvement in the quasi-trade-unionisation of the poetry scene. He had been among the first of the radicals to be elected to the Poetry Society's governing Council, in the late 1960s, and he was at the centre of most of the key developments, such as the link-up with his organisations *Writers Forum, Poets Conference* (no apostrophes in either), and the ALP (*The Association of Little Presses*), which together brought a form of 1960s left-wing collectivism to the highly individualistic business of writing and publishing poetry. Cobbing's recent death (in 2002) meant that his papers had not yet become available while this book was being written, but when they are, they will be a principle resource for the history of that strand of British experimental writing. Cobbing's fellow sound poet and performer, and fellow tactician, Lawrence Upton, as well as the poet and performer cris cheek, and the poet and artist Allen Fisher, were also important parts of that history. But I have not attempted to write that history here. I look forward to reading it in due course, when another researcher has undertaken the major task of filling that important gap in the cultural history of late twentieth century British avant-garde writing. Other aspects of the Poetry Society's operations in the 1970s which I make no attempt to cover here include the National Poetry Secretariat, which assisted in the organisation of poetry readings nationally, and offered subsidy to pay the reading fees of registered poets. The NPS was based at the Poetry Society's premises in Earls Court, and for most poets and local groups outside London it was in many ways a more important organisation than the Poetry Society itself. It was a highly successful and widely praised aspect of the Poetry Society, and helped to ensure that the work of poets who were not big stars continued to be disseminated. Its history is an important part of the sociology of recent poetry, and this history too awaits its historian. The same is true of the Education Section of the Poetry Society, which also operated in a state of quasi-autonomy within the organisation. The NPS and the Education Section make occasional appearances in this account, but, to repeat, this book is not a comprehensive account of the Poetry Society in the 1970s. I should also emphasise here, though it will be apparent to anyone who knows anything at all about the topic, that this is not a comprehensive account of the British poetry avant-garde of the 1970s: it is almost entirely confined to what was happening in London, with some references to the 'Cambridge' poets against which the London group is often defined. But there is nothing here about (for instance) Newcastle, Liverpool, Hull, and Belfast, all of which had lively and innovative poetry 'scenes'. A great deal of that activity is yet another history which still awaits its historian.

Muriel Spark writes that 'After leaving the Poetry Society I became aware of the value of documentary evidence' (*Curriculum Vitae,* page 185), and investigating these events has had the same effect upon me. Numerous anecdotes and myths about the Poetry Society in the 1970s have been in circulation for many years, but I have restricted this account to what can be documented. I resolved, therefore, not to repeat such stories as the one about Charles Osborne denying to the press that he had referred to 'those rag-bags down at the Poetry Society' and then issuing a correction saying that the word he used was 'rat-bags'. However, I then found documentary evidence for this story, so I do repeat it, in the appropriate place. When I sat down at the V & A's Archive in November 2004 to look at the Arts Council's 1970s files on the Poetry Society, the elastic bands often snapped as I took them off the folders, suggesting that they had not been touched *since* the 70s. Often I could look at the same crucial meeting as documented in several differ- ent sources, for instance, as minuted on the day, as described a little later in private letters, as reported by the Arts Council assessors, and as represented by newspapers at the time. In some cases there were also retrospective accounts in interviews and memoirs. One of the persistent anecdotes about the period (which I should *not* repeat) is that some of these meetings were secretly taped, but I have not come across any of these hot, and probably mythical, boot-leg recordings.

However, using only documented material does not mean that I have striven for complete and inert neutrality—if I did not believe that the work of the radicals had some interest and importance, there would have been no point in writing at such length about these events. I was taught by Eric Mottram as an undergraduate at King's College, London, and as a postgraduate at London University's Institute of United States Studies, and I was very much on the 'radical' side as a regular audience-member at Poetry Society events in the 1970s. But this is not a partisan account, and I have made no attempt gloss over self-evident faults and failings, whichever side they belong to. Both sides, I anticipate, will find much to dislike in the book, but as Iain Sinclair has said, the avant-garde poetry of the 1970s is not a topic one would choose to write about if simply looking for a few quiet years of academic calm before picking up a bus pass.[1]

In relating these events of the 1970s, my conscious generic affiliation is to a form of prose narrative, recently popular, which is known as the 'event history'. Works of this kind seek to explore and explain the nature of a specific era in cultural history—or a specific aspect of that era—by focusing on the causes and effects of a single key event or occasion.[2] The culminating 'event' on which this one focuses is the Poetry Society's General Council meeting of 26th March 1977 when the avant-garde group, which had been the dominant influence at the Society since 1971, walked out *en masse*. Investigating these poetic conflicts of the 1970s can help us to understand a significant epoch in recent British cultural history, when the relationship between high culture and popular culture in the visual and verbal arts was shifting rapidly, and Humanities academics were increasingly seeking a voice within contemporary culture, rather than being content just to comment on and evaluate the writing of the past.

One problem I have not solved is what best to call the two opposed groups, and I doubt whether any ideal solution exists. The various

[1] In the Preface to his *Conductors of Chaos* anthology, Paladin, 1996.

[2] Examples include Penelope Hughes-Hallett's *The Immortal Dinner* (Viking, 2000), about a dinner party in December 1817 attended by Keats, Wordsworth, and Lamb, and *Wittgenstein's Poker,* by David Edmonds and John Eidinow (Faber, 2002), about the clash between Wittgenstein and Karl Popper at Cambridge in October 1946.

possibilities are pairings of opposites such as: (1) *large press poets v. small press poets*: this is potentially confusing because small presses published more poetry in the 1970s than 'large' ones. The large presses are some-times called 'commercial' presses, but this, again, is a potentially misleading designation. (2) *'centre' v. 'margins'*: a dichotomy expressed like this, of course embodies a self-fulfilling prophesy about the exclu-sion of the 'marginal'. (3) *neo-conservatives v. neo-modernists*: I find this quite a useful way of formulating the grounds of the conflict; the impli-cation of this way of expressing the dichotomy is (as suggested earlier) that the former group continued the 'project' of the Edwardian and 1950s anti-modernists, while the latter continued that of the 1920s modernists. (4) *the 'Axis' v. the British Poetry Revival ('BPR') poets*: these are the terms used by Eric Mottram in his polemical writing (beginning with his 1974 essay in the programme book for the British Poetry Conference of that year at the Polytechnic of Central London), but they are clearly not suitable for a general chronological account of these events (though I do use the abbreviation 'BPR' poets, and find this a useful short-hand designation). (5) *Mainstream v. 'Other' poets*: these terms are used by Ric Caddel and Peter Quartermain, the compilers of the anthology *Other British and Irish Poetry since 1970* (Wesleyan University Press. 1999) and by Nicholas Johnson, compiler of the *Foil* anthology subtitled *Defining Poetry, 1985–2000* (Etruscan Books); again, the self-exclusion explicit in the notion of 'other' poetry makes this (for me) an unsatisfactory term. (6) *The Mainstream v. the parallel tradition*; the latter term is used today by the BEPC, the British Electronic Poetry Centre (a consortium of Southampton, Birkbeck, and Royal Holloway poetics groups);[3] I use the term 'the parallel tradition' occasionally in what follows; its intention of avoiding self-marginalisation is apparent, but 'parallel' is still essentially a negative definition of one thing in terms of something else, and in any case, this late 1990s term has an anachronis-tic feel when applied to the events of the 1970s. (7) *Empirical or 'Lyrical I' poetries v. 'LIP' poetries* (that is, 'Linguistically Innovative Poetries'); the term 'LIP' was first used by Gilbert Adair in Robert Sheppard's on-line journal *Pages*: It was also the subtitle of the anthology *Out of Everywhere: Linguistically Innovative Poetry by Women* (ed. Maggie O'Sullivan, Reality Street Editions, 1996). It distinguishes British work in this field from

3 The term 'the parallel tradition' was first used (in an e-mail discussion list) by the American poet and critic Ron Silliman, designating US 'language-centred' poetry: see Ken Edwards's article 'The Two Poetries', *Angelaki*, 3/1, April 2000, pp. 25–36, footnote 34.

American 'Language Poetry', and is, I feel, a useful term, though again, it seems to me somewhat anachronistic when back-dated to designate work of the 1970s. (8) *Mainstream v. Disjunctive Poetics*: the latter term is from the book of this title by Peter Quartermain (Cambridge University Press, 1992); it is an attractively expressive term, but again it feels anachronistic when applied to the poets of the 1970s. (9) *conservatives v. radicals*: this is my default solution, though it is complicated in the account which follows by positing such important sub-groups as: 'conservative conservatives', 'radical conservatives', 'radical radicals', and 'conservative radicals'; the second and fourth of these played a crucial role in the events I describe in this book. In general, I have used (9), *conservative v. radicals* as my shorthand designation, while well aware of its limitations.

The book is divided into three sections: the first section, 'Chronology', gives a chronological account of the events as they unfolded: the second, 'Themes', contains a series of 'thematic' chapters, each considering a specific theme, issue, or aspect of the situation, or the characters involved, in a more reflective way. Removing these from the basic narrative account helps to avoid blurring the account of how the events unfolded, and separates the retrospective 'placing' of the events from the events themselves. Readers could (if they wished to break up the uniformity of the chronological account) read a couple of chronological chapters and then dip into the thematic chapters, before returning to the chronological account, thereby giving themselves a 'non-linear' reading experience of the kind approved by Eric Mottram. Readers not familiar with the kind of poetry favoured by the radical side in the conflict might wish to begin with Chapter Six, which gives an overview of their work, possibly followed by Chapter Seven, giving an overview account of the work of controversial editor Eric Mottram. The third section, 'Documents', presents a series of background documents, the first four being from the period itself, while the remainder are new compilations of relevant data. The new data should make the story easier to follow: there is a summary of the circumstances of Mottram's initial appointment to *Poetry Review* and his four subsequent re-appointments, or 'extensions', as it might be more accurate to call them, (Document 5); then a summary in diagram form of the basic characteristics of the twenty Mottram issues of *Poetry Review* (6), a summary of the structure of the Poetry Society (7), a list of the shifting year-to-year membership of the governing General Council of the Poetry Society in the 1970s (8), a basic list of the most relevant poetry organisations of the period (9), and finally the longest document, an 'Alphabetical Who's Who?' (10) which identifies all the mentioned participants in these events on whom information could be found, listed in a form which I hope is more convenient than a footnote-on-first-mention would have been (well-known writers like Dannie Abse, Ted Hughes, B. S. Johnson, and Iain Sinclair are omitted). All the material in the 'Documents' section is designed to avoid the need for lengthy quotation and citation in either of the other two sections, while at the same time enabling the reader to view at first-hand some of the material in the primary sources.

PETER BARRY, ABERYSTWYTH, DECEMBER 2005

Chronology

1

The Back Story and Moving in: 1951–1972

The Road to Earls Court

To understand the events which took place at the Poetry Society in the 1970s it is necessary to begin with a little back-tracking. The Society in the early 70s was very much (to use Raymond Williams's terms) a 'residual' cultural and social organisation. It had been left behind by the major transforming poetry events of the era, events such as the great Albert Hall Poetry Incarnation of June 1965, organised by Mike Horovitz, when an audience of several thousand heard inspirational readings from the American 'Beat' poets Allen Ginsberg, Gregory Corso, and Lawrence Ferlinghetti, and from British poets such as Adrian Mitchell, and others. Peter Whitehead's half-hour film of the event, entitled *Wholly Communion*, quickly achieved iconic status, and Horovitz's related Penguin anthology *Children of Albion: Poetry of the 'Underground' in Britain* was published by Penguin in 1969. His *New Departures* magazine, founded to 'bring into the public readership in England the work of experimental writers and artists',[1] had been running since 1959. The outstandingly successful anthology *The Mersey Sound*, published by Penguin in 1967, had brought a new urban demotic flavour to poetry and made the 'Liverpool Poets' famous.

Given the recent context of the 1960s, then, it was obvious that poetry could not simply stand still, yet the becalmed world of the Poetry Society remained in some ways a bizarre survival from an earlier poetic age right into the 1970s. Its poetry readings, for instance, were still

---

[1] Gortschacher, *Little Magazine Profiles: the Little Magazines in Great Britain 1939–1993*, p. 347.

announced in the *Times* as part of the Court Circular, so that odd juxtapositions occurred under the heading 'Today's Engagements', like that
on September 29th 1972, where the announcement 'The Duchess of Kent
opens new wing at Dunford YMCA, Sussex, 2.50' is followed by 'Poets in
Person: Basil Bunting, The Poetry Society, 21 Earls Court Square, SW,
7.30'. When it needed a typist, the Poetry Society advertised discreetly in
the personal columns of the *Times,* alongside 'Domestic Situations', and
under the heading 'Women's Appointments'. So the Poetry Society,
founded in 1909, was the hub of a somewhat isolated poetry world,
typified by the verse speaking competitions which were then its major
source of income. Its premises—a Georgian terraced house in off-the-
beaten-track Earls Court Square—were slightly shabby, but genteel-
shabby and profoundly re-assuring. As Eric Mottram remarked later, it
was the representative organisation for the amateur poetry lovers and
weekend-poets who had never really recovered from the shock of the
new, as exemplified by T. S. Eliot, and were hoping that modernism
might one day go away and yield the ground again to *Palgrave's Golden
Treasury.* In Raymond Williams's terms, again, what was about to happen
was a head-on collision between poetry's 'residual' and 'emergent'
worlds, a kind of dialectical confrontation between the *thesis* of the old
and the *antithesis* of the new, out of which a new formation might (or
might not) emerge. Of course, all this is to present the Poetry Society in
somewhat stereotypical terms, and it could be argued that a different
picture emerges from a closer look at the narrative of events: the Society
in the late 1960s certainly showed signs of *wanting* to modernise, but
also of not really knowing exactly how to go about doing so, or which
direction to take. As will be seen in the narrative which follows, it began
the process of change itself by inviting some figures from the wider
poetry world onto its General Council. However, as we shall further see,
the momentum of this process increased beyond what it could cope
with, and it then pulled back in a kind of panic.

But let us return to the start of the modernising process: in 1951 a
part-time London 'experimental' writer called Bob Cobbing began a
fortnightly workshop and magazine under the title 'Writers Forum',
and by 1963 this had developed into a small press of the same name, run
by Cobbing, John Rowan (a poet, and later a founder member of the
Association of Humanistic Psychology), and Jeff Nuttall (later to become
well known as the author of *Bomb Culture,* the classic partisan account of
the 'counter culture' of the 1960s). In 1964 Cobbing gave up his job as a
teacher of art and poetry and joined the staff of the innovative

bookshop 'Better Books' on Charing Cross Road, where he developed the poetry section, and organised regular weekly poetry readings, paying poets a flat fee of £10 plus expenses. Several aspects of these activities provided a prototype for activities later at the Poetry Society, as will emerge.[2] Cobbing had established connections with Stuart Montogomery of Fulcrum Press—the biggest of the small presses.[3] Montgomery was a radical from Rhodesia and a qualified doctor, who taught a 'poetry anti-course' at the Anti-University of London (*Times*, 13 Feb 1968), that annual summer event which was a focal point of the 'counter-culture' of the day, and a major centre of Marxist and New-Left activity. Montgomery was profiled in the 'Pooter' column in the *Times*, 2 August 1969. He explained that he and his wife ran Fulcrum Press from a garage in Highgate, publishing Basil Bunting's *Briggflatts*, his best-seller (7000 copies by 1969), and doing initial print runs for all his titles of an amazing 3000 copies (Penguin had offered Bunting a meagre £50 for the paperback rights).[4] Early in 1966 Cobbing and Montgomery went to the Arts Council of Great Britain to talk with its then Literature Director, Eric Walter White, about the problems of subsidising literature. White had said that the problem of subsidising poetry lay in the absence of any suitable organisations towards which money could be directed. Cobbing took the hint, and together with Montgomery set up the Association of Little Presses (usually called the ALP) in the summer of 1966, with the

---

[2] The source for the foregoing information is Cobbing's 'personal statement' as Chair of Poets Conference, which was issued under the title 'The State of Poetry—Part Two' in January 1976 and again in September of the same year. The complete document is five A4 pages. There is a copy in Mottram, 4/3/36–46.

[3] Fulcrum Press folded in the 1970s as a result of a dispute with Scottish poet Ian Hamilton Finlay over the publication of his collection *The Dancers Inherit the Party* in 1968. This was wrongly described as a first edition, though it had previously been published by Gael Turnbull's Migrant Press, leading to a sequence of legal disputes which Fulcrum eventually lost, with costs. The relevant correspondence is in the Hamilton-Finlay papers at Northwestern University Library, Evanston, Illinois, 'Ian Hamilton Finlay: Correspondence 1968-1970'.

[4] The level of interest at that time in poetry and poetry writing was extremely high: when Charles Osborne and Peter Porter invited submissions for the Arts Council anthology *New Poetry* 1, published in 1975, they expected to receive about 5,000 poems: in fact 42,000 were sent, from 10,000 different poets. In contrast to Fulcrum's initial print runs of 3,000, a new book of poetry from Secker in the early 1980s, according to Blake Morrison, would have a print run of about 500 (see footnote 4, p. 10 in Hampson and Barry).

former as Secretary and the latter as Chair, to act as an umbrella organ-isation for the increasing numbers of 'non-commercial' or 'alternative' publishers of poetry. Montgomery was elected to the Poetry Society's General Council in 1967, and (with Norman Hidden) persuaded Cobbing to stand successfully for election in 1968, at a point when the more progressive members of the Council were seeking to extend the Society's scope and put it in touch with the rapidly expanding poetry world of the late 1960s.

The Arts Council, meanwhile, in line with its desire to establish subsidisable poetry institutions, set up a sub-committee in 1968 to examine the possibility of establishing a National Poetry Centre, which would have a bookshop, a mail-order distribution service, and a poetry-reading venue.[5] Advertisements were placed in the *New Statesman* and *Bookseller* in August and September 1968 for a person who would carry out a survey of opinion and investigate practicalities, and interviews of short-listed candidates were held in November. In December the writer B.S. Johnson was commissioned to do the job, the deadline for the completed report being 31st March 1969. He sought the views of 377 persons or organisations and received 229 replies. Those who opposed the idea felt (as summed up by Johnson) that 'Any Poetry Centre would inevitably fall into the hands of cliques and factions'—a prophetic judgement, from the Arts Council's viewpoint, in the light of what happened in the 1970s. The Literature Panel recommended to the Arts Council that the project should go ahead, envisaging that the Poetry Centre would be at the Roundhouse (the former railway building in Chalk Farm, North London, which had become a highly successful alternative Arts Centre in the 1960s). It would be run by a quasi-independent body, along the lines of the Poetry Book Society (Witt, 20c). The initial suggestion was for a committee of four people to undertake the day-to-day running of the centre, these being 'a well-known and responsible poet' (the first choice was Ted Hughes), a book-shop manager, and a representative each for the Roundhouse and the Arts Council.[6] But matters dragged on without final decisions being

---

5   These details are from paragraph 20b of the *Report to the Arts Council of Great Britain by the Assessment Committee on the Poetry Society,* published by the Arts Council in October 1976, and usually called the Witt Report (after its Chairman, Sir John Witt). Subsequent references will be given in-text in the style 'Witt, 20b'.

6   Minutes of the Arts Council Literature Panel, 12th June 1969, item 7 (ACGB/59/5, box 2 of 7).

taken, so much so that publishers and others invited to meetings at the Arts Council about the Poetry Centre project began to see the whole business as something of a joke.

By October 1970 no final decision on the matter of the National Poetry Centre had been made, and the Poetry Society launched a public appeal for funds to set up the Poetry Centre at Earls Court. There were now two rival schemes in contention, these being the Arts Council's proposal for a poetry centre at the Roundhouse, and the Poetry Society's own scheme for a centre at Earls Court.[7] In February 1971 the Arts Council's Literature Panel recommended backing this scheme, rather than the projected Roundhouse venture (Witt, 20d), on the grounds that the Poetry Society was an already established organisation which could bring the Centre into being more quickly and effectively. In retrospect, it can be seen that this was an error: at the Roundhouse, the Poetry Centre could have become a centre for radical, innovative, and performance poetries (a kind of ICA for the verbal arts, perhaps), leaving the Poetry Society free to represent something a little more conservative in poetic tastes. But it was not to be: in 1971–2 the Arts Council made funds available to the Poetry Society to implement its plans for a National Poetry Centre at Earls Court (Witt, 20e).

The kind of National Poetry Centre which the more radical members (like Cobbing and Montgomery) hoped to bring into being is indicated in Cobbing's later comments on the set-up at 'Better Books', where he had been working. In a footnote to 'The State of Poetry—Part Two' (issued by Poets Conference in 1976) he emphasises the vibrant and inspirational character of the activities there:

> 'Better Books' Paperback Department could have been regarded as the first National Poetry Centre, considering the wide range of activities carried on there. The Arts Council could have taken it over as a going concern—bookshop, readings, exhibition space, the lot—but declined to take it over when William Collins closed it down.

This radical bookshop, then, was the model for what was attempted by the radical poets at the Poetry Society in the first half of the 1970s:

---

[7] There had also been a proposal, from Professor Brian Cox of Manchester University, suggesting a national poetry centre be set up in Manchester, to be completed by 1975, and forming part of the university (see minutes of Arts Council Literature Panel, 15th November 1970, item 3b. 'Poetry Policy' (ACGB/59/5, Box 2 of 7).

'Better Books' ('BB' to the initiated) was run by the poets themselves—Lee Harwood, Bill Butler, Anthony Barnett, Paul Buck, and Glen Storhaug are all listed by Cobbing as having been employed there at various times, and it combined book-shop, mail-order, and reading venue, with an emphasis on avant-garde and experimental writing. Undoubtedly, as already suggested, this kind of mix and orientation would have seemed the natural and accepted character of the Poetry Society if it had been set up at the Roundhouse, which was closely identified with the 'counter-cultural' arts and music scene (the 'underground' newspaper the *International Times* was launched there in 1966 with a gig featuring *Pink Floyd* and *The Soft Machine*), whereas the more genteel-seeming surroundings of the Georgian town house in Earls Court Square raised a rather different set of expectations.

Also in 1970, as the Poetry Society launched its appeal for funds to set up the Centre, another key organisation was formed by Cobbing and Montgomery: acting with Jeni Couzyn, Asa Benveniste, Adrian Henri, and George MacBeth, they set up 'Poets Conference' as a professional organisation open to all poets. It held its first conference from the 3rd to the 5th July 1970, at the Poetry Society, attended by over eighty poets, who were urged to join the Society and make their influence felt:

> [Poets Conference] laid down minimum fees for poets' readings, called for the setting up of a National Poetry Secretariat, advocated well-stocked poetry bookshops in each region of the country (with an efficient mail-order service and poetry sales vans to visit universities, festivals, etc.) and decided to put its energies into helping to create a National Poetry Centre based on the Poetry Society, with the hope of regional centres as well.[8]

The trajectory envisaged here, which pushes towards a kind of trade-unionisation of poetry, represents an ideal of 'collectivist' action, and runs counter to the opposite ideal of individualistic isolation, which is inherent in long-standing Romantic notions of the poet. The regional centres, it should be added, never got going, and the 'metro-centric' character of Poets Conference, and its cognate organisations, weakened its long-term effectiveness. The London avant-garde had only informal links to centres of innovative poetry activity elsewhere in the country—it

---

[8] From 'Poets Conference: The State of Poetry—Part Two', issued in 1976 (copy in the Mottram Archive, 4/3/36–46).

wasn't a North-South divide, so much as a divide between London and the rest of the country.

At the beginning of the 1970s the Poetry Society's journal *Poetry Review* was edited by Derek Parker, whose tenure was from 1966 to 1970. Parker was by no means a stereotypical conservative editor. For instance, issue 60:3 under Parker had poems from Andrew Turnbull, Stevie Smith, Anselm Hollo, Alex Comfort, and Ronald Bottrall, a very eclectic mixture, and 61:3, his penultimate issue, featured concrete poetry, including work by Bob Cobbing himself (Gortschacher, p. 140), so the journal was already beginning to strain at its traditional parameters. Merely running a truly national journal like *Poetry Review*, to say nothing of attempting to set up a genuinely *National* Poetry Centre, needed resources and funding on a realistic scale, and Derek Parker clearly felt that these were not going to be made available to him at the Poetry Society, leading him to resign his editorship at the end of 1970. The *Times* 'Diary' (31st December 1970), under the heading 'Poor prices for poetry—a plea', notes Parker's expression of dissatisfaction with the post he was leaving—having to read 500 manuscripts a week (again indicative of the extent of the poetry boom of the period), working without any editorial fee for several years on a magazine distributed free to Society members (it accounted for half their £3 annual fee) and able to pay poets only small fees of from £2 to £25. Clearly, the vastly increased interest in poetry which was so evident at the end of the 1960s needed to be matched by substantial increases in funding to cater for it, and there seemed little prospect of that happening.

So there was now both a hiatus and a vacuum at the Poetry Society, and it must have been clear that the most likely outcome was that the Society would veer towards one or the other of the polarised constituencies it had been seeking (tentatively) to integrate. The result of the inaugural 'Poets Conference' in July 1970 was that a number of radicals were elected (or re-elected) to the Society's General Council, including, in 1970–71, Asa Benveniste, Martin Booth, Bob Cobbing, Stuart Montgomery, Eric Mottram, and Anthony Rudolf. Others would follow over the next few years, including Allen Fisher, Lee Harwood, Peter Hodgkiss, Pete Morgan, Tom Pickard, Elaine Randell, Ken Smith and Barry MacSweeney. As a consequence of these developments, and marking the significant shift which had taken place, Basil Bunting—the last survivor of the heroic age of modernist poetry—became President of the Poetry Society in 1971 and Eric Mottram became editor of *Poetry Review*.

'A Great Awakening'

The process which led to Mottram's appointment as editor of *Poetry Review* began with a brief letter dated 9th December 1970 from Michael Mackenzie, General Secretary of the Poetry Society, inviting him to apply for the post. He was asked to supply a statement of how he would see the magazine and its role, and was told that two other candidates had also been approached with the same request. If appointed, he would need to leave the General Council of the Society if he wanted to receive a fee for his editorial services.[9] In a subsequent letter, of 18th January 1971, from Norman Hidden as Chair of the Society, Eric Mottram was offered the post for two years, this being for eight issues, with an editorial fee of £50 per issue (Mottram, 4/3/1–11). Part of the successful candidate's statement about the magazine was subsequently attached to the minutes of the General Council for Wednesday 14th June 1971, as an appendix from the Publications Committee entitled 'from Editor's statement on taking office':

> There is an extreme need for a poetry magazine in this country which will represent centrally what is being created in poetry in our time. We simply do not have it, the existing outlets being provincial and partisan in the extreme. The *Poetry Review* must stand or fall on its ability to print a wide range of different kinds of poetry, so that each issue contains a collection which . . . contributes to our acknowledgement of what is in fact going on in poetry. Hopefully . . . the *Poetry Review* could lead rather than follow and thereby encourage people to consider the Poetry Society as a body committed to the development of poetry and nothing else.[10]

Between the departure of the old 'permanent' editor (Derek Parker) and the arrival of the new one (Eric Mottram) there were two guest-edited issues of *Poetry Review,* the first (spring 1971) by Adrian Henri. This issue produced some rumbles from the journal's traditional readership: the Chairman of the Society reported that a number of letters commenting

---

[9]   The letter is in folder 4/3/1–11 in the Mottram Archive at King's College, London. Subsequent references to material from the archive will, wherever possible, be inserted into the text in the form: (Mottram 4/3/1–11).

[10] In ACGB/62/103, box 1 of 10. References in this form are to the Arts Council of Great Britain archives, held by the Victoria and Albert Museum. Section 62 is for the AC's Literature Department, 1947–1994, of which box 102 covers the Poetry Centre, 1968–1976, and box 103 (with ten sub-boxes) the Poetry Society, 1966–1994.

on the latest issue of *Poetry Review* had been received. The majority were in the form of complaints (General Council minutes, 18th May 1971). The second of the 'inter-regnum' issues (Summer, 1971) was edited by Martin Booth and Anthony Rudolf, the latter editor choosing poems in translation. They added a note to the brief editorial to their issue:

> The editors, as members of the General Council of the Poetry Society, would like to take this opportunity to welcome, on behalf of the Society and the Council, the new regular editor, Eric Mottram, who takes over with the next issue.

On taking over, the new editor quickly put in hand changes to the way poets contributing to the journal were paid. A letter from Mackenzie (2nd June 1971) allocated £100 per issue for contributors' fees, to be distributed as the editor decided (4/3/1–11). Before the end of the year, Cobbing and Mottram had decided (very much in the spirit of the various poets' organisations run by Bob Cobbing) that the journal ought to be egalitarian and pay the same flat-rate fee to all contributors, rather than offering a higher fee to those considered to be 'stars': in a letter of 5th January 1972 the Society Treasurer, May Ivimy, agrees (with obvious reluctance) to the proposal to pay all contributing poets a £10 fee, if the editor so wishes. She had also to deny the accusation in the letter that the Poetry Society was reluctant 'to pay proper and very much increased fees to poets' (Mottram, 4/3/1–11).

The accusatory tone often evident in Mottram's communications with the Society's officials sometimes seems like a strategy, as if designed, almost, to give a sense that the Society and the journal are separate entities. There is a rather pained letter from General Secretary Michael Mackenzie on 24th February 1972 in which he writes: 'Incidentally, I am sorry you want to dissociate yourself from the Society's section of the journal [that is, from the pages at the back used for notices of readings and other events]. There has been no suggestion that this wish is reciprocated' (Mottram 4/3/1–11). Judging from correspondence in another file, this sense of the separation between the Society and the journal was an impression Mottram also conveyed to potential contributors: one letter to him begins 'Dear Eric Mottram, Thanks for taking the trouble to explain to me you have nothing to do with the Poetry Society' (Mottram 4/2/14). *Poetry Review* was roughly A5 size, and it is clear from the opening page of Eric's black editorial notebook (in Mottram 4/2/1–2) that the intention right from the start was to change as quickly as possible to a larger format. The page has jottings from a meeting with Bob Cobbing (who functioned throughout as a kind of unofficial assistant editor): the current volume would be completed in the present size ('2 issues same size'), but they would then introduce a larger format ('Bob's argument—better for visual poems & long poems'). In the event, the change could not be made until 1975, but when it was, the accompanying editorial note gave these same reasons for making the change (though not attributing them to Bob Cobbing).

The first Mottram issue of the journal was Vol. 62 no. 3, autumn 1971, which had a 'typewriter-art' cover by Dom Sylvester Houédard, and opened with a series of extracts from Lee Harwood's *The Long Black Veil*. Controversy broke out almost immediately: the first page of Harwood's contribution contained the words 'I fuck you', and a type-setter at the Ditchling Press, the Sussex printing firm used by the Poetry Society, objected to this: the printing was delayed, and a General Council member leaked the matter to the *Times* gossip columnist, who then phoned a number of people at the Society, including Mottram himself (who had not been told officially about what was going on). Eric wrote indignantly on 25th September 1971 to Denys Thompson (who had now succeeded Norman Hidden as Chair) asking which member had leaked the information and insisting that he be kept properly informed on all editorial matters (carbon copy of the letter in Mottram 4/3/1–11). His letter was read out at a meeting on the 28th at which the difficulties with the Ditchling Press were discussed, and Thompson was mandated to write formally to Mottram, re-assuring him that he would in future be kept fully informed on all matters relating to the editing of the jour-nal. Thompson also attached a hand-written note to the formal typed letter, explaining that 'feeling was very strong at the meeting that it had been wrong for the person unknown to contact the press.' Though the difficulty with the printing press had been sorted out fairly easily, it was an inauspicious beginning, and the evidence that there were enemies on the General Council with ready access to the national press would become a significant factor later on.

But external reactions to the new editor were at first very promising: Lyman Andrews wrote in the *Sunday Times* that 'the autumn 1971 issue of *Poetry Review* is an eye-opener. By far the most interesting issue of a poetry magazine to appear in a long while: it is a vital purchase for anyone interested in poetry'. The *TLS,* too, described *Poetry Review* as a 'steadily improving magazine'. The new editor made no editorial state-ment or manifesto in the first issue, but the notes on contributors were much fuller than had previously been the case. From the next issue (62:4) this was expanded into a formal 'Poetry Information' section at the back of the magazine, compiled with the aid of Nick Kimberley, then of *Compendium Books* in Camden Town, North London, the main UK stockist of small press poetry after the demise of 'Better Books': it incorporated the 'Notes on Contributors', and listed new booklets and magazines in the 'BPR' ambit.[11] This was continued until 65:2 & 3 in 1975, after which the 'Poetry Information' mission was transferred to Peter Hodgkiss's journal of the same name, which provided listings, reviews, and criticism of 'BPR' poetry, and became the major source of sustained explication and discussion of this kind of material. It was perhaps unfortunate in some ways that the 'educating' element, which might have contributed to building a readership, was hived off in this way, but as Mottram explained in a prefatory 'Editor's Note' to 66:1 in 1975, the space available in the journal ought to be devoted to the poetry itself, and a plan to issue *Poetry Review* and *Poetry Information* together under the auspices of the Poetry Society had had to be dropped 'partly owing to the refusals of public money to the Centre' (See Eric Mottram's 'Editor's Note' in the 'Documents' section, below). However, the space argument for dropping reviews was somewhat undermined by the fact that it really wasn't true that the space available in the journal was entirely devoted 'to the poetry itself', since the 'Poetry Information' section took up large amounts of space in the journal: it was never less than ten pages in the issues from 64:1 (spring 1973) to the double issue 65:2/3 (the last to contain listings) in 1975, in which no less than twenty one pages were devoted to the listings. Indeed, the 'Poetry Information' section (in my view) was symptomatic of a tendency to just give *lists*—of poets, presses, or journals—or mere enumeration, saying how many poets or issues had been published—at times when argument and cogent exemplification were needed. The generalist readership of *Poetry Review* surely needed reviews which explained some key aspects of the new poetries, rather than being bludgeoned in each issue with lengthy un-annotated reading lists.

[11] *Compendium* bookshop opened in 1968, at 240 Camden High Street, selling the works of 'counter-cultural' thinkers who had participated in such events as the Dialectics of Liberation conference at the Roundhouse in 1967 and the London Anti-University. Nick Kimberley ran the poetry department at the shop. *Compendium* closed in 2001. (http://www.indigogroup.co.uk/llpp/archive.html#comp).

The second Mottram issue (62:4, wrongly designated 61:4 on the title page) was for winter 1971-2 and had a cover which was described by Michelene Victor in *Time Out,* January 14–20th 1972 as 'a phallic-toad like cover by Jeff Nuttall which would make Kenneth Grahame blush with pleasure'. It did make some people blush, though (mostly) not with pleasure [see illustrations on page 26 and 27], for the complaining letters which were now being received at the Society often mentioned it—'perhaps the current cover design was the last straw', writes one correspondent on 10th January 1972, resigning his membership, and another (12th January) says that 'the cover 1971–72 is an insult' (Mottram 4/3/23–29). According to Bill Griffiths, the offending cover was actually an allegory of the state of affairs at the Poetry Society:

> Consider, if you can, the cover of *Poetry Review,* 62:4 (Winter 1971–1972). It is by Jeff Nuttall. The front and back covers each bear a single red figure, from trunk upwards. On the front is Mottram himself, identifiable by the crowns on his tie (for King's College). His strangely distorted face which bears a number of possible apertures plays a toy trumpet from which issues a wash of song prompted by some music clasped in a hand. In opposition, the back cover shows a frock-coated individual, whose horseshoe motif tie proclaims him a 'country member'. His hand holds a sonnet-like text, and his mouth issues a wash of colour aimed at the Mottram figure round on the front. It satirised the myth—current even in that day—that Mottram only represented a coterie of London members, and was alienating the 'country members' who so depended on a traditional 'Poetry Review'.[12]

At the other extreme of reaction, those who had previously despaired of finding any outlet for their work other than at the remote margins felt almost as if a new era had dawned; thus the poet Jeremy Hilton writes to Eric Mottram, 7th April 1972, 'It's difficult to get down in words the joy and enthusiasm I feel over your three issues of *Poetry Review*— what a great awakening they bring.' He then writes in detail with specific praise of specific aspects of the journal, mentioning Mottram's *Stand* essay on William Carlos Williams's *Paterson* as seminal on his own thinking (Mottram, 4/2/52).

---

[12]   This is a contribution to the British-Poets e-mail discussion list. The list (begun by Ric Caddel in 1994) is an invaluable source of information on British avant-garde poetries and can be accessed at: http://www.jiscmail.ac.uk/lists/British-poets.html The Griffiths contribution can be found at: http://www.jiscmail.ac.uk/cgi-bin/ webadmin?A2=ind98&L=british-poets&P=R141975&I=-1

But the voicing of opposition to Mottram's editing, by individuals and later by groups, became a persistent feature of General Council meetings. For example, the minutes for 31st May 1972 have an item headed 'The editorship of *Poetry Review*, an item raised by Mr Cox:

> Mr Cox asked that the General Council should thank the Editor for providing controversy and interest with his issues of the magazine. In his opinion the recent issue had contained some good work, but that overall the work included had often not been poetry, and was therefore not acceptable in the Society's magazine. He therefore suggested that the Editor be replaced. A number of differing comments were made, amongst which the auditor pointed out that the annual accounts were to show that there had been an increase in the sales since Mr Mottram's advent as editor. (ACGB/62/103, Box 1 of 10).

As with any editor of a journal attached to a Society, Mottram depended upon support from several different committees, including the Publications Committee (his most reliable source of support), the General Council (most strongly in his favour in 1975 and the first half of 1976), the Executive and Management Committee (of which the same is roughly true) and, ultimately, the Annual General Meeting (which might, in exceptional circumstances, consult the membership in a postal ballot). The first AGM during Mottram's editorship was on Saturday 10th June 1972, which was perhaps too soon for any organised opposition to form. But there were already sporadic outbursts from Council members against Mottram's editorial practice. Patricia Norris, a member of the General Council, wrote a sympathetic letter to Mottram expressing her view that 'the attack of yesterday afternoon was scurrilous . . . I have written to Michael Mackenzie in support of present editorial policy'. Clearly Mottram had described the meeting in fairly pessimistic terms to friends and potential-contributor poets, for on 13th July 1972 his friend Arnold Goodman of Sussex University writes 'Your account of the general meeting is heart-breaking' (Mottram 4/3/23–29). But it seems likely that aggressive and personalised attacks at meetings initially had the effect of increasing support for Mottram, rather than the opposite, so that even Council members of generally middle-of-the-road tastes in poetry tended to support him at this stage. All the same, from this point onwards Mottram told poet friends that his position at the Poetry Society was tenuous.

40p

Adding Up the Numbers

The Chair's report at the 1972 AGM commented on the membership figures, which remained at around 1200; this looks like stability, but actually there was a pattern of continually changing membership, even though the overall numbers remained pretty stable: thus, there were 399 new members between the end of May 1971 and the beginning of June 1972: likewise, 400 new members had joined between May 1970 and June 1971, but 'the usual fall-off of lapsed members—457 this year—which approximately matches new members' (Mottram, 4/3/12). Membership figures, of course, would always be an extremely sensitive issue: 736 of the 1179 members in June 1972 lived outside London, meaning that very few of them would ever come to events at the Poetry Society. Their main reason for joining was their quarterly copy of *Poetry Review*: sometimes disgruntled members who took a dislike to the journal would write to the Chair saying that they were not renewing their subscription to the Society, but most of the displeased, of course, would simply let their subscription lapse. The letters received were forwarded to the editor, and Mottram notes in his black notebook during 1972: 'Letters of complaint since I took over, 24, some referring to past issues' (mainly to the Adrian Henri issue between the end of Derek Parker's tenure and the beginning of Eric Mottram's). I will comment on some of this material later, in the section on the editorial postbag in chapter seven. Sometimes complainants wrote directly to the man at the top, as evidenced by a note from Lord Goodman (Chair of the Arts Council) to Charles Osborne (Director of the Literature Panel), 11ᵗʰ Jan 1972:

> Dear Mr Osborne,
>
> Can you let me have a copy of the current *Poetry Review*. I have had a letter about it from an enraged subscriber.[13]

Such letters raise the question of how the circulation of *Poetry Review* was affected by Eric Mottram's editorship—was there a boom in sales, did sales collapse, or did they remain more or less what they had always been? I will end this opening chapter with a detailed look at this important but tricky question.

According to Andrew Duncan, writing a review of Clive Bush's *Out of Dissent,* under the title 'Structures getting in the way of visions', in the autumn 1998 issue of the magazine *First Offense*:

[13] Folder 'Correspondence April 71- November 73' in ACGB/62/103, Box 1 of 10.

The truth is that it was the collapse of the sales of *Poetry Review*, under Eric Mottram's editorship, which provoked the crisis at the Poetry Society; sales allegedly fell from 1500 to 300; it was the broad poetry market which rejected the new formally dissonant world, and the Arts Council was following broad taste.

But Duncan doesn't say who made the allegation, nor on what evidence it was based. As *Poetry Review* was sent 'free' to paid-up members of the Society, of which there were about 1200, and was also available for individual sale, this is a very puzzling statement—it would imply about 900 resignations from the Society, and no applications to join, for which there is no evidence. Bill Griffiths (on the British Poets Archive) seeks to set the record straight:

> As regards sales figures, I can certainly bring forward my own testimony, as a member of The Poetry Society's General Council during the mid 70s, as well as a proof-reader of *Poetry Review* for several years, and the printer of one (not very elegant) edition of it. The print-run was consistently over 2000 copies during Mottram's editorship, to my observation. This comprised 1200 copies approx for members as part of an annual membership fee, and the rest as copies for sale, either to libraries or to private enquirers or via bookshops. Neither the number 1500 nor that of 300 fits obviously into this equation.

Griffiths cross-checked the data carefully, and reports further:

So I also checked with others concerned with the Publications Committee of The Poetry Society at the time and was provided with the following significant figures by the then Hon. Treasurer [Bob Cobbing]:

sales of *Poetry Review*　　　in 1967 – £397
　　　　　　　　　　　　　　　in 1971 – £411
　　　　　　　　　　　　　　　in 1975 – £1050
　　　　　　　　　　　　　　　in 1976 – £1151
　　　　　　　　　　　　　　　in 1977 – £1409

Quite contrary to the figure produced in the article, sales can be seen to have consistently risen during Mottram's editorship (1971–1977), and there is absolutely no question of any 'collapse' that I can detect, certainly not while the duly elected officers were able to retain their posts or prior to the Arts Council intervention.[14]

---

[14]　http://www.jiscmail.ac.uk/cgi-bin/webadmin?A2=ind9811&L=british-poets&
　　　P=R2416&I=-1

Elements of this broad picture are confirmed by the recollections of cris cheek:

> The first issue of *Poetry Review* that Bob [Cobbing] and myself printed was Volume 66 Number 1, 1975. It's priced on the cover at 40 pence (so placing that alongside the relevant sales figures you provided gives some measure of the print run, although my memory—and what a fickle and abject beast it can become—is of 2000 copies) and was the first issue to adopt the enlarged format (A4).[15]

These raw year-by-year figures suggest that income from the journal rose in the Mottram period, although they don't actually reveal unambiguously how many copies of each issue were being sold. To get a sense of that, we need to know the cover price of each issue for all the years in question and the number produced each year. But it should be noted that all the terms involved are tricky to handle. Firstly, does 'sales' (or 'circulation') mean the number of individual copies sold at bookshops, poetry readings, and individual mail order, as well as to non-member subscribers, but *excluding* the copies which went direct to members as part of their membership deal? Secondly, what is the *'income'* from the journal when members receive it as part of their membership package? Clearly, not all the membership fee can be counted as income from the journal; only a proportion of the fee can be so counted, but *what* proportion? Thus, all the basic terms—'income', 'sales', 'circulation'—need to be defined each time they are used, and obviously, too, knowing the 'print run' doesn't necessarily give reliable information about any of them. With these cautions, we can consider 1967 and 1977, the first and last years in Cobbing's list. In 1967, pre-decimalisation, the cover price of *Poetry Review* was 3/6d for the first two issues and then rose to 5/- for the last two. We can therefore take the average price to be about four shillings, or 20p. On the year's takings of nearly £400, this is around £100 received per issue, or about 500 copies. Do we take this to mean that around 500 copies were sold, over and above the copies distributed to members? 1977 is the year for which the largest income is recorded: in that year two large double issues were produced—66:3/4, and 67:1/2. An income of £1409 for the year means about £700 for each of these two issues, which would represent over 700 copies sold of each issue (at a cover price of 80p each for these two double issues), in addition to the

---

[15] http://www.jiscmail.ac.uk/cgi-bin/webadmin?A2=ind9811&L=british-poets&
      P=R2672&I=-1

(up to) 1200 copies for members, which is consistent with a print-run of about 2000. A slightly complicating factor is that single copies by post cost £1, and a year's subscription (for the four issues, or, in 1977, for the two doubles) was £2. Taking this into account, we might estimate that the income of £1409 in 1977 would represent about 600 copies sold of each of the two double issues, over and above the copies distributed to members.

This is a considerable achievement, but it doesn't represent the kind of increase in circulation which might be imagined on seeing a jump in income from £400 to over £1400 between 1967 and 1977, because, of course, this was a period of high inflation, so merely looking at sums of money will tell us very little—in fact, as just calculated, the jump was from around 500 to around 600 copies. For purposes of comparison, it should be noted that in 1975 the final issue of Peter Finch's *Second Aeon* (which did have subsidy) had a circulation of 2,600.[16] The sale of around six hundred non-member copies of *Poetry Review* would also need to be compared with the print-runs of the typical unsubsidised 'BNR' magazine during the same period. For example, the magazine *Alembic*, with which I was involved in the 1970s, printed 120 copies of its first issue, and then varied between 150 and 250 copies until the final (8th) issue (Gortschacher, pp. 163–4). Paul Buck, who ran the magazine *Curtains*, explained the scale and economics of the venture in a 1973–4 letter to Eric Mottram (Mottram, 4/2/51) thanking him for his subscription:

> Jesus, it's going up: printing, etc, about £35, postage £15. Of course the issue will be 150 pages long and I'll be doing 300. Everyone keeps asking me to go litho but when I'm spending £50 and getting back £10 an issue on a Roneo version, how could I do a litho mag? *Compendium*, 12 or so: *Turrett* 5: 6 to Larry: 6 to Ohio shop: 3 US libraries, + British Library: 10 subscriptions—doesn't make much, does it? I do 300 and give 250 or so away free.

By comparison, *Poetry Review*, with its national distribution to Poetry Society members, and its payments to contributors, existed in a completely different league, and it might be expected that the difference in circulation figures between *Poetry Review* and less privileged radical poetry magazines would be even greater than it was. But comparisons are difficult because of the major dissimilarities between *Poetry Review* and all other journals. However, it isn't important that the

---

16   http://www.peterfinch.co.uk./2ndaeon.htm

figures should have pin-point accuracy: in spite of their ambiguities, they do show that there was no 'collapse' in the circulation of *Poetry Review* under Mottram's editorship.

This conclusion is confirmed by another contributor to the 'British Poetry Archive' discussion site which had addressed Andrew Duncan's allegation about a collapse in circulation figures for *Poetry Review* during the Mottram era, as quoted above. The contributor is David Kennedy, co-editor of the successful Bloodaxe anthology *The New Poetry* of 1993, and author of *New Relations*, which is about British poetry from 1980 to 1994. His contribution quotes Peter Forbes, editor of *Poetry Review* from 1987 to 1992: this on-line discussion took place in November 1998, and it gives useful comparative information about the sales of the journal after the Mottram era: Forbes replied to Kennedy's enquiry:

> This is not an exact science and record keeping has never been the Po[etry] Soc[iety]'s strong point. The bare bones are that the print run was 3500 when I arrived, about 3000 of which were being sold. This was the Mick Imlah era [editor, 1983–87]. I think the run had increased somewhat in Andrew Motion's time [editor, 1981–83]. We've been selling around 4500–4700 for some time now. The 'New Generation' issue [spring, 1994] sold out 7500 but we've not found a way of repeating that. To go into further detail would be to invent.

He goes on to make the point that the circulation of a journal like *Poetry Review* tends not to react immediately to changes in content or format, and we could add that all such journals (those which are linked to a society or club, as well as most academic journals) have a built-in inertia factor, since many copies are taken by libraries or academic institutions, and there is a great reluctance to break the run of a journal which has been taken for many years, since doing so reduces both the value and the usefulness of the holding:

> Legend had it that the circulation collapsed in the Mottram period but I don't think it was that dramatic. The great truth is that the circulation of the *Review* isn't as responsive to contents as you might think. There's a kind of buffer of people who seem to subscribe irrespective of what we're doing and it's hard to bring new people in.[17]

---

[17]   David Kennedy, Archives of BRITISH-POETS@JICSMAIL.AC.UK, 19th November 1998

In the post-Mottram period, then, the journal had, by the mid 1990s, pretty well doubled its circulation, but only by becoming a very different kind of poetry magazine, one which used all the resources of contemporary printing and publication techniques, to produce a much more commercially-minded publication which included commentary, reviews, illustrations, publishing news, and gossip as well as the poetry itself.

2

Editing Under Pressure: 1972–1975

'Running into Some Hostility'

The third Mottram issue of *Poetry Review*, 63:1 in spring 1972, contained Allen Ginsberg's 'Bayonne Entering NYC', a great poem in his mature, epic, Whitmanesque manner (also included in his City Lights book *The Fall of America: Poems of these States, 1965–1971*). It is about returning to his home neighbourhood, and evokes the familiar inner-urban sprawl of East Coast USA with clear-eyed relish:

> Megalopolis with burning factories-
> Bayonne refineries behind Newark Hell-light
> truck trains passing trans-continental gas-lines,
> blinking signs KEEP AWAKE

Them in the autumn issue of 1972 (63:3) came one of the most significant 'finds' of the period—'Cycles on Dover Borstal', the first published work of Bill Griffiths, who went on to become a major 'BPR' poet, and later the cataloguer of the Eric Mottram Archive at King's College, London. Griffiths is usually said to be the only previously unpublished writer whose work Mottram published in *Poetry Review*, though this is only true if translations are excluded.[1] The typed manuscript is signed in capitals 'BILLY GRIFFITHS', varied to 'B. B. GRIFFITHS' on another copy. In response to Mottram's standard request to accepted writers for brief details of previous publications (to go in the 'Notes on

---

[1] See letter to Mottram from Adrian Clarke (in Mottram, 4/2/25–6), 21st October 1972: 'Many thanks for taking my Reverdy variations for *Poetry Review*. These will be my first published poems'.

Contributors'), he writes: 'How can I give you my publication history?—
having none. You can say if you want "Other poems have appeared and
will re-appear pasted on selected public walls."' But in the event the
contributor's note simply reads 'The poems in this issue are his first to
be published'. In the letter, Griffiths explains that he 'was a Hell's Angel
(Nomad) in Ruislip until, as you may know, they were busted after a fight
at Denham last year. Tom Saunders in the poem was a Ruislip
Angel . . . . "Cycles" is based on visits to Dover and a period inside
Brixton [Prison]'. Mottram's publishing of Griffiths may have given the
impression that he would be open to moral persuasion (or moral blackmail) in the case of other ex-offenders: on 16th January 1975 a probation
officer wrote to him; 'Enclosed please find copy of X's poems . . . he has
four previous convictions, exclusive of motoring offences . . . I do believe
that some encouragement at this stage could have a dramatic effect on
X and his future. . . There is an element of urgency in this matter, as his
case will be called in about three weeks' time.'

Issue 63:4 (winter 1972/3) contained more Lee Harwood, the first
appearance in a Mottram issue of Allen Fisher, and perhaps Mottram's
most surprising acceptance—a group of poems from children at Our
Lady's RC Junior School in Ellesmere Port, Merseyside. 64:1, in spring
1973, had the 'Romany' poems of Bill Griffiths, and also published
poems by Elaine Feinstein, Frances Horovitz, and Elaine Randell. This
was one of the three Mottram issues which contained three women
poets, and it may be apposite here to comment on the question of
sexism in relation to the Poetry Society and *Poetry Review* in the 1970s.
Over his twenty issues of the journal, Mottram published some two
hundred poets, of whom twenty, or around ten per cent, were women.
The women poets he published were: Carol Bergé (an important
American poet and avant-garde figure, born in 1928); Elaine Feinstein (a
major British poet and literary biographer); Katherine Gallagher (an
Australian poet, born in 1935 and resident in London); Barbara Guest (an
eminent American poet whose first book appeared in 1960); Frances
Horovitz (1938–1983, an important British poet whose *Collected Poems*
were published by Bloodaxe in 1985); Nicki Jackowska (a British poet and
influential teacher of creative writing); Ann Lauterbach (an eminent
American poet and academic, author of five books of poetry, including
And, For Example, from Penguin); Denise Levertov (1923–1997, a major
poet, resident in America since 1948); Lyn Lifshin (a prolific American
small press poet); Sharon H. Nelson (a Canadian poet, born in 1948,
author of eight books of poetry); Alice Notley (an important American

poet, born in 1945, whose papers for 1969 to 1997 are in the special collections library of the University of California, San Diego); Judy Platz (American poet and teacher of creative writing); Elaine Randell (born in 1951, important British small press poet and editor); Carlyle Reedy (performance poet and experimentalist, born in 1938); Muriel Rukeyser (1913–1980: an eminent American poet whose work has been influential on women poets such as Anne Sexton); Penelope Shuttle (a British poet, born in 1947, author of six books of poetry and a *Selected Poems* published by Carcanet); Val Torrance (her booklet *Earth heart almanack* was published by Cwm Nedd Press, West Glamorgan, in 1977); Diane Wakowski (a major American poet and academic, born 1937); Anne Waldman (an American poet, founder, in 1966 of the innovative St. Mark's Poetry Project, East Village, New York, and now at the Jack Kerouac School for Disembodied Poetics, which she founded with Allen Ginsberg); and Val Warner (a British poet and literary critic whose most recent collection, *Tooting Idyll,* 1998, is published by Carcanet).

What is immediately apparent here is the high percentage of North Americans, and the eminence of most of them. *On average*, the women poets published by Mottram were more successful, both at the time and since, and especially beyond the small press circle, than their male counterparts. It would seem to follow that it was probably more difficult for a relatively unknown female poet to be accepted by *Poetry Review* than for an unknown male poet, though it was difficult to a large extent for both, since very few writers were published for the first time in *Poetry Review,* with Bill Griffiths being the only undisputed example. At least four of the published women poets had a husband or partner who was also published in the journal, but I don't know to what extent, if at all, this influenced the decision to publish. Also, since there is no list of poets who were invited to submit work to the journal, I don't know whether women poets of similar eminence and orientation were less likely to be approached than equivalent males poets. Of the visual material used, it should be added, a slightly higher proportion was by women artists, with four of the seventeen Mottram covers being by women. The imbalance between men and women in the performance events at the Poetry Society during the period seems even more marked: comprehensive lists of events are not available, but, for instance, the list of readings for autumn 1975 (given later) features only one woman, the Glasgow playwright Marcella Evaristi, who shared the bill with two male poets on the second night of a special Scottish event, on Saturday 27th September. The regular Friday night 'showcase' readings that autumn had no women poets reading. Were the Poetry Society and *Poetry Review*, then, unusually sexist? To answer this, a comparison would have to me made with other poetry events or institutions of a similar kind in the same period: the Horovitz *Children of Albion* anthology, it has been noticed, has a lot more sons than daughters—sixty three of the former and five of the latter, which is a lower percentage than that of women contributors to *Poetry Review*, although it too is pretty close to the ten percent which seems to have been the going rate. *Poetry Review*, then, was of its time in this respect, but it was by no means a conspicuous offender.

In spite of some success and encouragement, Mottram remained most unhopeful about his chances of long-term survival as editor. The poet Dave Chaloner, writing on 22nd October 1972, says 'I am sorry you are meeting such aggravation and opposition from those in power at the Poetry Society' (Mottram, 4/2/46–7). Perhaps his pessimism was justified: the General Council of the Poetry Society met on 11th April 1973, and George Wightman, who was the most vociferous of Mottram's critics right through the 1970s, circulated details of an alternative candidate as editor of *Poetry Review*—Gavin Ewart.[2] Support had been unanimous for Mottram on the Publications Committee, and he had also been a majority recommendation by the Executive, but events would later show that these power-bases counted for little if control was lost in the General Council. The motion proposed, that Eric Mottram be reappointed for one year, was carried by twelve votes to one, and the word 'only' was not inserted after 'one year', as the counter-motion had demanded (Minutes for 11/4/73). The new Poetry Society Chair, John Cotton, informed Mottram of the decision in a letter of 13th April (4/3/1–11). Though the vote is minuted as twelve to one, this figure is not given in Cotton's letter, and Mottram seems to have gleaned a figure of sixteen to one from other sources, judging from Elaine Feinstein's reply to a letter of his of 26th April (responding to an invitation to contribute

---

2 Wightman ran the organisation 'Poets in Public', and is dismissively referred to in Charles Osborne's *Giving it Away* (pp. 161–3) as a frequent writer of 'long . . . and excruciatingly tedious letters' to him. Osborne sent an acknowledgement postcard to one of these, calling the letters (rather oddly) 'suicidally impertinent' and Wightman published a version of the correspondence in the radical paper (or 'hippy newspaper', as Osborne calls it) the *International Times*. This contributed to Osborne's status in the 70s as a cultural hate-figure: the *TLS* was already publicising controversy over Osborne's correspondence with novelist Anthony Burgess, a story which the *Daily Mail* had also taken up.

poetry to the journal): 'I'm delighted to hear your news about *Poetry Review*, not just to hear you're still *there* (though that's important) but sixteen to one: that's a triumph. A real turnabout. Whatever happens next?' And she adds a hand-written P.S. '*How* did you do it? You must tell me the inner story some time' (Mottram, 4/2/41–42). However, the figure was a little exaggerated, and the news was not all good: the Poetry Society was experiencing financial difficulties, and the decision had been made to reduce *Poetry Review* from four issues per year to three, to change printer, and to use the cheaper offset litho method of production. In recognition of the fact that the new method of printing would increase the editor's workload, the editorial fee for each issue would be raised from £50 to £75.

The Poetry Society AGM at 2.30 on Saturday 16th June 1973 was preceded by an Extraordinary General Meeting at 2.00 which considered and passed (*nem con*) a proposal to raise the number of General Council members from 21 to 30, the increase to be phased in over three years, with three extra vacancies in 1973, 74 and 75. The minutes of the meeting (Mottram, 4/3/12) record that Basil Bunting, the new President of the Poetry Society, made a brief opening address, expressing his appreciation of the present editor's work on *Poetry Review*: he said that there were poems in recent editions which the Society would be proud in the future to have published. The Chair's report noted that adequate bar records had not been kept, leading to a loss (this would become a recurrent item over the next few years). In the discussion which followed the Report some considerable time was spent on *Poetry Review* and its immediate future: the Chair commented that the *Review* had 'a lively and controversial editor—I have had my share of members' letters! Certainly many seem to have noticed that there *is* a *Poetry Review*. I would suggest that a journal ignored is the worst kind of criticism.' He also said that the General Council would be considering very early next year the question of who would be editor from the autumn of 1974. A number of differing views were displayed regarding the contents of the magazine under the present editor, and the point was made that the appointment of the editor was the job of the General Council, one third of whom were to be elected at the present meeting. Members should bear the magazine in mind when they considered the election slip. This discussion must have made the twelve to one victory of a couple of months before seem less than irreversible.

One of those elected to the Council at this AGM was Martin Booth (later the author of *British Poetry, 1964 to 1984: Driving Through the*

Barricades) who wrote to Mottram the day after the AGM, on 17th June 1973:

> Firstly, thank you for supporting me at the AGM: I was afraid I'd had it as far as re-election was concerned, as Wightman had been smashing me (with others), although, until Friday, he had been my proposer—he dropped me in favour of Lord Feversham . . . I'm glad to say that I seemed of greater worth and I don't work for the Thompson organisation, thank God . . . How sad none of GBHW's people got in, but for himself. My heart bleedeth. (Mottram, 4/2/32–3)

George (initials 'G.B.H.') Wightman will feature prominently later in this account, but at this stage he was more of a future threat than a clear and present danger. But, to repeat, Mottram certainly did not feel that his future at the Poetry Society was bright. On 10th July Philip Pacey wrote 'I'm not surprised your editorship has run into some hostility: it has spelled change, after all' (Mottram, 4/2/32–3), and to poet Chris Torrance he seems to have indicated that that the process of ejecting him had already begun, for Torrance replies (16th June 1973) 'Needless to say, there is a general feeling of regret that you are being pushed out of the editorial chair at *Poetry Review,* but I think in our hearts we knew it couldn't last anyway' (Mottram, 4/2/32–3). Issue 64:2, in summer 1973, contained a series of diagrams or designs for sundials by Ian Hamilton Finlay (presented as visual texts), and a photographic rendering of one of these as the cover. The presentation is crisp and stylish, but presumably expensive to set up (the journal was still being handled by the Ditchling Press), another theme which would soon become very prominent. The issue also contained work by Brian Catling, Iain Sinclair, and Barry MacSweeney.

By 1973 relations between the Poetry Society and the Arts Council (represented by the Literature Director Charles Osborne) had become distinctly difficult, with considerable evidence of a break-down in communications. An internal memo from Osborne to the Chair of the Arts Council reads 'I doubt if a meeting with the Poetry Society to discuss the literature allocation would serve any useful purpose. . . . we are not, however, entirely happy with the present management of the Society, and will be meeting them shortly to discuss the future.' ['not' inserted by hand into the typescript].[3] On 1st May 1973 Osborne wrote to Michael Mackenzie (the Secretary of the Poetry Society) 'Dear Mike,

---

[3]   ACGB/62/103, Box 1, folder 'Correspondence April 71-November 73'.

Thank you for inviting me to the all-day marathon on Friday at which the National Poetry Secretariat will be discussed. I am afraid I cannot spare the time to attend. Fortunately it isn't necessary that I should as there really is little to be argued about'. And in the autumn (17th September) he writes to Trevor Royle at the Scottish Arts Council, 'Dear Trevor, I would like to talk to you sometime about the dreadful Poetry Society. Will you be in London for the next meeting of the General Council on Oct 4th?' One of the symptoms of the problems at 'the dreadful Poetry Society' was an on-going financial crisis, particularly in relation to the management of the bar, which would rumble on through the seventies: The Executive and Management Committee, 29th August 1973, discussed it under 'Matters arising':

> The Hon Treasurer (Bob Cobbing) reported that the loss on the bar at March 31st which emerged from the auditor's investigation, was £2,394. As far as it was possible to ascertain, this resulted from the disappearance of stock and inadequate inspection of the invoices received from the brewers. The total loss (i.e., up to June 1st, when full-time bar tending ended) was £2,746.

The Committee agreed that the bar would only function in future if run by an outside firm.

During 1973 Charles Osborne had instigated a system of having significant Poetry Society committee meetings attended by an Arts Council representative who reported back to him. This development was not, of course, welcomed at the Poetry Society, and it was also unsatisfactory from Osborne's own point of view, as the representatives were only observers, not voting members, at the committees they attended. In the spring of 1974, therefore, he would propose that the Arts Council nominate three full members to the Poetry Society's General Council. For the time being, however, observer status had to suffice. The nine-to-five civil servants at the Arts Council were constantly irritated by the Poetry Society's habit of holding meetings in the evenings and at weekends, and all these observer reports have a somewhat disgruntled tone. Thus, Lawrence MacKintosh attended an Executive & Management Committee meeting on 29th October 1973 at seven in the evening:

> The agenda was completed in just over an hour and we then adjourned to the pub next door for the important social part of the meeting. I came away feeling rather depressed. The Society's dowdy premises present a rather shabby image and I imagine the Society would benefit by

recruiting some provocative and lively enthusiasts to its staff and committees. (ACGB/62/103, Box 2 of 10)

He needn't have worried, since plenty of provocation and liveliness lay ahead, though the shabbiness of the Earls Court premises remained a fixture.

'Those Rat-Bags Down at Earls Court'

Eric Mottram's academic career and reputation advanced considerably in the mid-1970s: he was promoted to a Readership at King's College, London, in January 1973, and began to receive many invitations to lecture abroad: he was at Kent State University, Ohio, from January to April 1974, lectured in Tunis, 10th–17th April, and was a speaker at the Melville Conference in Paris, 5th–9th May (information from the Mottram Archive). All this necessarily reduced his ability to take part in the on-going battles in the Poetry Society, effectively leaving the conduct of affairs to Bob Cobbing and Lawrence Upton. 'Between January 3 and April 1 1974 I went to America for the sixth time . . . . . I had three months in which to get certain matters fairly clear'. Thus, Eric Mottram at the start of his *Kent State Journal,* a record of his thinking during a three-month visiting professorship at Kent State University, Ohio. During his absence, the fort was held at the Poetry Society by Bob Cobbing, who wrote to him on 7th February with the news that 'Here the battle still continues. I *think* we have won you another year as editor of *Poetry Review,* but no official announcement has been made yet'. In fact the winter meeting of the General Council had been cancelled, owing to difficulties associated with the miners' work-to-rule, the power-cuts, and the resulting imposition of the three-day week. Hence, there was a postal ballot of General Council members on the editorship of *Poetry Review,* and the 'Decision was to re-appoint Mr Mottram for a further year (ending with the summer 1975 issue) by a majority of two' (Minutes of the GC on 27/3/74). This twelve to ten vote in Mottram's favour is a dramatic reduction in support since the twelve to one triumph of the previous April, and suggests a better organized opposition than hitherto. On the 13th April the Chair, John Cotton, sent a hand-written note acknowledging receipt of Eric's letter confirming his acceptance of the re-appointment, and making the plea that 'without lowering the quality of *Poetry Review* in any way you 'perhaps extend its catholicity'. Of course, it would be impossible for Eric to see any need to do that, and—if anything—the range of contributors became more narrow (or more 'concentrated') as his editorship progressed. Cobbing also tells of a stiff struggle to get approval for the kind of programme of readings the radicals wanted, and the depressing news that the proofs of the issue Mottram had left ready for press on departing for America had not yet appeared: 'The three-day week is slowing everything down. We shall be lucky if it's out by the time you are back' (Mottram, 4/3/15–22).

In June 1974 the Seventh International Festival of Sound Poetry was held at the Poetry Society in Earls Court. The previous six of these had been held in Stockholm, beginning in 1968, and organized by a group of Swedish artists and broadcasters interested in electro-acoustic music and related arts. The eighth and ninth were also in London, the 10th, in 1977, had several European venues, and the series ended with the eleventh in Toronto in 1978 and the twelfth in New York in 1980. Cobbing had been involved in these from the start, and was instrumental in gradually shifting the emphasis from the 'electro' to the 'acoustic', that is, towards voice and performance and away from the electronic manipulation of sound patterns. A press release was put out for the first of the London festivals, attracting a visit from the *Times* diarist, which was written up, in evident bemusement, though not un-informatively, in the issue of 30th May 1974, under the heading 'Noises':

The National Poetry Centre in Earls Court seemed deserted when I arrived yesterday for the press reception to announce next week's seventh international festival of sound/poetry. I wandered up the stairs and past the exhibits of concrete poetry but could not see a soul. Finally, I heard a mysterious wailing in the basement. Following my ears, I came upon half a dozen sound poets listening to records of their own work. Svate Bodin from Sweden, wearing a bright green corduroy jacket and clashing green corduroy trousers explained what sound poetry is. It is poetry built on sounds rather than on the meaning of words. Usually it is created through a tape recorder, which slows down, speeds up, or otherwise interferes with speech, breaking it down into components of meaningless pure sound. In Sweden, said Bodin, where much more sophisticated electronic equipment is available to sound poets, it is something created by computers synthesizing the human voice. Bob Cobbing, the festival coordinator, also in green corduroy, said he had been a pioneer of sound poetry in Britain, but started quite late, in 1965. The Daddy of sound poets is Henri Chopin, of France, who started in 1955. More records were played. One consisted of slow readings of words beginning with 'tan'— "Tan, tandininan, tandinanane, tanan, tandina, tanare", and so on. Bodin said one of the most interesting sound poems he had heard was where somebody had recorded a poem backwards, then reversed the tape so that it came out the right way. Bruce Cheyne, a Scot (there is always one Scot at these affairs), said that, though a sound poet, he was a voice purist who did not hold with all the electronic gadgetry. Lawrence Upton, an Englishman, said 'A few years ago I was a very normal poet, and then I suddenly took this up'.

The piece was noticed by *Times*-reader Charles Osborne, as reported by the diarist two days later, writing up another poetry event, this time one that the Arts Council approved of:

> It has been a poetic week. After my adventures with the sound poets in Earls Court on Wednesday, I repaired to the Martini Terrace yesterday to meet participants in next week's Poetry International '74 at the Institute of Contemporary Arts in the Mall. There must be something symbolic in the difference between the party venues—a damp Earls Court basement compared with a plush 16th-floor terrace room with views all over London. The sound poets are not much admired by the more conventional kind who I suppose could be called unsound poets. Charles Osborne, the Director of Poetry International, was rather brutal. I read your piece this morning about that ragbag down in Earls Court, he said. (*Times* Diary, 31st May 1974)

But Osborne, apparently, had been misquoted: when Poets Conference put out a long press release under the title 'The State of Poetry' on 5th January 1975, the accompanying Newsletter wrote of Charles Osborne:

> In the corridors of the Arts Council, he has been heard to say 'I will snuff out The Poetry Society within a year'. The *Times* reported him as describing the Poetry Society's National Poetry Centre as 'that rag-bag down in Earls Court.' He later took the trouble to 'phone the Society to say "I have been wrongly reported. I did not say 'That rag-bag down in Earls Court' I said 'Those rat-bags down in Earls Court'.

Osborne stood by this setting of the record straight, and in his memoir he quotes the above quotation from the Poets Conference Newsletter (without the first sentence) with evident approval (*Giving It Away*, p. 193). He also quotes from the *Guardian's* account of the argument, which is more trivializing and dismissive of the sound poets and their allies than anything which appeared in the *Times* during this period, tending to bear out Mottram's frequent assertion that no support was ever forthcoming from such supposedly 'progressive' quarters at the height of the hostilities:

The poets are threatening to confront Mr Osborne in his office at 105 Piccadilly and force him to listen to the words which he will not sponsor—such as a tape recording of 'Kurrirrurrirri', a sound poem by Bob Cobbing. Although in fairness it should be heard, not written, [sic] the sounds of 'Kurrirrurrirri' are something like 'Twonk, rol rol rol, twonk twonk rol rol rol twonk rol rol rol rol rol twonk rol rol rol rol rol rol. (Quoted by Osborne, p. 193)

Meanwhile, the more mundane day-to-day business of the Poetry Society continued. The 1974 AGM took place at 2.30 on Saturday 15th June, when the news of Mottram's re-appointment was formally announced to the Society membership as a whole. In his report the Chair said:

We have expressed the hope that now he has had time to establish himself as editor he will feel confident enough to re-introduce book reviews to the journal. As Mr Mottram's appointment is for a further year, the Council will have to consider the appointment of an editor again in September/October next year.

This is hardly a ringing endorsement, and is distinctly cooler than what had been said at the previous year's AGM, so there are definite indications of a coming climate change at the Society. Mottram's abolition of reviews in *Poetry Review* remained a sore point, since offering reviewing was a useful way of involving committee members in the running of the journal, and the presence of a review section, of course, used to bring in large numbers of new books of poetry for the Society's library. Mottram's stated position was always that the available space in the journal ought to be used for the poetry itself, but in fact the 'Poetry Information' section took up a good deal of space too, was extremely labour-intensive to produce, and, as already suggested, was surely less useful to the journal's readers, who were hardly likely to be persuaded to broaden their poetic tastes by long lists of poets, journals, and presses. Further, the 'training' mission that Mottram believed in so strongly could far better have been forwarded by judicious and informative reviewing of at least a few of the kind of works he favoured. Increasingly, the foregoing of this opportunity to put the case for the 'BPR' to the wider readership of *Poetry Review* was emerging as a serious tactical error.

The other indication that the climate was cooling was the fact that the 1974 AGM at 2.30 was preceded by an EGM (Extraordinary General

Meeting) at 2.00 (this was becoming something of a routine; when the crisis became acute the following year the EGMs became separate occasions). The purpose of this EGM was to consider a startling resolution:

> That the Society accepts the Arts Council of Great Britain's proposal that the Arts Council nominate three fully-serving members of the General Council, within the agreed maximum complement of the General Council's membership.

This indicates that those who were discontent with the status quo at the Poetry Society had the direct sympathy of Charles Osborne, the Literature Director at the Arts Council. This issue (of directly-appointed Arts Council nominees on the Poetry Society's General Council) would run throughout the next two years and would cause the final breakdown of the uneasy compromise whereby an essentially conservative organisation like the Poetry Society hosted the radical 'BPR' movement's reading programme and flagship publication. In a flanking move, Bob Cobbing (as outgoing Treasurer) tabled an amendment that Welsh and/or Scottish Arts Councils, plus at least one of the Regional Arts Associations, also be represented. This was a shrewd ploy, drawing attention to what might now be called the 'metro-centrist' tendencies of the original proposal, and answering a frequent criticism made of the radicals—that they did not meet the needs of 'country' members of the Society. The minutes of the EGM (Mottram, 4/3/13–14) record that during discussion it was established that no specific names had been put forward by the Arts Council (perhaps an indication of either the ineptitude or the arrogance behind this proposal), and it was agreed that the Society should safeguard its position from having unacceptable nominees imposed upon it, and should preserve its democratic constitution. The amendment was carried *nem con,* although it must have been obvious that the Arts Council was not going to give up on its determination to have a direct say in affairs at the Poetry Society.

The autumn 1974 Newsletter (two stapled, Roneod foolscap sheets) announced that 'the long-awaited *Poetry Review* (Vol. 65, No.1) is at last published: the next two will be as one doubled issue to make up lost ground' (Mottram, 4/3/12). This was the eleventh Mottram issue, containing material from Diane Wakowski, Gael Turnbull, Ivor Cutler, and David Chaloner. The struggle between the two camps continued, with increasing bitterness, into the autumn of 1974. The poet Roy Fisher, mild-mannered and self-effacing, and then teaching American Studies at Keele University, viewed the mutual rancour with evident distaste. (Years later, when the organisers of the Cambridge Poetry Festival asked invited poets to list others with whom they wouldn't appear, he was famously the only one to send in a nil return.[4]) On 1st October 1974 he sent Mottram a brief typed note letting him know that:

> I'll be in London very briefly on Thursday night, shooting in to Earls Court Square to help Bob the Cob, etc, repel the claw-like actions of the Arts Council. What a load of shit it all is up at the heights. *They're* still at it. And I'm feeling steadily paranoid about the amount of Calvinism that's still lurking around, injected into everybody's underpants by Puf-pak. I must be getting old to notice it! (Mottram, 4/2/48–49).

Now, for the first time, the Arts Council's Literature Panel raised the possibility of mounting a formal investigation of the Poetry Society, for at its meeting of 16th September 1974 (under 2b 'Matters Arising: Poetry Society') a proposal was put forward (presumably by Charles Osborne) to ask Professor C. B. Cox of Manchester to undertake an investigation of the Society. However, it was not implemented at this stage, on the grounds that his university commitments might not allow him enough time to do the job.[5] The double issue (65:2/3) came out in 1975 and was the last to include the 'Poetry Information' listings, plus poetry by Peter Riley, Carl Rakosi, Edwin Morgan, Hugh MacDiarmid, Anthony Barnett, Paul Brown, Joel Oppenheimer, and F. T. Prince. 65/4, also in 1975, was the last small format Mottram issue, and the first to appear without the poetry listings. It was also the first to be printed at the Poetry Society itself. The production standard of this issue was particularly poor, with a rather muddy appearance and poor contrast throughout, and with some shedding of ink across pages. Issue 66:1 in 1975 was the first in the new, enlarged format (A4 instead of A5), the change having been made to 'better accommodate the spatial forms of the wide variety of poems in today's poetry scene'. It was also (as number fifteen in the sequence of Mottram issues) the only one of his twenty issues of *Poetry Review* to carry any kind of editorial statement, for as he says at the start of this one-page 'Editor's Note', 'It has never been the policy to spout policy: the

---

[4] See 'The Thing about Roy Fisher' (an ironic self review by Fisher) in *The Rialto*, 35 (1996), and reprinted in the Bloodaxe Books catalogue for 1997–98, pp. 34–5.

[5] See minutes of the meeting in ACGB/59/5, Box 2 of 7.

poems and their juxtapositions were their own editorial'.[6] 66:1 was only the second issue to be printed 'at home', so to speak, in the Society's print workshop in the basement of the premises, and again the production standards and page design were poor: Mottram's statement was printed directly onto the page facing the inside cover (with no intervening 'Contents' page), and the almost edge-to-edge printing of the statement, with no spaces between paragraphs, had a particularly uncomfortable look. After this issue, however, production quality and page design were considerably improved, mainly because the type-setting was done out-of-house, with the material being returned to the Poetry Society for printing. But none of the five issues of *Poetry Review* printed at the Poetry Society (of which two were doubles) achieved anything like the professional appearance of (say) Peter Finch's poetry journal *Second Aeon*, the most prominent and best established avant-garde poetry magazine of the period. The poor production quality was especially evident in the printing of the covers, graphics, and visual poetry.

'An Apology is Due and Overdue'

1975 would prove to be a momentous and decisive year. Poets Conference met in London on 4th January and voiced its discontent with the Arts Council's Literature policy. Increasingly, it seemed, 'BPR' poets and presses were being refused subsidy, often with dismissive or abusive comments from the Literature Panel, and it was seen as a scandal that large amounts of money were being given to Ian Hamilton's *New Review*.[7] A document entitled 'The State of Poetry: a Preliminary Report' was sent to the Literature Director, Charles Osborne, on 5th January ('Poets are losing confidence in the workings of the Literature Department of the Arts Council'), a reply being received on the 24th. The reply read in part:

---

6   There were seventeen 'physical' Mottram issues, of which three were double issues, making twenty in all. In the *Poetry Information 20/21* piece Mottram mistakenly refers to '22 issues'. In both that piece and the 'Editor's Note' in issue 66:1 he refers with some irritation to the problems imposed by the insecurity of tenure involved in the editorship.

7   In the year ended March 31st 1976 the Arts Council made a total grant of £45,550 to ten poetry magazines, as follows: *The New Review*, £22,000; *London Magazine*, £6,600: *Agenda*, £4,600; *Ambit*, £3,000; *Modern Poetry in Translation*, £3,000; *Index*, £2,500; *Fireweed*, £2,000; *Poetry Nation*, £1,200; *Platform Poets*, £350; *Meridian*, £300. (Source: *The Poet's Yearbook*, 1977, ed. S. T. Gardiner).

The statement has now been considered by the Literature Panel of the [Arts] Council, but I am afraid that the general view was that it was really not worth answering . . . After all, its object presumably was not really to make any useful contribution to the continuing debate on methods of subsidy. (Poets Conference Newsletter, 4ᵗʰ February 1975)

Osborne also commented on the document to the press, telling the *Daily Telegraph* 'I can't say I've taken the report all that seriously'. The Poets Conference Newsletter announced a campaign to seek 'a fairer deal for poetry from the ACGB' (Mottram, 4/3/36–46). It also accused the Arts Council of having a 'closed' policy which tended to prejudice it against poetry in performance (rather than in print), poetry from small presses and journals, poetry from the provinces or from working-class poets, and poetry which is experimental (as opposed to more familiar kinds of descriptive or confessional verse). The 'State of Poetry' document was issued to the press on 7ᵗʰ January, and this was when the nation first realised that there was a dispute of some kind going on between the Poetry Society and the Arts Council. Comment began to appear widely in the press, and John Cotton, who was both a member of Poets Conference and Chair of the Poetry Society, felt obliged to issue a clarifying statement, emphasising that 'The views expressed in the Poets Conference Statement are those of Poets Conference, which is a separate body from the Poetry Society.'

In March the Poetry Society mounted a two-day 75ᵗʰ birthday event for its President, Basil Bunting. Mottram organised it, and wrote to Barry MacSweeney (16ᵗʰ February, 1975) inviting him to take part, and indicating 'length to be determined by the number of poets we can manage, and would you please accompany your poems with something for the occasion re Basil's work and your stance with it.'[8] A later note to MacSweeney (BM15/1/210) gives him the final shape of the event: 'We have nine poets reading on the Friday plus BB—which makes about ten minutes or less reading time'. Bunting himself read 'At Briggflatts Meeting House', about the simple Quaker meeting house near Sedbergh, Cumbria, which he had been coming to since he was twelve years old. The event was a great success, a defining moment of the radicalised Poetry Society, and by paying homage to Bunting the radicals celebrated their own lineage, linking themselves, through Bunting, to the pioneer modernists like Yeats and Pound. However, against the

---

[8]   Letter in the Barry MacSweeney Collection, Newcastle University catalogued as BM15/1/214.

mention of the event in his copy of the Chair's report at the 1975 AGM Mottram has written 'few Council members turned up'.

Poets Conference met for the thirteenth time on 3rd May, and invited Charles Osborne (as Chair of the Art's Council's Literature Panel) to attend. At first he declined the offer, owing to a projected trip to Israel, but when this was postponed, he agreed to attend, but 'as a member of Poets' [sic] Conference.' He had not been asked to attend for the Arts Council, and they would not be sending a representative (Mottram, 4/3/13–14). There were to be sessions at 10.30, 2.30, and 6.30, held at the Poetry Society; Osborne said he would attend the first, and was 'impressed that you have so much to discuss that you intend to go on talking far into the night'

The 1975 AGM was on Saturday 14th June. Those elected to the General Council on this occasion were Alan Brownjohn, Peter Finch, Allen Fisher, Bill Griffiths, Adrian Henri, Eddie Linden, George MacBeth, Barry MacSweeney, Pete Morgan, Angus Nicolson, and Elaine Randell. Only the first of these would be considered a potential opponent of the radical side, so the latter now had, for the first time, a clear majority on the Council. The Chair reported that the General Council had decided to continue the present editorial policy, and had invited Eric Mottram to remain as editor for another year, which he had accepted. (This was the fourth renewal of Mottram's tenure as editor). He went on to say that there had, unfortunately, been extended delays with the printing, which had resulted in a somewhat irregular publication pattern: 'These difficulties with the printers, together with the continually rising costs, have brought about the decision to do our own printing, as outlined earlier in this report' (Mottram, 4/3/13–14).

As a result of this meeting, the radicals reached their strongest point, and seemed pretty well invulnerable within the Poetry Society, but the meeting also had the effect of increasing their opponents' sense of helplessness and frustration. At this AGM, for instance, 'a motion was put forward asking for a poll and then a show of hands on the editorship of *Poetry Review*', but the Society's auditor told the meeting that 'such business required prior submission'. In fact, the reformers believed, 'it only needs seven members to ask for a poll on any matter.'[9] The radicals perhaps made the tactical error of leaving no outlet at all for dissent, no

---

[9] These points are from the document 'Explanation of the Movement for a Reformed Poetry Society', issued by the Reform Committee for the EGM of January 1977 (See 'Documents').

form of safety valve through which opposition might pursue its legiti-
mate ends and activities and dissipate its energies. Hence, those who
were discontent with what was happening sought a hearing elsewhere,
by developing sympathetic contacts in the press.

Within the Society, those who were dissatisfied with the editing of
Poetry Review continued to press for change. At the General Council of
13th September 1975 the editorship was item 9: three candidates were
nominated—Peter Finch, Gavin Ewart, and Eric Mottram, who were
asked to provide details of their 'platform' for the next meeting on 13th
December when the vote would take place. In addition, a motion was
put forward about the maximum tenure of editorial office:

> Mr Upton, seconded by Mr Cobbing, proposed that the editorship of *Poetry
> Review* should be for a maximum of 5 years (i.e. 20 issues) and this should
> apply to the present editor as well as future. GBH Wightman's counter-
> proposal of three years was defeated, 7 to 5. Original motion carried
> *nem con.*

This motion is the source of the mistaken view that Mottram wasn't
sacked from *Poetry Review* but simply came to the end of his allotted term
of twenty issues. In fact, the new ruling applied to him only retrospectively, and he had never had the luxury of tenure for so many issues.[10]
The statements by the two new candidates were duly supplied: Gavin
Ewart would change present policy by excluding American poets, but
would continue the policy of not publishing reviews or criticism in the
journal. Peter Finch explained his desire to take on *Poetry Review* as
having its source in the sense of loss he felt at having to give up his
journal *Second Aeon* when he joined the Welsh Arts Council (which could
not give a grant to one of its own employees, meaning that the magazine had to cease publication). He would aim for catholicity of range,
and would seek to include both experimental and traditional poetries,
so long as they were both of this age (his underlining).

In September 1975 the opposition to the Mottram/Cobbing faction
became more formally organised, setting up a 'Committee for the

---

[10]   The late Ian Robinson, for instance, states in an interview that 'a lot of people now
believe that Eric Mottram was sacked as editor of *Poetry Review*. This is not true. He
served out the full term of his appointment—I forget how many issues this was'
(see *Contemporary Views of the Little Magazine Scene*, ed. Wolfgang Gortschacher,
Salzburg, 2000, p. 167). But Mottram himself was one of the people who believed
he had been sacked, for a correspondent in April 1976 replied to one of his letters
with the words 'I'm sorry to hear you have been sacked'.

reform of the Poetry Society', and issuing its 'Manifesto for a Reformed Poetry Society' (reprinted in the 'Documents' section of this book). The Committee consisted of six people: Irving Weinman (Chair), Denis Doyle (Secretary), James Sutherland-Smith, (Treasurer), Tim Coxe, David Lovibond, and Padraic MacAnna. Only the first two and the last of these were actually members of the Poetry Society (as they indicate by putting the letters 'P.S.' after their names), something their opponents would later exploit. They indicate that their concerns about the condition of the Society were sparked by the exclusion of a group called 'Poetry Round' from the Society's premises, and lament the impact of 'an all too influential and vindictive group of Council members.' This group is interested only in 'sycophancy and nepotism', and they answer any criticism with 'spite and rank vindictiveness'. In order to achieve the 'essential openness' (strikingly, both sides accuse the other of a lack of 'openness') they make five demands: *firstly*, that the Society should 'seek out, encourage and present the work of the many groups practising in Great Britain. *Secondly*, it should extend its work beyond the premises and 'initiate community events, whether centred in a village, a commune, an adventure playground, or even where poetry is merely an element in a festival': *thirdly*, to avoid continuity of control, 'the entire General Council [should] stand for election each year' (with postal votes being acceptable): *fourthly*, *Poetry Review* should be edited by 'an editorial board of five' (to reverse its current status as 'an anthology of bad verse'), and *fifthly* the Poetry Society should 'support the publication and distribute to its mailing list an alternative review which would be representative of the best poetry in the British languages.' The first two of these demands are unexceptionable, if perhaps somewhat quixotic (the 'Merrie Britain' of villages, communes, adventure playgrounds, and festivals sounds like a vanished idyll), but the last three seem a rather amateurish recipe for permanent destabilisation—re-electing the whole Council every year, editing the journal by committee, and setting up an alternative journal which seems to have exactly the same aims as the first are not moves likely to bring about 'stability. The frequent mentions of 'Great Britain' and 'British' are presumably a reaction against the perceived dominance of *Poetry Review* by American poets.

Meanwhile, the Arts Council's monitoring of the Poetry Society's activities continued, involving the counting of attendances at readings: of course, the absolute reliability of these figures cannot be verified, but all the same, these documents give some insight into the nature and scale of the Society's activities. On 8th October 1975 Michael Mackenzie sends a note to Charles Osborne giving attendances at the early part of the autumn programme:

> Dear Charles, Thank you for being so kind as to remind me that we had agreed to keep you informed of the attendances at readings. Numbers for 'Scottish double event':

> Fri 26 Sept
> Sorely MacLean / Iain Crichton Smith   65 people

> Sat 27th Sept
> DM Black/Marcella Evaristi/Angus Nicolson   40 people

A further letter (22nd December) details the attendance at the remainder of the year's programme:

3/Oct Pierre Joris/Robert Vas Dias	75
10/Oct Allen Fisher/Bill Griffiths	36
17/ Oct Ulli McCarthy/Neil Oram	40
24/ Oct Roland John/Stan Trevor	45
25/ Oct Jeremy Adler/Andrew Lloyd/John Rowan	30
31/ Oct R.D.Laing	85
7/ Nov John Hall/Martin Thom	52
14/Nov David Tipton/Jeremy Hilton	45
21/ Nov Brian Morley/Paul Brown	43
22/ Nov Paul Selby/David Miller/Ian Patterson	32
28/ Nov Nikos Stangos	80
5/ Dec Basil Bunting	75
12/DecPeter Redgrove	38

Also 'Celebrations' (Thursday series): upwards of 60 for Harwood's 'Langland'

In October 1975 the *Times* journalist Philip Howard began his coverage of the story of the disputes within the Poetry Society with a page two piece headlined 'Nation's poets let slip the dogs of war' (7 October 1975). It announced that 'unpoetic and discordant things' had been going on at the 'official organisation of English bards' and that a reform committee had produced a four-point manifesto intended to 'democratise the society and prevent its being run by an unrepresentative clique'. The chair of the reform committee was David Lovibond ('who works for IPC magazines') who declared 'our intention is to bring poetry back to the people'. The group wanted to 'replace six specific people on the general council', and to replace Eric Mottram as editor of *Poetry Review* with 'an editorial board of five'. They claimed that in retaliation for publishing the manifesto 'two groups of poets, 'Poetry Round' and 'Poets' Workshop', had been forced out of the society's headquarters' and 'forced to take refuge with their rhymes and assonances and dissonances in the Black Bull public house at Fulham'. The Society's chair, Laurence Cotterell was reported to be maintaining a stance as an 'ecumenical chairman' and remaining neutral amidst this 'mixture of noble aspirations and emotional talk'. In a letter to the *Times*, 1st November 1975, from George Wightman, some detail emerged about how exactly the Reform Group proposed to 'take poetry to the people': he wrote that 'the Poetry Society' (though actually it was the reform committee within the Poetry Society) had recently put forward the recommendation that the Arts Council 'should fund one or more poetry sales vans which would call on colleges, libraries, and other potential customers'. It is pleasant to imagine teachers and librarians rushing out into the street with their cheque books on hearing the chimes of the poetry van, but the idea is less practical than the second recommendation, which is that a public Poetry Resources Centre be set up. The rules of the Poetry Society allowed for an Extraordinary General Meeting to be requisitioned if desired by 'members of the Society constituting no less than 10% of the membership' (around 96 people, as the membership now stood at around 960). The Reform Group achieved this (a considerable achievement, in fact), and notification and papers for an EGM were sent out by Secretary Michael Mackenzie on 20th November 1975, the meeting being fixed for 10th January 1976 at St Luke's Church Hall in SW10, a walk of about ten minutes from the National Poetry Centre at Earls Court.

While the plot was thickening in these summer and early autumn months at the Poetry Society, the work on *Poetry Review* went ahead. On 16th June Basil Bunting sent a brief typed note to Mottram with the beautiful short poem 'At Briggflatts Meeting House': his note says 'I sit anxiously, waiting for the editor-regrets note', and he adds of the poem that 'It's been read to the meeting, otherwise virgin'. The 'meeting' in question was his 75th birthday celebration at the Poetry Society, mentioned earlier. It appeared in *Poetry Review*, 65:4 in 1975, the only piece by Bunting to be published in the journal, and it is a poem that ranks alongside Wordsworth's 'Lucy' poems, with which it has affinities of both theme and scale. The speaker, seated within this tiny building which was built for reflection, reflects on the passage of time, or rather, feels the passage of time, and the self sifted through and by it. The poem in Bunting's *Collected Poems* (OUP, 1978) is printed as the last of an eleven-poem set called 'Second Book of Odes', and the last two of its three verses read:

> Stones indeed sift to sand, oak
> blends with saints' bones.
> Yet for a little longer here
> stone and oak shelter
>
> silence while we ask nothing
> but silence. Look how clouds dance
> under the wind's wing, and leaves
> delight in transience.

Perhaps its tone and sentiment could equally be described as 'Hopkinsesque', the Hopkins who said of himself in 'The Wreck of the *Deutschland*' 'I am soft sift/ In an hourglass-at the wall/ Fast, but mined with a motion, a drift.' The poem is like the last echo of that intensely stark Poundian lyricism which Bunting was heir to, a lyricism which had its roots deep in the nineteenth century. Certainly this is one of the poems which (in Bunting's own words, though he did not say it of his own work) *Poetry Review* should be proud to have published.

65:4 also contained Barry MacSweeney's 'Black Torch', a longer piece on the Durham Miners' Strike of 1854. The typescript (in Mottram, 4/2/54–55) is accompanied by a note in red ink arranging to meet Mottram 'at Eltham Well Hall Station at 7.5 p.m. [sic] on Thursday . . . for a good natter and maybe listen to *Blood on the Tracks* over some after-dinner scotch.' Though the end was actually not far away, there were widespread feelings of general optimism on the 'BPR' side of the poetry divide, and indeed, some felt that a genuine breakthrough had been achieved and that really significant things were happening in British poetry. On 14th August poet Chris Torrance wrote to Eric Mottram:

> The new issue sounds really great. The names really ring through. What a platform *Poetry Review* has been for the *real* new poetry in the last few years, and Sinclair's book *Lud Heat* due any moment, to do for London again, from a different but essentially linked angle, what Fisher's book [*Place*] did—is—doing. For years London has been crying out for an 'open field' work, and now two of our best men are at it . . . I do feel more and more, especially after the conferences, that something is really happening here, and that a force is emerging. (Mottram, 4/2/52)

The conferences referred to here are those at the Polytechnic of Central London in 1974 (the occasion of Mottram's defining 'British Poetry Revival' essay). Iain Sinclair's *Lud Heat* and Allen Fisher's *Place* were the 1970s antecedents of the 'cult of London', as it might be called, which developed into the 1990s phenomenon of London 'psycho-geography', notably Sinclair's own later prose writing, and that of Peter Ackroyd, the 'biographer of London', who was much influenced by *Lud Heat*. But the editorial pressures continued: on 8th October, in a note accepting poems from Lyn Lifshin, Mottram wrote 'the hassles are appalling, but it's partly my own having been abroad' (Mottram, 4/5/52). This refers to his most recent trip, to Salzburg University in September, as a Faculty member for the long-established Salzburg Seminar in American Studies. Mottram had first participated in this in 1953, in Harry Levin's seminar on the symbolic novel.[11] On the same day (8th October 1975) a small box advertisement headed 'NATIONAL POETRY CENTRE' was placed in the *Times* seeking applications for the post of 'Director of the National Poetry Centre (and General Secretary of the Poetry Society) to implement directives of the Poetry Society's elected General Council and to initiate developments in accordance with the Council's policies. Salary by negotiation.' The American-born (but British-resident) writer Robert Vas Dias applied for the post, and at his request, Mottram agreed to be one of his referees (there is a copy of the CV in the Mottram archive in folder 4/3/1–11), but there isn't actually a Mottram reference in the Arts Council files. But Vas Dias's referees were illustrious: Allen Ginsberg sent a hand-written letter of recommendation from PO Box 582, Stuyvesant Station, NYC; British poet Michael Hamburger wrote from a residency at Boston University, and American poet Jerome Rothenberg sent an enthusiastic typed and professional recommendation from the University of Wisconsin. But within a year of Vas Dias's appointment, as he strove with some desperation to juggle the warring factions, Mottram and Vas Dias had fallen out, and the disagreements between the two became a theme of the final days. Meanwhile, an embarrassed letter of 12th November from Laurence Cotterell (Chair of the General Council) gives an indication of the extent of the 'hassles' Mottram had

---

[11]   John Gillard Watson, addendum to the John Calder and Clive Bush obituaries of Mottram in the *Independent*. The Salzburg connection with experimental British poetry was maintained by Salzburg lecturer Wolfgang Gortschacher's work on *Poetry Review* in his *Little Magazine Profiles: the Little Magazines in Great Britain 1939–1993*.

mentioned in the note to Lifshin. The letter expresses 'continuing confidence and support in the exacting task of editing *Poetry Review*', and continues:

> An apology is due and overdue for the offensiveness to which you were subjected when taking the chair at a recent meeting here. This sort of thing on our premises shames us all . . . I am told that you soldiered on and rode it all out admirably. (Mottram, 4/3/1–11)

A press release announced that Robert Vas Dias would take over from Michael Mackenzie as General Secretary of the *Poetry Society* and Director of the National Poetry Centre on Monday 29th December 1975. The new year of 1976 would take the conflict at the Poetry Society to new levels of bitterness and ferocity.

3

The Empire Bites Back: 1976

'Frizzled Lampshades to the Socket Harvest'

Poets Conference scheduled its fourteenth meeting to take place on 9th January, going into Saturday 10th, when they would meet at 10 a.m. to discuss the Poetry Society EGM, which was due at 2.30 p.m. on the same day. The Reform Group hoped to achieve its four aims at the EGM, these being, firstly, to remove six Council members (Jeremy Adler, Bob Cobbing, Allen Fisher, Bill Griffiths, Roger Guedalla, and Lawrence Upton) and, secondly, replace them with their own nominees, these being listed as:

James Sutherland-Smith, poet, teacher, Poets' Workshop member

David Jones, poet, economist, free-lance journalist

Julian Roberts, poet, film-director

David Lovibond, poet, works for IPC magazines, leader of Snowdonia Poets

Tim Coxe, poet, accountant, founder member of London Poetry Co-operative

Irving Weinman, poet, university lecturer in Eng. Lit., Committee [member] of Poets' Workshop.[1]

---

[1] Taken from a document in Mottram 4/3/13–14, headed 'Explanation of the movement for a Reformed Poetry Society', which had been sent out to Poetry Society members before the EGM.

The third aim was to replace the current editor of *Poetry Review* with an elected Editorial Board of five members, each of whom would require nomination by at least ten other members, with the names of the proposed Board members being circulated in advance of the relevant meeting. Members of the Editorial Board would not be allowed to publish their own poetry in the journal. The final aim was that half the members of the General Council should stand for re-election each year. This was the main 'platform' of the reformers.

Members arriving on the day for the afternoon's AGM found North London anarchist poet Bernard Kelly handing out his Dada Manifesto to those going in to St Luke's Hall; it was headed 'Split Peas for Hair-Brained Door-Mats'; it asks:

> Precisely who leads you, *en masse*, holding your frizzled lampshades between your false ears, to the socket harvest?

In the event, much of the socket harvest of the day would turn upon the significance of articles sixteen and twenty of the Poetry Society's constitution. When the reformers at the June 1975 AGM had demanded a poll or a show of hands on the matter of the editorship of *Poetry Review,* they had been told that such business required prior notification, but in fact article sixteen says that a resolution dealt with at a Council meeting by a show of hands may be decided by a poll if seven members present demand it. And article twenty says that if such a demand is properly made, then voting papers must be sent out to all members within seven days of the meeting, for return within a further fortnight. This is a very large procedural loophole, which made it inevitable that the day would not be decisive, and the only resolution put forward by the radicals sought to close the loophole, by proposing that 'All expenses incurred in taking a poll shall be borne by the persons demanding it.' Such persons would have to deposit a sum deemed adequate by the Secretary before the poll could be taken. The radicals urged members to vote 'Yes' to that resolution and 'No' to all the rest. In the event, the radicals won the day, since that resolution was carried and all the rest were defeated. Thus, all six proposed removals of radical members from the General Council were lost: all six of the sitting members being challenged were voted on separately, and the *closest* vote was 'Yes' (for removal), thirty one, and 'No', seventy nine. Hence, the proposed substitutions could not be voted on as there weren't any vacancies. The voting pattern on the remaining resolutions put forward by the reformers (showing the margin of defeat in each case) was:

1. An editorial Board, not an editor, for   'Yes', 34: 'No', 71
   Poetry Review?
2. Half the Council members to stand   'Yes', 33: 'No', 62
   down each year?
3. Limit continuous term on General Council to   'Yes', 31: 'No', 59
   four years?
4. Members to have right to inspect and make   'Yes', 41: 'No',47
   copies of accounts?
5. Elect Council members by poll, not show of hands? 'Yes,' 41: 'No', 47

However, the voting on the Radicals' own resolution (on making the proposers of membership polls pay for them) was very close: seventy two voted in favour and seventy against. The Chair proposed to carry this item to the next AGM, rather than referring it to a postal vote, and this was carried by ninety eight votes to twenty. However, all the voting which took place that day was immaterial, (as must have been foreseen by both sides) since the reformers had sufficient strength to ensure that a postal vote was demanded by seven members on all the resolutions put forward at the meeting. So the agony was to be prolonged, for another three weeks at the very least.

Both sides could send out information and argument to members in preparation for the postal vote (separately from the mailing containing the ballot papers) so a new flurry of activity now ensued. The reformers sent out a letter on a single side of foolscap, and the radicals sent a two-sided document, more densely argued, which went out on the 15th January. The reformers' document is undated, but must be later, since it seems to be written in answer to the points made by the radicals. The issues raised and contended can be set out under the various headings, as follows:

(1) *On cost*: the radicals say that what the reformers propose (a poll now, then another EGM, then another poll) will cost the Society more than £600: the reformers respond that it will cost no more than £100 in the present year.

(2) *On breadth of representation*: the radicals say that the Council has already been increased from twenty one to thirty; ten are already from

outside London, and a sub-committee is looking at ways of increasing this. Reformers respond that the radicals seem to believe in 'money first, then democracy', since charging for polls is a way of disenfranchising members.

(3) *On sacking six Council members:* the radicals say that no reasons are given or charges brought against the members they seek to oust—all six have been extremely active in putting on events, etc. The reformers respond that their 'strenuous' activities do not justify their disregarding members' wishes.

(4) *On editing:* the radicals say that the reformers' proposal to edit the journal by committee will render it worthless, and the proposed machinery is cumbersome, especially when there are 'some thirty thousand poems a year' to be edited. The reformers reply that what they actually intend is to rotate the editorship around the Editorial Board, so that each issue has a single editor.

(5) *On the term of office of Council members:* the radicals say that members of Council need to be able to follow through longer term projects and hence require a longer term of office; but in any case, the present average term is only three years. The reformers reiterate points about spreading democracy and avoiding 'packed' meetings making crucial decisions.

(6) *On the availability of information:* the radicals say that members are already free in practice to examine accounts and minutes, but concede that communicating with the wider membership has sometimes been inadequate—a new system of regular newsletters is being instigated.

The outcome of the postal vote was reported in the *Times* on 6 February 1976 ('Vote settles dispute in Poetry Society, by Our Arts Reporter'): about a third of the membership had taken part, and with 319 votes received, the vote for change was lost by 195 to 124. So there would be no gang of five to replace the editor of *Poetry Review,* and the six radical Council members would not be unseated and replaced by conservatives. However, the Council's counter-proposal, that any group requiring a postal ballot should pay for it themselves, did not get the necessary seventy five per cent majority required for any change in the Society's constitution—only fifty eight per cent voted for it. The Chair, Laurence

Cotterell, now optimistically proposed that the Society should get on with satisfying the nation's vast appetite for poetry readings. So the first serious attempt by the conservatives to retake the citadel of the Poetry Society had been beaten off. Effectively, this meant the end of the Reform Group, which had made a number of significant tactical errors. For instance, its platform seems (in retrospect) unpromising: seeking to replace specific Council members without debating or specifying any charges against them is not a very persuasive ploy, and the idea of a committee-edited journal sounds unconvincing. But the radicals' victory was a Pyrrhic one, since it merely ensured that a more effective oppositional body would later emerge.

While the outcome of the reformers' activities was still unresolved, another letter to the editor was published in the *Times* (24th January 1976): this referred to reports in the national press about 'a dispute at the Poetry Society between an extremist oligarchy on the General Council and a Reform Group which opposes them'. But the writers of the letter professed to draw back from taking sides, publicising their wish 'to dissociate ourselves from factions of any kind' (though I suppose that calling one of the parties in the dispute an 'extremist oligarchy' indicates pretty clearly where their sympathies lay). They wish (as 'long serving members of the General Council') to devote their energies instead to 'excellent work in schools, arts centres and regional arts associations throughout the country', which is clearly the 'poetry to the people' agenda of the Reform Group. The signatories are Alasdair Aston, Alan Brownjohn, John Cotton, Clifford Simmons, and George ('GBH') Wightman. This distinguishing of themselves from the Reform Group by evident sympathisers seems to anticipate the failure of the postal vote to secure the original group's aims, and signals the commencement of the second wave of opposition. In February, in accordance with the new policy of regular updating of the membership, the Poetry Society's Newsletter went out, giving the results of the ballot, and expressing the hope that the Society could now devote its major energies to its core business of promoting poetry, starting with a children's festival weekend in the first week of March.

The Arts Council's concerns about the Society were increased by the EGM and the subsequent postal vote, and a fresh proposal for a formal investigation (the first since 1974) was put forward at its Literature Panel meeting of 2nd February 1976. Instead of the £99.000 grant it was asking for, the Society would be offered £23.000, plus an allowance for inflation, and Alan Brownjohn (the only one of the three Arts Council

representatives which the Society's General Council had ratified) would
be asked to submit a report on the situation. Very sensibly, Brownjohn
hesitated (and eventually declined), daunted by the amount of work
such a report would involve, and the degree of hostility it was bound to
encounter.[2]

The meeting of the General Council on 28th February was too late to
be reported in the Newsletter: it was a significant one: the editorship of
Eric Mottram was confirmed for the next four issues, until spring 1977
(the maximum possible extension under the new rule which limited
editors to a term of twenty issues) and Peter Finch, formerly editor of the
journal *Second Aeon* (by the far the largest and most regular 'BPR' magazine) was elected as his successor.[3] The voting figures on the editorship
given in the General Council minutes are: Ewart, two; Finch, ten;
Abstentions, three. A now poignant-sounding note from poet Paul
Matthews to Mottram on 10th April 1976 reads 'Yes, do use those poems.
I'm sorry to hear you have been sacked' (Mottram, 4/2/61–63).

Meanwhile, David Lovibond continued his campaign against the
General Council in the press: on 1st March 1976 the *Times* had reported
(under the heading 'New aim to reform the Poetry Society') that, with
his followers, Lovibond 'has announced plans to take poetry to the
people'. The idea of the poetry van had been revived ('He plans in
the next few weeks to buy a van and start a countrywide tour'), but the
intention now seemed to be to bypass the municipal infrastructure of FE
colleges and libraries and make a direct assault on the public 'including
people at their factories and offices'. The group had also produced a
poetry magazine 'at a cost of £450', evidently an alternative *Poetry Review,*
which is criticised for devoting sixteen pages of a recent issue to the
work of three Council members. By contrast, his group would encourage
'the budding poet' with comments and criticism—perhaps something
was envisaged like the Poetry Society's current (2005) 'critical service',
known as 'Poetry Prescription', in which 'a team of established professional poets send you constructive advice, specific to your personal abilities', as evidenced in up to one hundred lines of poetry sent in by the
user of the service. The group also hoped to set up regional branches of

[2] On one occasion, he reported to the Witt Panel later in 1976, the atmosphere at a
Council meeting was such that he had suggested to George Wightman that the
two of them should leave the Poetry Society premises together rather than singly.

[3] This information comes from the Chairman's Report at the June 1976 AGM of the
Poetry Society.

the Society 'from which members would be elected to serve on the council', thus lessening the possibility of power being seized by an unrepresentative group. These efforts were clearly aimed at devolving power in the Society away from the centre and re-emphasising the 'pedagogic' mission: the 'poetry school' and the 'workshop' operated by the group are mentioned again, and there is a sense that the piece mainly serves to remind the public that there is unfinished business at the Poetry Society: the electoral system requires a third of the Council to stand for re-election each year (that is, seven of the twenty one members): the Council had noted points for discussion and action at its last meeting, and 'at the annual meeting in June they will try again to push through their reform proposals.'

A further *Times* piece a few days later (5th March 1976), this time over the signature of Kenneth Gosling, has the same basic material, but a somewhat more belligerent tone. It expresses Lovibond's view that 'the recent upheavals over the composition and management of the Poetry Society are by no means over'. He and his supporters 'intend to keep the war going on a number of fronts until they can push their reform ideas again at the annual meeting in June'. The Society has become 'too esoteric', poetry has to become 'more accessible to the public, including workpeople at their factories and offices'. In the next four weeks they hope to make a start, 'to buy a van, visit places like Aberdovey and hire a hall, get people like Ford's interested in our work'. Lovibond 'and his group of adherents, working from the 'Black Bull' in Islington [had this pub migrated from Fulham?] and operating a poetry school and workshop, insist that they are not trying to bring down the Society . . . Poetry, they hope, will never be the same again.'

Laurence Cotterell, as Chair of the Poetry Society, was alarmed at the pattern of publicity which was giving the impression that the Society had no interest in an agenda concerned with bringing poetry to the people, and he responded with a letter in the *Times* of 8th March 1976 emphasising the 'outreach' elements of Poetry Society work: he mentions the Society's 'National Poetry Secretariat' which 'arranges about a thousand poetry readings and events each year, involving groups of every conceivable kind, and employing most of the leading poets of our day as well as a host of young, emerging writers.' He comments on the Society's work in schools and 'the Association of Little Presses, housed at this centre, since they now produce seven-eighths of all the new poetry issued in this country': he welcomes anyone interested to Poets Forum, 'which takes place here at 7.30 pm . . . every alternative Thursday', and invites aspiring poets to 'use the facilities of the print-shop at this centre to produce their own book, at no cost except that of the materials used.' He ends by calling for a record turnout at the AGM on 12 June, and saying that the Society can only achieve representative administration of its affairs by the votes of its members, 'not the rhetoric of dissidents, who have been defeated in their aims by the very postal poll of the entire membership they were so insistent on demanding—after losing every resolution at the extra-ordinary general meeting they had also demanded.' On 19th March, Lovibond published an article in the weekly journal *Tribune*, criticising what had been happening at the *Poetry Society*, and reiterating the points and demands already described here (of course, it may have been sent to *Tribune* before the January EGM or the February poll had taken place). Bob Cobbing published an article in reply a fortnight later (*Tribune*, 2nd April), under the heading 'The Poetry Society *is* doing its job'. He outlined the range of activities (printing, publishing, readings, etc) being put on at the Society, emphasised the cost and time-consuming nature of the reformers' challenges (all of which had been debated and defeated both at an Extraordinary General Meeting, and in a postal ballot), and stressed that the leader of the Reform Group 'joined the Society less than six months ago, and since then has not attended any activities or events of the Society apart from the occasional Poets Forum meeting. This is equally true of other members of that Committee.'

'Sabre-Toothed Politics'

It will be remembered that the EGM of 1974 had rejected Charles Osborne's demand that three Arts Council nominees be installed on the General Council of the Poetry Society. The Arts Council seems to have held fire while it remained possible that the Reform Group might succeed in wrenching control of the Poetry Society from the radicals, but after the January 1976 EGM, and the February postal vote, it was evident that this was not going to happen, so the Arts Council pressure again became more direct and overt. Further, from the Arts Council's point of view, not much could be hoped for from the forthcoming June AGM, since there was little likelihood that what had failed after an all-out effort in January would succeed in June. Charles Osborne was convinced that the only solution was to mount a formal investigation of the Society, and when Alan Brownjohn finally declined to undertake this (in April), he wrote to cultural historian Richard Hoggart (then Warden of Goldsmith's College), asking him if he would do it. Hoggart wanted more information about the scale of work likely to be involved, but finally declined, in a brief hand-written letter of 29th April.[4] Osborne then went back to the idea (first mooted in 1974) of asking Professor C. B. Cox to do it (even though his university duties had presumably not lessened since then), and when Cox had agreed over the phone to take on the job, the request was confirmed in writing on 19th May.[5] Osborne, in his capacity as Chair of the Literature Panel of the Arts Council, therefore announced an enquiry into the affairs of the Poetry Society to be chaired by Professor C. B. Cox of Manchester University. An Extraordinary General Meeting of the Poetry Society's Council took place on Sunday 23rd May to discuss the threatened investigation.[6] However, Osborne had neglected to secure the agreement of the Literature Panel itself, nor had he cleared the enquiry with the Arts Council first, and at the Literature Panel's meeting of Monday 24th dissent was expressed, again, by Elizabeth Thomas, who felt that 'this was jumping the gun', and that 'the matter should have been referred to the Panel for a decision on how to proceed . . . [An] investigation by outsiders ought to have approval of the Arts Council'.[7] Consequently, the Arts Council's own meeting, on Wednesday 26th, did not endorse Osborne's decision, and the enquiry had to be called off. Unfortunately, Cox had already started work: in a letter of 1st June 1976 he writes that he:

> Went through files on the Poetry Society and spent two hours at Earls Court Square last Wednesday afternoon. Poetry Society's journal *Poetry Review* is of low quality. I should recommend a system of guest editors such as Stephen Spender or D. J. Enright . . . . . Building is dilapidated and needs thousands of pounds spent. (ACGB/62/103, Box 2 of 10)

[4] The letter is in ACGB/62/103.

[5] The letter is in ACGB/62/103.

[6] See the document by Roger Guedalla headed 'the Report of the Arts Council of Great Britain in Mottram, 4/3/36–46.

[7] Minutes in ACGB/59/5, Box 2 of 7. Elizabeth Thomas was the Panel member responsible for literature in the regions, and she had opposed Osborne on a number of issues, including the heavy subsidy awarded to Ian Hamilton's *The Review* and *The New Review* (as reported in the satirical magazine *Private Eye*, and quoted in Osborne's *Giving it Away*, pp. 185–7).

Shortly after this, when the enquiry was discontinued, he wrote in irate terms about how badly he had been treated, claiming expenses for three London trips, and suggesting that he ought to be paid a fee for work he had already done. All these requests were quickly acceded to, with an air of embarrassment and cover-up.

So another announcement had to be made to the press on the 27th, stating that no such invitation had been extended, and this was reported in the *Times* of Friday 28th May 1976 under the headline 'Arts Council halts inquiry into Poetry Society'. The statement announcing that the Cox inquiry had been halted, however, also stated—somewhat ominously—that the Arts Council 'will now consider alternative measures'. Poets Conference registered all this in an information sheet about the Poetry Society AGM, due on Saturday 12th June. Sponsored candidates for the General Council (of those already members and seeking re-election) would be: Anthony Rudolf, Paige Mitchell, Ian Robinson, Roy Fisher, and Jeremy Adler. In addition, first-time candidates would be cris cheek, P. C. Fencott, Steve Clews, and Stan Trevor. Though it is not now going to investigate the Society, the document said, 'one wonders from which direction the [next] attack may come. Eternal vigilance is the only answer.' But before being duplicated, the sheet has had written on it large letters 'The investigation is Now On Again!' (Mottram, 4/3/36–46). Evidently, the 'alternative measures' had been considered very quickly by the Literature Panel, for it now announced—on 5th June, just a week before the Poetry Society AGM—that instead of an *external* enquiry there would be an *internal* enquiry, by a three-person panel consisting of Sir John Witt, Vice-Chair of the Arts Council, and Paddy Kitchen and Christopher Sinclair-Stevenson, both members of the Literature Panel. It is presumably because of these formal procedural moves against the radicals that Charles Osborne sees 1976 as marking the outbreak of civil war in the Poetry Society, but hostilities had, as we have seen, been going on for some time without a formal declaration of war. He writes in his memoir: 'It was during 1976 that a form of civil war broke out in the ranks of the Poetry Society. *At my instigation*, the Arts Council had investigated the Society and its affairs, and had produced a highly critical report' (*Giving it Away*, p. 204, my italics). Laurence Cotterell, as Chair of the Society, voiced his regret at Osborne's intervention, but was obviously finding the task of steering a middle course a hopeless one, and had already decided he would resign from the Chair and the Council at the AGM the following month.

As the date of the AGM approached, there was an acceleration in the pace of opposition to the radicals on the Society's Council. The essence of the next phase of development is that both these failed and distinctly 'amateurish' attempts to dislodge the radicals (namely, the failed Reform Group attack and the aborted Brownjohn/Hoggart/Cox Report) were re-constituted and renewed, but in a much more professional way. Firstly, the Reform Group (or Reform Committee), with its quixotic notions of driving its poetry van round the country (a kind of Ken Kesey fantasy), was replaced as the main opposition group by the Poetry Action Group, and secondly, the Cox inquiry, which had been instigated in a maverick and unconstitutional way, was replaced by the [Sir John] Witt Panel, which would investigate and report upon the Society's affairs. These developments were reported in two pieces in the *Times,* from Philip Howard on 1 June 1976, and Kenneth Gosling on 5 June. Howard's front page piece was headed 'Society in search of poetic peace': the Society has had a year of 'sabre-toothed politics and factionalism', he begins, but 'five long-serving and distinguished members of the society's General Council are launching a last-ditch effort to save the society from devouring itself and losing most of its members, what reputation it has left, and its Arts Council grant'. The 'five peacemakers' were sending out a postal appeal to all the Society's members to elect a 'moderate, tolerant, poetry-loving council' at the AGM on 12 June. The five Action Group members are the signatories of the *Times* letter of 24th January, showing that they had already lost confidence in the Reform Group at that early stage, and had determined to set up a more effective opposition. The five are identified as Alasdair Aston, poet and inspector of English for the Inner London Education Authority: Alan Brownjohn, poet and lecturer: John Cotton, poet and headmaster of Highfield School: Clifford Simmons, deputy director of the National Book League: George Wightman, poet and businessman.[8] This group, when compared with the five members of the Reform Group, has a distinctly 'professional' feel, and there is an emphasis upon their status as both practitioner poets and responsible professional individuals with strong affiliations to various cultural organisations. The letter sent by the 'Peacemakers' to the members concludes (as quoted by Howard):

> No one would deny that the extremists possess dedication. Nevertheless it is a stark fact that under their management the general council of the Poetry Society has lost the confidence of members, poets, poetry lovers, and sponsors.

[8]   As listed in Howard's Times article of 1st June 1976.

In response, Laurence Cotterell wrote again to the paper on 5 June, urging members to make their views felt by attending the AGM (at St Luke's Hall, Ifield Road, Chelsea) on 12 June: he again stresses the Poetry Society's record, hoping that it will not be obscured by 'unpoetic, humourless and ugly recrimination, whatever quarter it comes from.' Members should take 'an independent look at the candidates and their conduct' before deciding which are more concerned with poetry 'than with partisan philosophies and the scoring of sectarian points'. On the same day, a piece on an adjacent page in the same paper announced the Witt enquiry, adding that 'it is expected to report fairly quickly', which rather suggests that it had in fact already made up its collective mind on the major issues.

This, then, was the highly charged atmosphere in which the 1976 AGM took place. There were twenty five candidates, put up by the various factions, for the nine places available on the General Council: in addition, there were two Arts Council vacancies, for which there were three nominees. Some two hundred members were expected to attend (The *Times,* Saturday 12 June 1976, under the heading 'Poetry Society's council election today'). There are various accounts of the nature and outcome of this meeting: Andrew Duncan implausibly presents it as a victory for the radicals, because it saw the final defeat of the Reform Group (Duncan, p. 175): this is technically true, for in Philip Howard's *Times* report ('Victory for compromise at the Poetry Society', 14th June, 1976, p. 4), David Lovibond, founder of that group, is quoted, expressing 'his disappointment that none of his group's candidates was elected'. But the largely ineffective Reform Group, as we saw, had been superseded anyway as the main opposition group, and the five new members elected to the council were all nominated by the new opposition, these five being: 'Mr Laurence Baylis, Literature officer of the Greater London Arts Association; Anne Beresford, poet; Mr Gavin Ewart; Mrs Betty Mulcahy, examiner in the verse-speaking examinations run by the society, and author of books on speaking verse; and Mr Will Fulkin, editor of the poetry list at Penguin Books.' Additionally, two of the four council members re-elected 'included two poets who are founders of the Pacific Poetry Action Group [sic], Mr Alasdair Aston and Mr George Wightman.' So seven conservatives were elected, but only two radicals. The radical majority of 1975 was too big to overturn completely in a single year, but on Laurence Cotterell's calculation (in his written evidence to the Witt Panel a couple of weeks later) the 1976 AGM produced a Council with fourteen 'broadly activist' members (the 'radicals', in the terminology used throughout), and fourteen 'broadly centrist' (the 'conservatives'). On this basis, the balance of power would be held by the two Arts Council nominees. On the other hand, in place of the 'moderate' Chair, Laurence Cotterell himself, the poet Jeff Nuttall was elected, a man 'associated with the militant and exclusive modernists who rally around the flag of Mr Bob Cobbing, the concrete poet, and Mr Eric Mottram, the editor of *Poetry Review.*' So the day ended with a decisive win for neither side, but rather in a score draw, producing what Howard called 'a council that is better balanced between moderates and extremists of all varieties.' The balance was to prove a very precarious one, but however one looks at the events of this day, the unambiguous situation at the end of it is that the radicals are no longer in control. In retrospect, it can be seen that excluding 'Poetry Round' and 'Poets' Workshop' from the Poetry Society in 1975 (as described in detail in chapter eight) was perhaps the decisive event, because it ensured that the ineffective Reform Group opposition was superseded by the much better organised Poetry Action Group, which in turn secured a more evenly balanced Council in 1976. This reading of events, which sees the treatment of 'Poetry Round' as the deciding factor in the struggle is confirmed by a paragraph near the start of the Reform Group's 'Manifesto for a Reformed Poetry Society', which reads:

> The foundation of concern over the condition of the Society originated with fears that 'Poetry Round' might be closed—closed certainly to non-members of The Poetry Society. This incident gave rise to an examination of the whole structure of the Society, particularly the degree to which a small cabal is able to influence or control the direction and nature of functions as vital to the Society as is, for instance, *Poetry Review.*

The first meeting of the General Council after the June AGM was on Sunday 27th June at 2.30pm. This was the first GC chaired by Jeff Nuttall. The three officers were all radicals (Nuttall, Upton in the disputed role of Deputy Chair, and Cobbing as treasurer). In addition there were nineteen Council members, and four observers—two representatives of the Poetry Society's accountants, Robert Vas Dias as General Secretary, and Marjorie Barton as Director of the National Poetry Secretariat. The Chair opened with an uncompromising statement about the historic and political potency of poetry, now in a state of emergency because it was in danger of censorship by the literary establishment. In advancing the cause of neglected poetry, the Society had done some good things, 'an example of which was Eric Mottram's editorship of *Poetry Review.*' It had become clear that the majority of the General Council 'had the massive support of the membership, as indicated by the EGM and the postal vote.' The situation was that 'we have a militant position supported by the membership, and we owe it to the majority to support the membership's faith in us.' The Chair's speech is rather like the hurled defiance of the Thanes at the Battle of Maldon. Actually, the situation had changed a great deal since the EGM and the postal vote early in the year: the opposition were winning the propaganda war, and had outflanked the radicals at the AGM: the Witt investigation was already in train, and electing a Chairman who lived in distant Yorkshire was arguably another tactical error on the part of the radicals. Bickering over retrospective modifications of the minutes of the April General Council (mainly over allegations of financial irregularities) was another sign of weakness. The auditor pointed out that the audited accounts should have been circulated 21 days before the AGM (at which they had only been passed by the device of linking them up with the Chairman's annual report). Then 'Mr Cobbing expressed his resentment of the innuendo by Mr Wightman at the AGM and in the press that the treasurer's statement regarding the preparation of monthly accounts was "unsatisfactory."' It was proposed, seconded, and carried by ten votes to nine with four abstentions that Mr Wightman be publicly asked to retract the statement, but Mr Wightman refused. Mr Brownjohn proposed that written accounts be attached to the Executive and Management Committee meetings, and this was agreed. Clearly, then, in spite of the Chairman's heroic speeches, the reality of the situation was that the radicals could no longer secure the outcomes they wanted. In the elections which followed for Chairs of sub-committees, the radicals won those which were contested, as follows:

Publicity Committee: Angus Nicolson (eleven votes to seven)
National Poetry Secretariat Committee: Lee Harwood (twelve to nine)
Development and Fundraising Committee: Jeremy Adler (sixteen to seven)
Education Committee: Elaine Randell (thirteen to ten)

This seemed to further the pattern of the radicals controlling sub-committees, but beginning to lose control of the General Council.

The meeting then reverted to discussion of the disputed 1976 Treasurer's Report, and the ongoing feud between Cobbing and Wightman over the latter's accusations of financial irregularities against the former. Roger Guedalla proposed that Council members' fees and expenses be separately listed but this was defeated (by ten votes to seven). Following George MacBeth's resignation, candidates were put forward for co-option and cris cheek was elected (by eleven votes to six): there was further discussion of the role of Deputy Chair: George Wightman said the position didn't exist and a postal ballot of all members would be required to bring it into existence: Jeff Nuttall said the role was needed when the Chair lived far from London. Under 'AOB', Barry MacSweeney proposed that 'no Council member write, produce, or submit any article concerning the Society for publication without first securing the approval of the Publicity Committee'. In the discussion which followed a number of speakers objected to the proposal on the grounds that it 'represented a move to suppress dissent.' Mr Guedalla proposed that discussion be postponed, which was agreed. The meeting closed at 6.15pm. From the radicals' point of view this was a highly unsatisfactory and symptomatic day: none of their major proposals were carried through, and the only gain for them concerned the chairing of sub-committees. They were bogged down in retrospective wrangling, and over financial issues rather than issues of principle: their frustration had led them to seek to impose authoritarian restraints on free expression at the very time when they were opposing the Arts Council investigation on the grounds that it sought to do precisely that. The meeting, then, marks a significant turning point in the struggle.

Meanwhile, the poetry magazine produced by Lovibond's Reform Group 'at a cost of £450' as an alternative to *Poetry Review* had evidently been sent out to members, and was causing confusion in some quarters: Mottram received a letter from Tim Fletcher, sent on 8th June:

Dear Eric Mottram,

There seems to be some conflict amongst your editorship. I received a red *PS* as an alternative (?) to *Poetry Review*. Well, the red *PS* had some pleasant lyrical material which one can find in numerous booklets of its kind but the book was hardly embracing the frontiers of the poetic art. I would very much prefer the *Poetry Review* to carry on as it is, giving us a chance to read the more avant-garde poets. (Mottram, 4/2/52)

There is a copy of the 'red *PS*' referred to here in the Arts Council archive[9]: it is about four inches by six, with a plain red cover with

[9] In ACGB/62/103 (Box 3 of 10) in the folder 'Poetry Society Assessment, Miscellaneous papers/Press cuttings'.

the letter 'PS' in the lower right corner. The title page identifies it as 'PS (A Collection of Poetry) Edited by Padraic MacAnna assisted by an editorial board'. Published by the Reform Movement 1976'. The most notable pieces are by Jamaican poet James Berry (including 'Lucy's Letter', the title poem of his 1982 book *Lucy's Letters and Loving*) and Carol Rumens. The production of a '*Salon des Refusées*' in the form of this 'little red book' was symptomatic of the growing resistance to *Poetry Review* as it then was.

4

The Witt Investigation: 1976

'Then we had to Stand Trial'

The main effect of the upheavals of the first part of 1976 was the setting up a new system of sub-committees, with the particular aims of involving members in regions outside London, and keeping a much tighter rein on finances. The practice of staffing key elements of the Society, such as the print-shop and the bookshop, with volunteers from the membership was felt to be unsatisfactory, and it was agreed that new paid appointments would be made to carry out these roles. Also, a series of regular newsletters for the membership was instigated. In this sense, various important kinds of 'reform' were already underway before the Witt Panel investigation began.

The announcement of the new enquiry came too late to be included in the Poetry Society Chair's 1976 annual report (which had already been sent out to members ahead of the AGM), but the investigation had been announced at the meeting, and members were urged to forward comments on the Society to the Witt Panel. Robert Vas Dias, as General Secretary, sent out a general invitation to members on 2nd July to send their comments to the Arts Council HQ at 105 Piccadilly by 19th July. Members were invited to 'submit written comments on the nature and quality of the Society's activities generally, including in particular the following:

a) the poetry readings and events at Earls Court Square
b) the society's publications: *Poetry Review* and the *Newsletter*
c) Facilities available to members: e.g. Library, Print-shop, Bookshop, Bar
d) Information services

It was added that 'The Assessment Committee may subsequently wish to invite certain individual members to supplement their written statements by giving oral evidence.' The six terms of reference of the Witt Panel were to offer the Arts Council advice on:

1. The nature and quality of the society's activities, how competently these activities are carried out, and which of them are proper objects of Arts Council subsidy.
2. The degree of public and membership support for these activities.
3. How far the society's constitution is workable.
4. How it is run.
5. The number and quality of its staff.
6. How the Council's grant is applied.

As part of the 'fact finding' process, Witt Panel member Paddy Kitchen attended the workshop event run by the radicals and known as 'Poets Forum' on 24th June 1976, and sent an account to Sir John Witt the following day. She noted that twenty people attended the event, of whom thirteen read out a sample of their work; there was one American present, and the rest were amateurs (!):

> The work ranged from perfectly acceptable to execrable. Bob Cobbing was chairing the evening, and was courteous to everyone. He seemed rather good at getting shy people to read a poem for a second time if they made a bosh shot the first, or asking them to repeat one that was rather difficult to take in. We had a break in the middle, and since the bar was closed (I don't know why), went to the hotel next door [where] there is a small run-down bar worthy of a scene in a William Trevor novel. I rather liked it, and everyone was friendly. A lot of people were there for the first time. There was no evidence of a hard core of regulars representing any particular style. Indeed, what style there was (and there wasn't much) was just like any other British amateur poetry gathering.

Whether this should be taken as re-assuring evidence of the absence of hard-core bullying, or as a disturbing indication of a lack of excellence and dedication at Poetry Society events she does not say. The radicals' 'Poets Forum' was the series which had been made way for by ejecting 'Poets' Workshop' (a similar series run by the conservatives), and forcing it to conduct its business at the 'Black Bull' in Fulham. These matters are discussed further in chapter eight.

At the Arts Council, meanwhile, a programme was speedily drawn up for the 'hearings' which would supplement the written evidence which

members had been invited to send in. An internal Arts Council memo
set out the 'Time Table for Oral Evidence':

Monday 26th July
Michael Mackenzie (Former Secretary of the Poetry Society)   10.00
Robert Vas Dias   (Current Secretary)   10.45
Marjorie Barton   (Director of the National Poetry Secretariat) 11.30
Barbara Hill   (Assistant to the Secretary)   12.15

An additional memo ordered a 'cold luncheon to be served in the 6th
Floor dining room at 105 Piccadilly for the 4 panel members' at 1.00,
followed by:

Mrs Walsh, with Mr Walsh (Housekeeper at 21 Earls Court Square) 2.00
Eric Mottram   (Editor of *Poetry Review*)   2.45
Peter Finch   (Editor-elect of *Poetry Review*)   3.30
Charles Osborne   (Literature Director, Arts Council)   4.15

Most of those to be interviewed on this first day were selected 'ex officio',
so to speak, whereas the list for the next day mainly comprises members
of the various conservative groupings within the Society:
(G.B.H.Wightman, John Cotton, former Secretary, Muriel Austen,
Margaret Baylis, and Robert Vas Dias recalled). The hearings concluded
on Monday 2nd August with Alan Brownjohn, followed by a joint meeting with Lawrence Upton and Bob Cobbing.

The timings, again, were tight: the letter asking Mottram to attend on
the 26th was sent on the 16th July: his reply, typed on King's College,
London notepaper, makes his views clear: his feelings about poetry and
professionalism have evidently been affronted by the fact that there is
little evidence of relevant expertise on the part of the panel members:

Dear Sir John Witt,

Thank you for your letter of July 16. I accept the Arts Council's invitation,
but I would like on the occasion of my visit to be able to speak to a good
deal more than *Poetry Review*, and I would also be grateful to you if you
could ask your secretary to forward me details of the professions and
interests of the members of the assessment panel, since I have no idea
who they are or what they do for a living: i.e. why they have been chosen
for such an important task.

Yours sincerely,

No response was sent to this request. The Arts Council's own record of the meeting begins with Sir John Witt's reference to Mottram's letter of acceptance:

> The Committee had been a little surprised at the tone and content at Mr Mottram's letter of acceptance of the Committee's invitation, and of his questions of the Committee's credentials. He then asked if he was right in thinking that Mr Mottram had worked in American universities from time to time. Mr Mottram showed anger and reluctance to answer the question but Sir John Witt went on to say that as they were conducting an enquiry into the Poetry Society, and one of its activities was the *Poetry Review,* of which Mr Mottram was Editor, the Committee would like to know the background of the Editor. Mr Mottram then agreed to reply and told the Committee that he had been a Visiting Professor at the University of New York, a guest of the State Department, and on the strength of that he was invited to be Visiting Professor of the University of New York at Buffalo in 1968 and again in 1972. These positions had been concerned with American and English Literature. He himself had been educated at Cambridge.

Mottram was then asked 'to expound a little' on his philosophy as editor: he gave the usual figures about the number of issues he had edited, the numbers of British and American poets published, the number of different presses which had published their work, and the list of languages from which translated poems had appeared. It seemed to him, he said, a fair coverage and quite an extraordinary variety. Again, it must be said, this kind of numerical totting up doesn't really seem the best strategy in these circumstances. He went on to stress the fact of the insecurity of his tenure: he was not given any mandate by the Society, and sometimes he was working on a three months' notice basis, and had then inconsistently been asked to be editor for three years, and was finally told he 'had got the boot' and had only a few more issues left—the five years/twenty issues tenure had only recently been adopted as policy: 'Mr Mottram appeared not to know that an editor (Mr Peter Finch) had been chosen to succeed him'. He went on to say that the magazine had been in a bad state when he took over, with a handful of poets in power: Paddy Kitchen interjected to ask which poets these were, and he named Anthony Thwaite, Peter Porter, George MacBeth, and Charles Osborne. These poets were published in hard covers by Chatto and Faber and appeared in MacBeth's BBC poetry programmes, but 'did not adequately represent the poetry of the world.' He went on to reiterate his conviction of the strength of the current British poetry scene, and his feeling that *Poetry Review* had only 'had a stab at it' as far as representing it was concerned.

Sir John Witt then cited some of the criticisms that had been made of the journal under Mottram—it 'covered too local a field and lacked more traditional work', it 'contained American propaganda' [sic]; it was criticised because it 'included a remarkable number of people from the General Council', 'people greatly regretted the exclusion of reviews', and 'a number of them deplored the present format as being shoddy'. In reply, Mottram attributed the shoddiness to lack of finance, insisted that he printed work because he thought that it was good, not because it was by members of the General Council. Paddy Kitchen asked what assistance the editor most needed, given ideal circumstances, and he replied that he thought the relationship between paid and voluntary workers was one of the problems—it was impossible to ask voluntary workers to do something by certain dates. Josephine Falk wondered what contact he had with the General Council, and Mottram said that he mainly went through the Publications Committee. He had recently proposed printing four poets in each issue, 'under the editorship of someone selected by the Publications Committee, because this would give the Editor a break and make the range bigger. A good idea, he felt, would be to publish six or eight pages of each poet so that people could get to know what the poet was about. Sir John Witt then cut in, saying that he felt the National Poetry Centre should reflect public taste, and did it worry Mr Mottram that there was no space for reviews? Mottram referred again to the idea of publishing two magazines 'in harness' (one with the poetry and the other with the information), but there hadn't been enough money to do it. He concluded by saying that the fact that there was a print-shop and a bookshop at the NPC was something that was not happening anywhere else in the world, and he deplored the Arts Council setting up an investigation of the NPC.

Mottram's own accounts of this hearing are—as would be expected—extremely embittered. In his diary for that day he wrote:

> At 2.45, interrogated rudely by Sir John Witt and his band [?] at Arts Council at 105 Piccadilly. I've never been treated so vulgarly and rudely. Apart from that, the whole affair was badly conducted and the questions showed no homework done at all. Peter Finch was asked [?] & Bob Cobbing and Lawrence Upton both [?] met him and were waiting for me—which was comforting. . . . I fear the Arts Council grant is lost, though.[1]

[1] Mottram Archive, BM1/1/22.

He replied to a letter from Roger Guedalla on 4th January 1977, referring back to the June 1976 hearing:

> At the investigation, that committee knew nothing about British poetry, nothing about *Poetry Review*, nothing about my own qualifications—which they began by actually questioning. When I asked them precisely what their qualifications were, they became extremely angry and vulgar. . . . You must also know that I was personally treated like dirt off the street by Witt and the other two members of the investigatory inquisition; their questions were of the utmost insolence, and the presence of Falk was permitted even when I asked that she should be removed, since she was not a member of the committee and only there as Osborne's secretary and spy.

Mottram talks again about this hearing, years later, in his 'North and South' interview, making very obvious his undiminished feeling that he had been insulted and belittled by people he regarded as nonentities:

> Then we had to stand trial. We were required to appear before Sir John Witt, some lawyer or other, Paddy Kitchen, an obscure children's writer, who became Chairman of the Poetry Society afterwards, and some other hireling, and answer questions. I had to appear before this board, and was treated like dirt. I was accused of only publishing my friends. I said 'You mean all 121 of them? Some of whom are dead?' What exactly do you mean?' But the idea was just that I was to be treated like filth. In fact I was very unnerved by the occasion. Fortunately Bob and somebody else were downstairs at 105 Piccadilly, where the Arts Council hangs out, and were very supportive. I was feeling very shaky after this nastiness.[2]

The bitterness at the way he had been treated remained with Mottram and remained unchanged. In 1978, while it was all still raw, he went along to the launch of the Oxford University Press edition of Basil Bunting's *Collected Poems,* and an unfortunate encounter took place:

> A ghastly person called Josephine Fox [Falk], who was Charles Osborne's assistant, and was at that trial that interrogated me, was there. She comes marching across and says 'I wonder if you remember me?' I said 'Yes I do. Fuck off, you bitch!' 'Oh' she says. I said 'Yes, oh'. (*Prospect into Breath,* p. 40).

The Witt Panel took oral evidence from twenty people: these individual hearings were set up after the 223 written replies had been received,

---

[2] *Prospect into Breath,* North and South, 1991, p. 38.

when the Panel 'invited certain people to supplement their written replies by coming and giving oral evidence to us'. Most of these invitees were also office-holders, people who would naturally and quite properly be the core of any investigation: the list given on page three of the report reads:

Laurence Cotterell	(Chair, 1975–6)
Jeff Nuttall	(Chair, 1976–7)
Lawrence Upton	(Deputy Chair)
Bob Cobbing	(Treasurer)

Members of the General Council
Laurence Baylis
Alan Brownjohn
John Cotton
Roger Guedalla
Clifford Simmons
George Wightman

Robert Vas Dias	(General Secretary)
Michael Mackenzie	(Former General Secretary)
Marjorie Barton	(Director of the National Poetry Secretariat)
Barbara Hill	(Assistant to the General Secretary)
Mary Walsh (with Mr Walsh)	(Housekeeper at 21 Earls Court Square)
Muriel Austen	(Part-time librarian at the Poetry Centre)
Eric Mottram	(Editor of *Poetry Review*)
Peter Finch	(Editor-elect of *Poetry Review*)
Charles Osborne	(Literature Director of the Arts Council)

The six non-office-holding members of the General Council form the slightly anomalous group here: in his written evidence to the Panel, former Poetry Society Chair Laurence Cotterell tentatively listed the General Council elected at the June 1976 in two groups, one headed 'Broadly Activist' and the other 'Broadly Centrist', both containing fourteen names. Of the six interviewed by the Witt Panel, only one—Roger Guedalla—is on the 'Activist' side of the division, and he was in fact an office-holder, being 'Chairman of the newly formed Regional Activities Committee' (as his written evidence to the Panel had indicated); indeed, later bitter correspondence between Mottram and himself (which I will discuss) makes it clear that Mottram regarded him as a 'collaborator' rather than an activist. Hence, all five non-office-holding members of the General Council interviewed by the Witt Panel were conservatives (or 'centrists' in Cotterell's terminology), and indeed one of them (Alan Brownjohn) was the Arts Council's own nominee on the Poetry Society's General Council. It could be argued that there was an element of imbalance in the range of sources from which oral evidence was taken. Of course, part of the reason for the imbalance is that many of the activists distrusted or despised the investigation which had been set up: the investigating panel had no recognisable expertise in contemporary British poetry and two of the three were members of the Arts Council's literature panel with which the Poetry Society was in dispute. Many, therefore, believed that they would compromise their principles by giving their views to the Panel, either in writing or orally. All the same, one might argue that the Panel still had a duty to ensure that both viewpoints were adequately represented in all categories of evidence taken.

Cotterell goes on to make shrewd comments on a number of the main protagonists—Cobbing he sees as having 'a streak of an early Quakerism in him. I believe him to be absolutely sincere and, like Robespierre, a sea-green incorruptible. On the other hand, he is capable of a considerable Machiavellianism to gain ends which he truly considers best for poetry and the poets and the poetry lovers.' Another former Chairman invited to provide written evidence was John Cotton, who had been Chairman for three years: he had stayed on partly to act as a buffer between the paid staff and the elected officers: 'For example, I can vividly remember a long and acrimonious meeting demanding the dismissal of the Director of the National Poetry Secretariat when she had only been with us for a few weeks. Her "crime" being that she had expressed some ideas of her own'.

A Scottish member (himself running a small press) responded to the invitation to give evidence by making particular reference to the printing facilities supposedly available to poets at the National Poetry Centre. He writes:

> It is quite unacceptable for the output of the 'Print Workshop' to be almost exclusively that of Council members and their friends or published by their presses. On two occasions friends of mine who live in Scotland wrote in advance to the PS saying that they would be in London on particular dates and asking that they be allowed to use the equipment. This is supposed to be permissible and is widely held up to be one of the things the PS do for the good of poets everywhere. Both friends wrote on more than one occasion, rang up, etc, yet got no answer by post or

satisfactory answer by phone. On arrival in London they went to the PS and were told that they couldn't use any of the equipment till 'next week'. Needless to say, they were unable to do so, though one did come back 'next week', only to be told to come back 'this evening'—the PS was closed that evening.

Waiting for the End

In the strange atmosphere of the period when the Witt Panel had completed its investigation but had not yet published its findings, the Poetry Society met again, on Saturday 11th September, chaired by Jeff Nuttall, and the strains evident at the June meeting were now even more apparent. There was some confusion about the minuting of this meeting: the minutes in the Arts Council's archive[3] are signed by 'E.P.' and dated September 20th 1976, but 'E.P.' notes that 'I attended the meeting in the belief that I was only an observer' and was only later asked to take on this role. It is noted at the start that 'the atmosphere of aggression and abuse in which the meeting was conducted was not helpful to a clear memory of the proceedings but such notes as I have been able to make are, I hope, accurately recalled.' Again, there were disputes about the minutes of the previous meeting: the resignation of Peter Finch was accepted (he had resigned in order from the Council in order to be able to take up the editorship of *Poetry Review*); the two vacancies on the Council were contested by Carol Buckroyd, Roy Fisher, and Ken Smith, with the latter two being elected (both sympathisers with the radicals). Under the heading of the Editorship of the *Newsletter*, it was recorded that the last meeting of the Publication and Media Committee had decided that Robert Vas Dias's editing of this had been 'unsatisfactory' and that in future he should edit it in conjunction with Ian Robinson and Lawrence Upton. 'This he declined to do, contending that his position as Secretary should allow him independent action in this matter. After much discussion the Chairman suggested that for a trial period Mr Vas Dias should edit the newsletter with the advice and assistance of Mr Robinson. This Mr Vas Dias agreed to do.' This, of course, continued the pattern of the radicals seeming to want to stifle any dissent, and is indicative of their unawareness of the negative effects of using the newsletter for partisan purposes. On the next item of the Chairman's Report, there was further discussion of the amount of independence the

3   In ACGB/62/103.

Secretary should have. The Council wanted him to consult them on every action taken, and they went further, arguing that 'It was decided that the title of Director of the National Poetry Centre was a misnomer, that such a title should never have been bestowed, and that Mr Vas Dias should act only on the resolutions of the General Council.' This, of course, would quickly make the Secretary's position untenable—he had been appointed to a salaried post which included 'Director of the National Poetry Centre' as part of its role and title.

The Chairman then put forward his idea of a manifesto for the Poetry Society and read out the draft to the meeting:

> General and animated discussion followed the reading of this manifesto, criticism being especially directed against item 6, in its political aspect, and item 9, by Messrs Simmons and Ewart and Mrs Mulcahy. There were many extremely prejudiced statements as to the sort of poetry the Society should encourage. In the charming phraseology of Mr Barry MacSweeney 'We want no Kingsley-f . . . ing-Amis here.' It was finally decided that a Manifesto should be published, based in principle on the Chairman's draft proposals, but possibly modified by suggestions from members of the General Council, to be received within two weeks from the meeting.

Yet the final Manifesto (see 'Documents, 3') is a document of some stature: its crisp and austere rhetoric carries conviction, it seeks memorable ways of expressing large aspirational principles, and it does not confine itself to parochial aspects of the Poetry Society. Indeed, its strength lies in the way it relates those apparently parochial struggles and rivalries to these bigger and more abiding issues. The (to some Council members) worrying item 6 of the manifesto (on the political function of poetry) reads in the final version:

> That poetry enjoys a direct social function in the perpetual alteration of the status quo; that it is the source of philosophical, moral, aesthetic, and therefore political change; that in order to function as source it must remain free of existing ideologies and dogma.

Here it is perhaps the word 'direct' which would make one pause: not even Shelley in 'An Apology for Poetry' went that far, contenting himself with the view that poets were the *unacknowledged* legislators of the world, and never (so far as I know) suggested that his fellow poet Lord Byron ought to be taking his seat in the House of Lords as an *acknowledged* legislator. Likewise, Coleridge distrusted literature which has a 'palpable design' on us, and Matthew Arnold, in 'The Function of

Criticism at the Present Time', wanted an aloofness from practice, which he saw as the source of the moral authority of literature. It simply seems a contradiction to impose a 'direct social function' on poetry, and at the same time to say that 'it must remain free of existing ideologies and dogma.'

Item 9 is about poetic form, and in its final version it reads:

That the belief in the absolute validity and predominance of traditional forms be granted its rightful place in the Society as the interesting and unique reaction against poetry which it is.

This is a somewhat baffling formulation, but it seems deliberately calculated to be so: at first it seems to be a resounding and surprising proclamation of faith in traditional poetic form: then, on second reading, it seems to be saying merely that the belief in traditional poetic forms must be tolerated and respected in the Society, on the grounds that such beliefs and their concomitant practice have their place: but on third reading, it seems to be making the uncompromising radical proclamation that the belief in traditional poetical forms is actually a reaction *against* poetry. But if this is so, it isn't clear how such a reaction can be called 'interesting'—what *interest* could it have?—nor is it clear in what way it could be said to be 'unique'. Elsewhere, the document uncompromisingly equates innovation with value, and puts forward a useful notion of the 'usable past'. It enthrones the individual imagination as the ultimate court of appeal, describes poetry as a 'visionary art', and extends its realm beyond the merely verbal. In short, there is plenty in it which remains worthy of detailed discussion, and it is, in all these respects, far superior to the Reform Group's Manifesto of the previous year.

On the other hand, it would be difficult to come up with a less suitable time and place for launching such a document, and the whole episode reinforces the sense that the Battle of Earls Court is now following the pattern of the Battle of Maldon—the radicals already know that the battle is lost, and they are pushing their demands and their rhetoric to extremes so as to provoke the final end. But the meeting wasn't yet over:

In the midst of this animated discussion about the nature of poetry and poets, a small man who had been sitting mute during the whole of the meeting, now rose to his feet and declared that in his opinion as an expert, the dry rot had advanced to such a point that he would not be surprised if the entire building collapsed! He proved to be a surveyor co-opted to attend the meeting to give his professional views on the dry rot, and was clearly unable to restrain his impatience until Any Other Business was reached.

It is a richly elegiac and emblematic moment, as the poets carried on their animated discussion about the role of poetry in society, oblivious to the fact that the whole building might collapse around them at any moment. It was followed by the report of the Deputy Chairman:

> Mr Lawrence Upton, in the course of a hectoring and aggressive report, said that all the members at that moment present at the Meeting could not be friends; that the members elected at the AGM to give a better balance to the Council would not do that; and that he felt that many people would resign if things continued that way. He attacked members of the Council for not helping with the work of the Society, and suggested a rota scheme whereby all Council members could assist in the work.

The events prophesised here (the mass resignations) would be fulfilled within a couple of months, and the new Chair's speech on the occasion of that final walk-out would reiterate some of Upton's points about the impossibility of holding a 'balanced' Council together. For today, there was yet more to come, with the Treasurer's report:

> He said that in the event of the Arts Council deciding against any further support of the Poetry Society, a sum almost equivalent to the grant could be saved by cutting out the National Poetry Secretariat readings and the salary of the General Secretary, thus allowing the Society to continue in business. At this point the Chairman mentioned that he had heard rumours that the Arts Council might remove the NPS and its Director from the Poetry Society and bring it to the Arts Council. What, asked the Chairman, would be Miss Barton's reaction to that suggestion? Miss Barton cannily replied that she would wait until such a suggestion were actually made to her.

The attacks on Robert Vas Dias and Marjorie Barton seem designed to provoke *their* resignations, and there was another sting under 'AOB'. Bob Cobbing asked how much had been spent on printing that could have been done in the Poetry Society print room if the staff had not gone on strike.' Mr Vas Dias gave the figure of £55.' Roger Guedalla proposed that a record be kept of how much Council members claimed in expenses. 'At this point Mr Cobbing bellowed "NO!!" But too late; the motion had been passed.' So ended the meeting.

A press release about the 'New Manifesto of the Poetry Society' was issued by Robert Vas Dias on 1st October. It was presented as 'a bid to rally members of the Poetry Society to the progressive position which characterised it in its early days, when it published the work of such figures as Ezra Pound . . . The Manifesto represents a constructive effort to resolve recent partisan disputes by emphasising aesthetic objectives for the Society in years to come.' But the Manifesto itself was never circulated to members as the Council meeting had agreed, and this was later seen as evidence that hidden influences were now in control of policy. Poets Conference re-issued the document in November 1977, called for a poets' boycott of the Poetry Society and adopted the manifesto as its own, stating that 'This Manifesto was passed by the Society's General Council at its meeting on September 11th 1976 and circulated to the press on October 1st. Yet it has never been published to Society members. Why not? Who took exception to it? The answer to this lies in the acceptance by the Society of the Report of the Arts Council's Assessment Committee.'

Judgement Day

The early drafts of the Witt report were being circulated between the three panel members by mid August 1976, with Josephine Falk at the Arts Council as the intermediary. On 9th September a letter from John Witt in Scotland to Josephine Falk indicates that it is in an advanced state of preparation, and puts a series of questions, to which she has pencilled in responses: for example '(2) We should find out from Vas Dias the result of his demarche over the editorship of the Newsletter', against which she has written: 'Vas Dias + 1 Council member, but attempt to demote his status—not Director'; her pencilled reply to Witt's question was obviously written after the 11th September Council meeting, to which it refers. Then '(3) We need to have details of expenses paid to voluntary workers', against which is pencilled '£717 as against £250 last year'. (5) Asks whether they have seen all the Chairmen of committees: 'We have seen Guedalla; ought we to see more, and if so whom?' The pencilled note mentions Ian Robinson, Lee Harwood, Allen Fisher, Angus Nicolson, and Elaine Randell. These are all Chairs who were supporters of the radicals, and seeing them would have redressed the imbalance evident in the list of oral interviewees. In (10) he asks for a list of forthcoming meetings and readings of the Society so that he can attend some, and suggests a panel meeting for 20th or 21st of September. The report must have been finalised then, even though this letter seems to envisage the investigation continuing (with further data being collected by attending events, for example), for a final draft is sent to the Head of the Arts Council in late September, producing a slightly puzzled note from him to Josephine Falk on 1st October 1976:

> Internal memo from Secretary General (Roy Shaw)
> In general, report seems to be excellent. Surprised that after all the fuss we should be recommending increased financial aid.

The Arts Council formally approved the report at a meeting of 27th October 1976, and on the 28th a letter to Robert Vas Dias informed him that the Society's subsidy was to rise from £32,000 to £54,000, but 'I am instructed to ask for an assurance that your Society accepts in principle the recommendations contained in the report.' News of the Report appeared in the press a few days later. The *Times* reported on 3rd November (headlined 'Poetry Society told to end discord or risk Arts Council subsidy') that the Arts Council had accepted its report. The outcome was a kind of ultimatum to the Society: if, in a year's time (1st April 1978) the Arts Council considered its management able to present 'the tolerant and reasonably united front necessary to ensure the efficient performance of its activities', then it would increase its annual grant in line with the panel's recommendations: 'Otherwise the council would not hesitate to withdraw its subsidy on 1st April, 1978.'

~

So the Witt Panel did indeed report 'fairly quickly', as had been expected, sifting rapidly through its 223 written replies, 'in some cases, an elaborate dossier with appendices [in others] just a few lines'. I will comment firstly on the general character of the Report, and briefly list its main recommendations, and will then discuss some of the internal disputes surrounding it. The report consists of seventeen typed pages comprising fifty numbered paragraphs. The terms of reference are first set out, the Constitution of the Poetry Society is summarised (paragraphs 3–8), the procedure followed by the Panel is described (9–18), the main conclusions are listed (19–31), then more detailed comments are made on various aspects of the Poetry Society, namely its Constitution (32), the role of its Director (33), its voluntary workers (34–35), the

Newsletter and *Poetry Review* (37–38), the Bookshop (39), the Print-shop (40), the Premises (41), the Bar (42), the Library (43), the Education programme (44), the readings and events at Earls Court (45), the regional activities (46), and the National Poetry Secretariat (47). Finally, the general recommendations are summarised in a lengthy paragraph 48 (i–xvii), and the financial recommendations in paragraph 49. The last paragraph (50), headed 'OVERRIDING CONDITION', is the one calling for a 'tolerant and reasonably united front' to be set up within the year.

The findings of the report can be briefly summarised as follows: The Poetry Society (. . .) is capable of performing a valid service to the cause of poetry (19i), but its work has been 'seriously handicapped by internal dissension' (19ii): the Society is underfunded (19v), the Arts Council [should] continue financial support of the Society, and indeed expand it to some degree' (23), subject to the 'overriding condition' that 'there should be an end to the internal strife within the General Council' (24): in the meantime financial support should be 'specifically earmarked' to 'certain categories of the Society's activities', 'as opposed to a block grant' (26). However, 'the requirement that the Arts Council should be entitled, as a condition of its grant, to nominate three members of the General Council of the Society, should be withdrawn. It has worked badly in practice, has failed to achieve any satisfactory measure of control, and has been bitterly resented by the Society' (27). Instead we 'recommend control through an effective Assessorship, backed by close financial scrutiny through the Finance Department of the Arts Council' (28). We further recommend 'that the Assessor should be consulted over the appointment of any new editor of *Poetry Review*' (29). We recommend that the terms of reference of the Society's General Secretary, who also combines the function of Director of the National Poetry Centre, be redefined to give him much greater executive authority' (33): following on from the above 'we wish to express our disquiet at the involvement of voluntary workers in the day-to-day running of the Society although we realise that this has largely been brought about through lack of finance' (34). The *Newsletter* . . . [we agree] 'has been misused as a vehicle for the dissemination of propaganda by certain members of the General Council'. Also, 'we are in agreement with the view (expressed in a proportion of about ten to one cases in the written comments we received on the subject) that the magazine, under its present editorship and in its present format, is not what the sole poetry publication of the National Poetry centre should be' (38a). 'We are concerned to note, too, that notwithstanding the magazine's title, articles and reviews of poetry are excluded from it' (38b): 'We believe that the decision to print the *Poetry Review* in the print-shop at Earls Court Square (a decision taken mainly for reasons of economy) has proved unsuccessful, and the result has been the production of a physically shabby looking magazine' (38e): we recommend that, at the end of the present Editor's tenure, the printing and production be placed on a professional footing; and that the Arts Council, in 1977/78, should make available a special grant for this purpose' (38f). 'We consider it essential that the bookshop be established on a professional basis' (39c), [with] 'a bookshop and mail order service on a firm footing before embarking on further projects such as a mobile Bookshop' (39e). On the question of readings and events, 'We have come to the conclusion that, during the recent past, a disproportionate amount of time, space and facilities at the National Poetry Centre has been devoted to the new, the unknown, the experimental, all of which should be represented, but not to the exclusion of the traditional, the famous, the "middle of the road"' (45c). 'We consider, too, that the Society has done itself a serious disservice by excluding from its premises two independent groups (Poets' Workshop and Poetry Round) which formerly rented rooms there for regular meetings' (45d). 'We consider that the Poetry Society has so far failed to establish itself as a National Poetry Centre, providing, as it purports to do, a nationwide service for poets and poetry' (46d), but 'The National Poetry Secretariat, which acts as an agency for arranging and grant-aiding poetry readings up and down the country, has emerged in the course of our Assessment as the jewel in the crown of the National Poetry centre' (47a). The financial recommendations, summarised in paragraph 49 for 1977/78 are for a block grant of £20,000, £8,500 for new staff, £3,500 for the production of *Poetry Review*, and £22,000 for the operation of the National Poetry Secretariat. In the current year (1975/76) the basic subsidy should go up from £28,000 to £32,000 to enable changes to be started as soon as possible.

On the whole, the report contains very little that is surprising: there is hardly anything specific on the contents of the 223 written replies or the oral testimony from twenty two people, but then the business of such a report is to convert the particular into the general. The specific points made concern the most controversial elements of the behaviour of both sides, for example, Charles Osborne's insistence on the three direct Arts Council appointees to the General Council, which had merely exacerbated the rift between the Poetry Society and the Arts

Council, the radicals' exclusion of *Poets' Workshop* and *Poetry Round* from Earls Court Square, and the use of the *Newsletter* for what was seen as partisan propaganda.

Debating the Word 'Control'

In response to the Witt Report a meeting of the Council of the Poetry Society was called for Saturday 13th November. A resolution rejecting the findings of the report was put forward by Jeff Nuttall (Chair), Lawrence Upton (Deputy Chair), and Bob Cobbing (Treasurer). But the resolution itself was rejected by the new 'balanced' Council (by eighteen votes to twelve), and it was agreed instead that the Society would seek a meeting with the Arts Council to discuss the criticisms made in the report. Nuttall, Upton, and Cobbing resigned in protest (that is, they resigned as office-holders, but not yet as members of the General Council). At this point, a split on the radical side became apparent which mirrored that on the conservative side between the Reform Group and the Poetry Action Group: *that* split had been between the (so to speak) *radical* conservatives (Lovibond and his followers in the Reform Group) and the *conservative* conservatives (Wightman and his followers in the Poetry Action Group). On the radical side, the split was between the *radical* radicals (Nuttall, Upton, Cobbing) and the *conservative* radicals, who now stepped into the breach. Rather than leave an unresolved vacuum (which would effectively hand power to the conservative conservatives under Wightman) the conservative radicals were able to exert their residual control of the General Council by replacing Nuttall with Lee Harwood, as Acting Chair, and Cobbing with Roger Guedalla, as Acting Treasurer, while Robert Vas Dias (General Secretary of the Society) would act as spokesperson, these arrangements being until the next General Council meeting on 5th December. Robert Vas Dias (who seems to have assumed the Laurence Cotterell role of would-be peace-broker) explained that the new situation 'enabled the society to present a much more united front': he said (the *Times*, 16th November, 1976) that the issue was 'either to reject the assessment, which most of its members felt would result in the society's becoming an impotent fringe organization without a grant, or to accept it in principle and work to ameliorate the several objectionable points raised in the report.' Only one issue of *Poetry Review* (66:1) carries a 1976 date, perhaps reflecting the difficulty of maintaining business as usual under these wartime conditions.

Power now hung in the balance: the General Council would not reject the Witt Report, thereby provoking resignations from the radical radicals, while the conservative radicals mounted a damage limitation exercise. Eric Mottram regarded it as an unforgivable act of treachery and betrayal (these terms are in no way exaggerated or over-dramatic) to have any further involvement with the Poetry Society once it had accepted the Witt report in principle. Those who did so were, in his view, endorsing the insulting judgement of his editing of the journal which had been made by the Witt Panel, so that they were effectively colluding in the destruction of the true energies of contemporary British poetry. In consequence, he now rejected the friendship of several former allies, including Robert Vas Dias, Lee Harwood, and Barry MacSweeney. The three resigning officers (Nuttall, Cobbing, and Upton), with Mottram, sent a circular to all Council members, criticising the six (Baylis, Brownjohn, Cotton, Guedalla, Simmons, and Wightman) who had given evidence to the Witt Panel. In response, Roger Guedalla circulated a detailed defence of his own actions, reiterating the timetable of events, and refuting the suggestion that he had acted in any way clandestinely. What chiefly emerges from this is that the radicals had no co-ordinated strategy for responding to the investigation: after the event, they tended to see those of their own side who had volunteered evidence as collaborators, by the mere fact of having done so, but at the same time they accused the panel of being biased in its findings. Clearly (in retrospect, at least), only two responses to the Witt investigation were possible: either the radicals should have campaigned with vigour to ensure that *all* their supporters wrote to the panel, so that the bulk of the evidence sent in would have been in their favour; or else, they should have instigated a tight and total boycott of the proceedings by all radical supporters, publishing what they were doing, and perhaps setting up a counter-committee of investigation with international representation and public debate and hearings. This would have meant that Cobbing, Upton, and Mottram would not have agreed to appear before the panel at all. As it was, the actions of the radicals between May, when the investigation was put in train, and October, when then findings were announced, were contradictory and uncoordinated, giving the lie to the myth that they were a tightly disciplined and ruthless group of agitators. Likewise, the period between the two walk-outs (November 1976, when the three officers resigned, and March 1977, when the mass walk-out of the radical Council members took place) had no clear overall radical strategy, and was based on the act of wishful thinking that the word 'control' in the Witt report didn't really mean what it said.

After the Council meeting of 13th November Robert Vas Dias contacted the Arts Council, which agreed to a meeting and asked him to supply an agenda—he sent one on 16th November, a brief document with stark headings such as 'The Principle of Accountability (the difference between accountability and control)' and 'Artistic Integrity and Independence of the National Poetry Centre'. It wouldn't do, of course, and he was asked to supply an explanation of the agenda. He sent an 'explanation', running to four closely typed pages, commenting in detail on particular paragraphs of the report, but I will not discuss this document (there is little evidence that it was very closely read at the Arts Council) and instead move straight to a description of what happened at the post-Witt meeting between representatives of the Poetry Society and the Arts Council.

The meeting took place at 105 Piccadilly at 8.00pm on the evening of 2nd December 1976: on the Arts Council side were Roy Shaw, the Director, Sir John Witt, Chair of the investigating panel, Charles Osborne, Literature Director, and Josephine Falk, Literature Officer. On the Society's side were Lee Harwood, Acting Chair, Roger Guedalla, Acting Treasurer, Alan Brownjohn, as a General Council member, Robert Vas Dias, as General Secretary of the Society, and Marjorie Barton, as Director of the National Poetry Secretariat. Firstly, on the notion of accountability, it was made clear that (i) the word 'control' in paragraph 28 of the report did not mean that the Arts Council wished to dictate to the Poetry Society, 'it was, rather, a shorthand term to describe the guidance, council and advice which an Arts Council assessor ordinarily made available to client organisations.' At the same time (ii) the assessor must be entitled to attend all Society committees and his advice must *regularly* be sought, but (iii) the assessor had no vote at the meetings and the Society was not obliged to accept his advice. But if his advice was consistently disregarded he would report this situation to the Literature Panel, which would take it into account when assessing future subsidy. The Secretary General could not agree to the Society's proposal that it should choose its own assessor. The assessment committee felt that the post of bookshop manager should take precedence over that of print-shop manager: the Society would have to realise they could not do everything at once. If the sum of £3,500 was not enough to produce four issues of *Poetry Review* they would have to reduce the annual number of issues again from four to three.

The outcome of this meeting was conveyed to the Poetry Society General Council meeting of Sunday 5th December, which Josephine Falk attended as Arts Council Assessor (with Maureen Duffy), reporting on it in a memo to Charles Osborne:

> Unpromising start: Bob Cobbing proposed prefix 'Ms' be abandoned: this provoked Eddie Linden to bawl an obscenity at Mr Cobbing. Resignations of Adler and Cheek reported: Harwood proposed that a delegate from the paid staff be on the General Council—'It's all very well talking about worker participation, what about having it?' He suggested that the staff be unionised, possibly in the TGWU: door keys had disappeared and as a result staff did not feel they could take responsibility for the building. Harwood gave an account of the meeting between representatives of the Society and the Arts Council on 2/12/76. He placed the Arts Council report in the context of general cut-backs in the arts and stressed that the Society must be able to account for the use made of public funds. 'Assessorship' did not imply dictatorship—Sir John had apologised for the use made of the word 'control'. Bob Cobbing left the meeting after an altercation with the Acting Treasurer over the expenses claimed by Council members. Elections to Chair: Barry MacSweeney 9, Aston 6, Robinson 5. Roger Guedalla elected Treasurer unopposed. 'Poetry Round' was allowed a Wednesday evening meeting room (MacSweeney voted against).

At this stage there was little that could usefully be said, and the voting figures make it clear that the election of a radical Chairman is merely a gesture, since the combined strength of the anti-radicals would ensure that no business which advanced the radical cause was likely to be passed. Hence, the scene was set for the staged and ritualistic walk-out of the radicals which would take place at the General Council meeting in March 1977.

1977 began with the matter of the successor to Mottram as editor of *Poetry Review* suddenly being thrown open again: Robert Vas Dias received a letter from Peter Finch, the editor-elect, declining the editorship: 'I feel I can now neither dedicate myself to the task in the way I once could nor can I feel an enjoyable commitment to the Society and its magazine, again, as I once could', as Robert Vas Dias quoted him in a letter to Mottram on 4th January 1977 informing him of this development. He adds 'given Peter's current attitude, I suppose I should feel relieved. Nevertheless, it's strange to me why poet/editors are so passive and non-supportive. The schism in British poetry is destructive in more ways than one. Let's hope Allen is able to accept.' This indicates that the intention was to offer the editorship to Allen Fisher, although that would never have been acceptable to the Arts Council 'assessors', and in any case, the radicals were no longer in a position to secure Poetry Society approval of such an idea once it got beyond their last bastion of the Publications Committee.

Finch's appointment as Mottram's successor had been announced in the Chair's report at the June 1976 AGM, but Mottram seems not to have known about it until his appearance before the Witt Panel, as indicated earlier. His letters in 1976–77 contain frequent mentions of the pressures of his university work, and he presumably just wasn't reading Poetry Society papers. A letter to Barry MacSweeney of 14th March 1977 (BM15/1/8) makes it clear that he believed some act of deceit had taken place over the editorship. He writes 'The affair of the editorship was incredible, or rather, it wasn't. Finch lied and Vas Dias of course lied. Only when under my pressures, and then of others, the files were looked into, did the truth of the matter appear. And then, as you know, Finch owned up.' I don't know of any evidence for Mottram's accusations, and by the time he wrote the letter he had already been told (in the letter from Vas Dias in January 1977) that Finch had subsequently written to decline the editorship. The period from late 1976 through the early months of 1977 was clearly a bad time for him: one factor was his mother's death on 16th November 1976, and the subsequent demands of family business, which required several trips to clear the family home. But he seems to refer to more than that when he writes in the same letter 'The last months of 1976 and the first of 1977 were horrible, and there are a number of people still shaken. It is not over, and coming on top of the Poetry Society nastiness, also not over, by a long chalk, as I'm sure you know.' Reading this (written less than a fortnight before the decisive walkout of the radicals) it might almost be imagined that Mottram is unaware that MacSweeney had succeeded Jeff Nuttall and Lee Harwood as the Chair of the Society at the Council meeting of 5th December 1976.

In this difficult period, Mottram had disagreements with several old friends, including Lee Harwood, whom he accused of betrayal, and I will quote at length from one of Harwood's letters, in which he explains the actions he took during the crisis, actions which have frequently been criticised since by former members of the radical side. He is writing to Mottram on 9th April 1977, less than a fortnight after the final walk-out, and complaining about Mottram's reliance on un-nuanced accounts of events:

Most of all, I wish you'd been actually present at the Poetry Society
Council meeting [13th November 1976] when Jeff resigned [as Chair], and
the one when Barry was elected Chairman [5th December 1976], and also
the meeting with Roy Shaw & ACGB representatives [2nd December 1976].
If you had you would have heard all the arguments, and discussions, and
got an idea of the tone of these affairs. As it is, I feel that your informants
on these meetings, whoever they are, were not the most accurate or objec-
tive . . Starting with the meeting when Jeff resigned—there was a question
of tactics, approaches to a problem. To reject the ACGB, its report, and its
money, or to accept the cash and some of their report but to insist on
negotiation & changes in the report. Jeff, Bob, etc wanted a total rejection. Myself, Roy Fisher, Barry MacSweeney, Elaine, Roger Guedalla, Ken
Smith & some others favoured negotiating, that is fighting from within. I
would think you'd agree both these groups of people are sensible, not
crazy, and have reasons for voting the way they did. For myself, the
National Poetry Secretariat is the most important service the Poetry
Society provides—it helps poetry <u>outside</u> London in a very real way. With
the atmosphere of Arts Bashing going on last autumn (ICA, etc), it seemed
very necessary to keep the NPS funded—and the ACGC seemed to be looking for any excuse to withdraw these funds. As chairman of NPS and
therefore responsible in a way to people all round the country hoping to
organise readings, I couldn't let NPS go down the drain. As a trade union-
ist I've never believed in resignation as a useful political weapon—it
always seems best to work from inside an organisation. I mean the basic
principle—in unity is strength. The old dictum of divide and rule has
certainly proved right if you look at the Poetry Society now in the sham-
bles it is. I obviously don't agree with Jeff's resignation nor the recent
block resignations—they seem more a selfish act than an act by people
who care. . . . What I'm getting at is that I considered the way I voted the
best course at that time. I may have been wrong, I don't know, nor can
one ever know for sure, but I sincerely believed that the approach the
majority of the Council decided on would be the most effective.[4]

In the meantime the policy seemed to be to proceed, as far as possible,
as if the Witt Report had never happened—that, at least, is the implication of putting forward Allen Fisher as next editor of *Poetry Review*, for he
was no less radical than Eric Mottram. John Cotton (MacSweeney's
successor as Chair, and not a radical sympathiser) described the period
as follows in an April 1977 Newsletter:

New staff were hired, consultations were held with the Arts Council
finance officers over accounting and financial procedures, Arts Council
representatives began regular attendance at Society meetings, and so on.
Regrettably, however, the minority did not cease in their efforts to
prevent certain of the recommendations from being put into effect. There

---

[4]   Letter in Mottram Archive, 5/103/1–41.

was resentment over the hiring of extra staff. There was reluctance to adhere to economy measures and to new methods of financial reporting— arising not only from suggestions in the Arts Council Report but also from emergency measures imposed due to the Society's critical financial position towards the end of the financial year. It began to be clearly evident that a few members of the minority group were still actively opposing the acceptance and implementation of the Report's recommen- dations. It was also quite clear that an atmosphere of distrust and suspi- cion was thereby engendered, and it became increasingly difficult to hold orderly meetings.

The new staff positions included the post of Bookshop/Print-shop Manager. Advertisements were placed, and interviews of three short- listed candidates took place at the Poetry Society on Saturday 12th March 1977, the interviewing panel being Robert Vas Dias, Barry MacSweeney, Ian Robinson, Roger Guedalla, and Elaine Randell, with Elaine Pomerey observing for the Arts Council. In spite of the Witt Report's recommen- dations, the job specification was almost entirely concerned with the print-shop: the successful candidate would have to 'maintain and oper- ate all the print-shop machinery, print the quarterly *Poetry Review,* organ- ise a booking system for extra-mural clients, advise them and prevent them from wrecking the machinery, keep accounts, order supplies, run the bookshop. The first candidate was a poet and academic, but had no knowledge of printing or printing machinery, and was thought to be 'far too gentle and altogether too nice' for the battles the job would require: the second was a good poet and had printing experience but 'was not considered to be tough enough to render him invulnerable to the currents he would meet'. The successful candidate had no poetry knowledge, but did have the right kind of practical experience, and presumably the 'toughness' to counter those mysterious 'currents' swirling round the Poetry Society print-shop. The Arts Council's filed copy of the document giving these details has exasperated marginal annotations in red ink by Josephine Falk: 'But the Witt report recom- mended the appointment of a bookshop manager with only incidental responsibility for supervising the Print-shop and a salary for this appointment was earmarked.' The successful candidate has experience of running a 'distribution system', 'but does this actually include experience of running a bookshop?' the annotator asks. At the end of the document she has written 'It seems to me that the Poetry Society has disregarded the recommendation of the Witt Report, which was very firm about wanting to establish a Bookshop as a first priority.'

If the policy being followed really was that the radicals should continue for as long as possible as if the Witt Report had never happened, then MacSweeney's letter to Mottram on 22ⁿᵈ March 1977 shows that he was reaching the end of his tether, and nobody who knew MacSweeney would imagine him temperamentally capable of following a conciliatory Lee Harwood line for long. He expresses his intentions and his feelings in his letter to Mottram of 22ⁿᵈ March 1977:[5]

> I will be resigning as chairman and from the Council—as I say, I've done too much compromising and my skull won't take any more. By a fatal error, I accepted what Lee had to say about his meeting with Roy Shaw [on 2ⁿᵈ December 1976]—that we cd 'take the money and run'. This was a gross misreading of the true facts and my (and others') acceptance of his advice was a gross miscalculation. . . There is a meeting of interested parties (i.e. Bob [Cobbing], Lawrence [Upton], Cris [cheek], Allen [Fisher], Ken [Smith], Tom [Pickard], me, Ian [Patterson]) on Saturday morning so something shd come from that.

Presumably, MacSweeney's advice at that crucial pre-meeting was to recommend that there should be a mass resignation and walk-out on that day.

'One Saturday Afternoon'

The decisive meeting of the General Council took place in March 1977, when 'the fourteen modernist members of the Council all resigned, in protest against the Arts Council's pressure on them' (Duncan, p. 175), the fourteen being: Barry MacSweeney, Peter Hodgkiss, Jeremy Adler, Peter Finch, Bill Griffiths, cris cheek, Lawrence Upton, Allen Fisher, Bob Cobbing, Jeff Nuttall, Tom Pickard, Pete Morgan, Ian Patterson, and Ken Smith (Gortschacher, p. 510). In fact, though, the big issue of Arts Council control of the Poetry Society had come to a head in the previous November, and the initial flashpoints in the March 1977 meeting were to do with on-going accusations of financial irregularities. There are a number of accounts of this meeting; firstly, the official minutes; secondly the formal account sent as a memo to the Director of the Arts Council by Tony Field, Finance Director of the Arts Council, who had attended it as an assessor with Charles Osborne; thirdly, Osborne's own account, as given in his memoirs; and finally the accounts which

5 Mottram Archive, EM5/151/1.

appeared in newspapers. The following extracts from the minutes give the gist of what happened:

General Council minutes of 26/3/77 (Sat. 3.00pm)—Present:

Jeremy Adler, Vicky Allen, Lawrence Baylis, cris cheek, Bob Cobbing, John Cotton, Gavin Ewart, Allen Fisher, Peter Hodgkiss, Eddie Linden, E.A. Markham, Pete Morgan, Betty Mulcahy, Angus Nicolson, Ian Patterson, Elaine Randell, Ian Robinson, Clifford Simmons, Ken Smith, John Stathatos, Lawrence Upton, G.B.H. Wightman. Barry MacSweeney (Chair), Roger Guedalla (Treasurer). *In attendance*: General Secretary, NPS Director, Education Secretary. M. Lawford, Barbara Hill, Charles Olson & Anthony Field for the ACGB, M.P. Ryan

Chair's Report: Chair wished it to be minuted that he intended to resign as Chairman and as a member of the General Council at the conclusion of this meeting because the Council was fragmented and was too big and unwieldy; an attitude of distrust had been in evidence over the past several weeks in which confidences had been broken, most Council members were unacquainted with the rules of order for holding meetings, there were certain Council members he considered to be 5th Columnists in that threats of prosecution were made in respect of acts undertaken in good faith by officers; decisions of the Council and Executive were not being adhered to; he had no confidence in the Poetry Society; he felt that approval of the Arts Council report had been a mistake, and he was no longer willing to compromise his principles. . . . After a short discussion of the contents of the letter by GBH Wightman referred to above, the Chairman proposed, seconded by Ken Smith, the following motion:

'that the Council believes George Wightman's action in threatening Council members with legal action is mischievous and detrimental to the Society, and that his threats are based on malice against members of the Council.'

An amendment was then proposed by J. Stathatos, seconded by I. Robinson, that the motion be not voted on. The amendment being put to the vote, those in favour were ten, opposed eight, and abstaining five. The amendment was carried. The Chairman [MacSweeney], Bob Cobbing, Lawrence Upton, and several other members of the General Council then offered their resignations and left the meeting. J. Cotton was elected Chairman pro tem, until the AGM, by acclamation. The

Treasurer proposed the buy-out of the ALP share of the offset litho machine for £750—agreed. ALP and CoLP [the Consortium of London Presses] to remove their equipment (11 in favour, 1 abstention). General Secretary to write to them to remove their equipment in a week. A secret ballot elected the following to do one issue each of Poetry Review from 67/3: Edwin Brock, Harry Chambers, Douglas Dunn, Roger Garfitt.

AOB: Write to MacSweeney accepting their resignations. The rest would be asked to clarify their position within seven days. They would be presumed resigned if there was no reply. [this was to Adler, cheek, Fisher, Hodgkiss, Morgan, Patterson, Pickard, Smith, Upton] 5 in favour, 4 opposed, 3 abstained—carried.

Field's account is more lurid: he and Osborne had attended the meeting, having been 'told they would be on their best behaviour! It transpired to be the most unbelievable meeting I've attended since joining the [Arts] Council. They were all spoiling for a fight from the outset, when the agenda itself was challenged':

> The minutes of the last meeting caused an argument and one member of the Council walked out. On matters arising from the meeting it was reported that the print-shop manager would start work on 4th April 1977. Charles and I had to point out that Sir John Witt's report had recommended the appointment of a bookshop manager who might "devote some time to the supervision of the print-shop" and that they appeared to be getting the emphasis wrong. There were cries of "Arts Council interference in policy" although I pointed out that this was one of the recommendations in a report which they had accepted. Half an hour was then spent arguing about why a 2nd-hand desk for the use of the Association of Little Presses had not been bought . . . I do not consider that Charles's "Impatient interjection" (today's *Guardian*) was in any way unjustified.

He then recorded the substance of the Chairman's speech, as given in the minutes, ending:

> They had been mistaken in accepting the ACGB's [increased] subsidy and they should have fought the Witt report and not accepted it. He then announced that he was leaving there and then and asked any others to follow him who so wished. He was followed by [names listed]. Some of them orally declared their resignations as they left.

It was agreed that John Cotton should take the chair for the remainder of the meeting and for the other Council meeting before the AGM, and the meeting resumed.

In his memoir, *Giving it Away,* Charles Osborne offers a more facetious and rather self-regarding account of this meeting. The Witt Report, he says, had given him the 'assessorship' role at the Poetry Society, and as such 'it was my duty to attend meetings of the Executive Council, which were not only absolute torture but were usually held on Saturday afternoons. The level of debate was subterranean, and it was only rarely about poetry. Usually they were arguing and shouting at one another about the most inconsequential matters imaginable' (p. 204). I will quote the remainder of his account in full:

> One Saturday afternoon, I found myself yet again at a meeting, waiting for it to begin. . . . They were nearly half an hour late in starting, because they were too busy shouting accusations at one another about the Chairman's desk being moved without permission, or something equally ridiculous. Finally, having had enough of this, I took a deep breath, projected my voice as though I were declaiming at the Theatre Royal, Drury Lane, and managed to make myself heard above the clamour. 'For Christ's sake pull yourselves together and start the bloody meeting,' I yelled. 'I have better things to do than waste my weekends here.'
>
> What the Arts Council's investigating team had failed to achieve in months I accomplished in seconds. One of the poets, Jeff Nuttall, stood up. 'I am not going to bow down to this kind of official censorship ,' he exclaimed. 'I resign in protest.' 'So do I,' said another, Bob Cobbing. And, one by one, their followers did the same. They marched out of the room, and I asked the Secretary to be certain to record their resignations in the minutes, for fear they should come to what senses they possessed and march back in again. But they didn't return. Was ever a victory so easily, so inadvertently achieved? (pp. 204–5)

Osborne also quotes from the *Guardian* report of this meeting 'when 12 [sic] of the members resigned from the 30-strong Council of the Society'. It continues:

> The affair seems to have been brought to a head by an impatient interjection at Saturday's Council meeting from Mr Charles Osborne, Literature Director of the Arts Council and charged with overseeing how the Society spends £54,000 of the Council's and taxpayers' money.
>
> The initial sticking-point was apparently whether a desk and chair should be provided for the secretary of the Association of Little Presses at Earls Court Square. 'It was really a matter of great principle,' said Mr McSweeney [sic] (Chairman of the Poetry Society). 'I discovered after instructing the General Secretary to do this four or five weeks ago that it still hadn't been done. There was an argument . . .' Mr Nuttall and Mr Cobbing said that they feared Mr Osborne taking control of the Society. (p. 205)

Both Osborne's memoirs and the *Guardian* report give the impression that the walk-out was a rather shambolic, spontaneous act, provoked by Osborne's goading, but a letter now in the MacSweeney Collection at Newcastle makes it clear that this course of action had been contemplated for several months, and linked with a plan to set up an alternative *Poetry Review*. The letter (to MacSweeney) is from Ian Patterson who had been co-opted onto the Council in late 1976 and had taken over as Chair of the Events Committee.[6] I transcribe the crucial parts of the letter, below:

> Thurs [deleted] Wednesday 17 [deleted]16[th7]
> Dear Barry,
>
> Thanks for the cheque and the letter. . . Very hurried thoughts on NPC in time to catch tonight's post. Approve the idea of breakaway review 100%: but still haven't mastered the current situation at Earl's Court. . . . I'm still, at heart, most strongly in favour of setting up a programme of central London readings and magazine independent of all the shit. . . . depending, as I say, on my impressions hardening on Saturday, I think that if a group of people did resign en masse, and with the intention of running regular, accessible, good readings + producing a magazine, then I would be all in favour and offer as much support to such a group as I could.

There is evidence here, then, that (albeit belatedly) a strategy for securing impact and publicity was being devised.

Another letter in the Mottram archive gives an indication of the strategy decided upon in the morning pre-meeting of the radical Council members (mentioned in MacSweeney's 22nd March letter to Mottram) which took place before the afternoon Council meeting. This letter is from Ken Smith to Mottram, written about ten days after the event and dated 'April (dammit) 5th':

> As you'll no doubt know a third of the Poetry Society quit. I'm aware that it leaves the field wide open to schmucks that wanted it all that way, that *Poetry Review* is now the creature of [Douglas]Dunn [and Roger] Garfitt [two of the four editors elected to produce an issue each of *Poetry Review*], that the centre will be rapidly dismantled. I'm aware that all the work you chiefly and others did there to transform a moribund enterprise into a national centre has gone beneath the bridge. Tactically MacSweeney forgot

6 BM/4/6/76: Item in MacSweeney Collection (wrongly described in the hand-list as a letter from Clive Bush).

7 Probable date of writing is Wednesday 15th or Thursday 16th September 1976.

himself, and led the walkout <u>before</u> the editorship of the *Poetry Review* had come up. That was daft, but then, they'd have overturned it anyway.[8]

The plan, then, had been to stage the walk-out when the editorship of *Poetry Review* came up on the agenda, but in the event, MacSweeney's impatience and the tension of the atmosphere, led to his making his own departure early, and the radicals then followed, but somewhat raggedly because of this deviation from the plan. After the walk-out, the radicals (presumably in the White House bar next-door to the Society in Earls Court Square) may have composed a press release which was issued the following day—or does the fact that this document was put out so speedily stand as further evidence that the action had been planned long before?

PRESS STATEMENT MADE ON 26TH *[in fact]* 27th MARCH 1977:

Twelve additional members of the poetry Society's General Council resigned at yesterday's meeting, making twenty in the last twelve months. The mass walk-out was led by the Chairman, Barry MacSweeney, the third Chairman of the Society to resign in eight months. The two basic issues on which the twelve resigned were FIRSTLY that the [General] Council is no longer in control of Council policy. Policy is being controlled by the Arts Council of Great Britain and the Society's paid staff led by its director, Robert Vas Dias. It is a matter of bureaucracy versus poetry, and the censorship of a democratically elected body by a state agency. This is seen in the refusal to grant-aid the Society's magazine *Poetry Review* while it is under the editorship of Eric Mottram, who is not approved by the Arts Council, though he has had the overwhelming support of the Society's Council expressed over the past five years. SECONDLY, the dissenters object to the more than doubling of expenditure on staff and office expenses, while at the same time the amounts going to poets for readings at the Society, for readings throughout the country under the national Poetry Secretariat, and the Society's Poets-in-Schools scheme have been drastically cut. The Council members who resigned hope that their resignation will spotlight these issues and alert poets everywhere to what is happening.

So ended the decisive day in the Battle of Earls Court.

'Moderates Win Fight in Poetry Society'

The Witt report had given the Poetry Society a year to put its house in order, and Josephine Falk made an oral report to the Arts Council on

---

[8]   In box EM5/222/1–20

27th April 1977, approximately six months after the publication of the Witt findings:

> Following the acceptance of the Witt Report ... we were assured a new dawn had been heralded. Nevertheless, under the chairmanship of Barry MacSweeney, meetings of the Society's General Council have continued to be acrimonious and conducted to the accompaniment of mutual recrimination and abuse. A further set of resignations occurred at the end of March, when Barry MacSweeney and 10 Council members resigned (in the middle of a meeting). An interim Chairman was elected to serve until the A.G.M. in June when, we are assured, moderation will prevail. However, similar assurances which we have received in the past proved to be without substance.... The situation half-way through the year is that the management of the society through its General Council is still far from achieving the overriding condition which the Witt Committee considered should be the *sine qua non* of continued subsidy, namely the tolerant and reasonably united front needed to ensure the efficient performance of its activities and those of the national Poetry Society. Officers of the Literature Panel will continue to assess the Society very closely, but the present indications do not give grounds for optimism.

The formal restoration of the old order at the Poetry Society took place in the summer at the AGM in June. 'Moderates win fight in Poetry Society', Philip Howard reported in The *Times* on Monday 27th:

> The entire panel put up by the moderate and tolerant Poetry Action Group were elected to bring the council up to twenty one. They were: Vicky Allen, literature director of the East Midlands Arts Association; Mr Bernard Brooke-Partridge, chairman of the Greater London Council Arts Committee, Mr Norman Buchan, Labour MP for Renfrewshire, West; Lord Gowrie, poet, and opposition spokesman on the arts in the House of Lords), Mr [sic] Paddy Kitchen, member of the Arts Council literature panel and member of the Witt assessment committee that examined the troubled affairs of the Poetry Society; Wes Magee, poet and teacher, Mr Jon Silkin, poet and member of the Arts Council literature panel, George Tardios, poet, and Mr John Stathatos, poet and translator.

Bob Cobbing is reported in the same piece to have written to John Cotton raising the possibility of legal action against the Arts Council:

> It seems to me that the present troubles of the society—including the boycotting of the society by a very large number of poets and others— stem from the acceptance of the Arts Council's report. I am taking legal advice on whether this acceptance is not in itself a breach of the society's articles, in that a measure of control passes from the general council, and therefore the membership, to the Arts Council.

It seems doubtful that such a legal challenge could have been mounted with any possibility of success, but there were more substantial grounds for arguing that what happened at the 1977 AGM was unconstitutional. These grounds are stated in a retrospective document entitled 'How the Poetry Society lost its democratic status' which was issued by Poets Conference, as their 'State of poetry, supplement no.2' on 23rd January 1979. In the course of a useful account of the whole saga of events at the Poetry Society is this paragraph:

> Came the Annual General Meeting, and the Society, to ensure that those who had resigned [in March 1977] had no chance of making a come-back, at least twice broke its own constitution (a) by not requiring one third of its Council to resign (thus enabling two conservative members of Council to serve illegally for an extra year), and (b) by voting to make up the number of Council members to only twenty one rather than to thirty as stated in the Constitution (without the constitutional change having been agreed).

Some of these points are arguable: for instance, the Society could not be said to be intent on ensuring that those who had resigned 'had no chance of making a come-back', since the Council wrote to those who walked out on 26th March 1977 asking them to confirm in writing their intention of resigning, which did give them an opportunity to change their minds.[9] Also, since more than one third of the Council had walked out, it might seem unreasonable in such unprecedented circumstances to expect two of those remaining to resign and seek re-election. The second point, though, seems stronger: raising the Council membership from twenty one to thirty had been passed at the EGM in June 1973, the increase to be phased in over three years. The proposal to reverse this should therefore have been notified in advance in the papers for the 1977 AGM, and then, if passed, phased in in the same way, with stepped reductions in 1977, 1978, and 1979. Of course, even if these challenges to constitutional legality could have been sustained, they pass over the fact that the radicals too had countenanced procedural irregularities, such as instituting the post of Deputy Chairman without consulting the membership. However, no legal challenge was made in the event, and the most contentious division in the Poetry Society's history was now effectively over.

---

9 At least, that is what the Council agreed to do—I have not actually seen these letters, or any replies, in the files.

5

Endgame and Aftermath: 1977–2005

The Last Mottram Issues of *Poetry Review*

The Witt Report, having noted the shoddy appearance of recent issues, recommended a special grant of £3,500 in 1977–78 'to enable the printing and production of *Poetry Review* to be placed on a professional footing' (48 (xi)). It wasn't clear how much of this could be used on the backlog of Mottram issues, but at the General Council meeting on 9th January 1977 Roger Guedalla as Treasurer 'authorised with Council approval, the expenditure of almost any amount of money necessary to get the June issue and the two subsequent double issues printed, bound, and distributed as soon as possible' (letter to Mottram, 10th January 1977 [wrongly dated 1976]). On 20th April Guedalla wrote again to Mottram, following the inevitable disputes over amounts and figures: he recapped the situation: on 21st January he had agreed a figure of £650 with cris cheek and Bill Griffiths for 'this issue just finished,' and mentioned this in a letter to Mottram on the 8th.. The agreement was amended on 15th February to a revised figure of £900. Since his take-over as Treasurer in December 1976, two Mottram issues had been brought out (66:2, in December 1976, and the double issue 66:3/4, 1976-7, completed in April 1977). He remained committed to getting the final Mottram issue into print (the double issue 67:1/2, 1977). There was a problem with the copy for that final issue—namely, where was it?—'Apparently cris cheek has the typescript but we have never seen it and would be most grateful if you could arrange for it to be sent to us'. At that stage, so Guedalla understood, Griffiths and cheek felt that the collating should be done by an outside printer. The matter was not quickly resolved: on 11th May Ian Robinson (as Chair of the Publications Committee) wrote to Mottram at

[104]

the request of the Executive Committee to ask for the copy of the 'forth-coming double issue within the next ten days'. The Executive's view was that there was now adequate printing equipment, and a manager in post, to do the issue in-house. Ian Robinson added a hand-written note to the typed formal letter to say that the formal one had been written under the executive's instruction. Robert Vas Dias also sent a long typed letter to Mottram replying to Mottram's questions to him in a letter of 22nd April: like several by Guedalla in the same period, this is mainly a letter of defence against allegations Mottram had made about his role in the   situation ('I don't know why you accuse me of keeping the printer out of the print-shop'): he stresses that he had fought for the original agreement (for the production of the double issue) as well as for the current arrangement of having it produced in-house by cheek, Cobbing, and Griffiths. In early June the situation was still not resolved, and Mottram wrote to John Cotton as Chairman 'Now, I am privately informed that the last double issue is not to be printed on the premises', he writes (3rd June). John Cotton sent a hand-written note on 11th June, making it clear that he would 'advise against raising the matter again, for the arguments it will raise might well delay publication. . . . That we have agreement that the issue be published, and that the setting is to be done by someone in sympathy with your editorship is in itself quite an achievement'. And on the 15th he wrote again: 'following our conversation yesterday evening I had a word with Bob Cobbing in order to find out what is meant by "supervising" the printing. Bob told me it was usually the practice to visit a printer working on *Poetry Review* to see if any problems or snags had come up, and to offer help in solving them'. This would involve Brian Mitchell (the new print-shop/bookshop manager) and Bill Griffiths going to Bristol to deliver the copy to the printers. Mottram's reply on 21st June threw up a final point which Cotton takes up in a response in early July:

Dear Eric,

Thanks for your letter of 21st June. I should, however, like to take up your mention of Robert Vas Dias and point out that Robert is one of those who strived to ensure that your last issue of *Poetry Review* came out, and came out according to your wishes. I thought I ought to put the record straight. Yours sincerely,[1]

[1] All the material relating to the final Mottram issues of *Poetry Review* is in Mottram, 4/2/64–66.

This belated Mottram double issue (67:1/2) finally appeared in August 1977. The next one, Volume 67:3, which reverted to full commercial printing, and to the old A5 format, was edited by Edwin Brock. It is prefaced with a 'Note':

> As readers will see, this magazine now has a new editor as well as a new size. But before saying anything about this, the Poetry Society at the National Poetry Centre would like to thank the retiring editor, Eric Mottram, who has now completed his allotted span of issues, for his dedicated service to the *Poetry Review* and the Poetry Society. His tenure of the editorship has succeeded in making the Review an internationally recognised journal of poetry.

The note adds that the four issues starting with the present one will each be edited by a different editor, pending the appointment 'of an editor for a longer period'. The note courteously gives a kind of 'official' endorsement of the value of Mottram's tenure, but it sounds a cautious note for the future in not stating precisely how long the next editor's term of office will be.

The Failings of the New Order

The Arts Council's Literature Advisory Panel met on 5th September 1977, with the Poetry Society as its sixth agenda item (ACGB/62/103, box 2 of 10), and Charles Osborne reported on the state of play:

> 'It has been my task, as the Council's Literature Director, to assess the Society's performance since publication of the Witt Report. . . . Up to and including AGM, the auguries for the future were distinctly unfavourable: the atmosphere continued to be distinctly acrimonious, which perhaps mattered less than the coarse and illiterate standard of the abuse flung about by members of a General Council incompetently chaired. However, at the AGM a General Council (sensibly reduced from 34 to 21) was elected for the twelve months ending July 78 whose membership is certainly an improvement on the past. . . The Arts Council will have to decide whether this is good value for money. My view has always been that, as a method of subsidising poetry, our involvement with the Poetry Society has been both conspicuously extravagant and highly unsatisfactory, and we ought to devise a more efficient way of using £54,000 in support of poets and poetry.'

This indicates that Charles Osborne's long-cherished desire to end direct subsidy to poets is now nearer to fruition. On the other hand, the Arts

Council was in fact no more satisfied with the conduct of General Council meetings under the new regime than they had been under the old, for the following day Josephine Falk attended the Executive and Management Committee as Arts Council Assessor, accompanied by Martyn Goff (Director of the National Book League and a member of the Literature Panel). The meeting was conducted by Paddy Kitchen, who had been a member of the Witt Panel and had now become Poetry Society Chairman (unwisely, one would think, if the perceived impartiality of the Panel were a consideration). The meeting was conducted 'in an excessively long-winded manner and was tedious in the extreme.' 'Matters Arising' took nearly an hour, the minutes of the last meeting were gone through sentence by sentence. From the 'haze of repetitious triviality' she extracts a few points: one was the untactful re-instatement of the post of Deputy Chairman (instigated, the reader will recall, by Jeff Nuttall because of his Yorkshire residence, and the bone of considerable contention): the Society intended to revise upwards and re-submit its £86,000 grant application to the Arts Council for 1977–78: a great deal of time was wasted discussing which room in the Society should be re-painted first. After two and a half hours only five of the thirteen agenda items had been dealt with: an interval was announced and she made her excuses and left.

Martyn Goff sent a briefer account in the same vein: he was 'very distressed by both the substance and the conduct of the meeting': 'trivia were discussed exhaustingly'. The matters under discussion were mainly things which could have been dealt with by permanent staff, such as the arrangement of an office or the position of book-shelves— little seemed to have changed, then, since March, when Charles Osborne's outburst had been provoked by wrangling over the desk in the Chairman's office. The Treasurer, Vicky Allen, 'seemed to have no understanding of the figures or finances', and the Chairman 'seemed barely in control of the meeting'. He concludes that as the Arts Council is providing the Society with quite large sums of public money, they should expect affairs to at least be 'professionally conducted'.

Further worrying signs were apparent in the General Council meeting of 9th December 1977, attended for the Arts Council by Josephine Falk and Lawrence Mackintosh. The Secretary Robert Vas Dias had resigned, with effect from 13th February 1978, so the major business was the making of arrangements for appointing his successor. But the tabled job description only mentioned the role of General Secretary of the Poetry Society and not the conjoined role of Director of the National

Poetry Centre (echoing the situation earlier in the year when the second half of the conjoined roles of print-shop and bookshop manager was ignored in making the appointment). When this was mentioned 'George Wightman immediately dismissed my objections as merely a question of semantics'. When asked if they no longer saw themselves as a National Centre, Paddy Kitchen replied that they were not yet ready to undertake this, and that the building was not suitable for the role. They needed to mark time, she said. Falk wondered what was happening to the Arts Council's £54,000, which was being given to the Society to run a National Poetry Centre. The Education Secretary had applied to become half-time, and this was discussed, though Falk noted that the Witt Report had recommended an expansion of the education activities. George Wightman made a proposal that only corporate members of the Poetry Society should be allowed to use the services of the National Poetry Secretariat, but the Chairman and Treasurer discouraged further discussion of this. Valuable printing equipment had recently disappeared from the print room during a Friday evening reading, but Robert Vas Dias was not able to give a satisfactory answer about the insurance cover for such an event. Vicky Allen, the Treasurer, instigated a lengthy discussion about which cheques she should sign first.

I have quoted these rather depressing accounts of late 1977 meetings of the Poetry Society to show how far from the truth was the Arts Council's assumption was that all would be well at the Society once the radicals had been evicted. These accounts seem to show that, on the contrary, from the Arts Council's point-of-view, everything got worse. Paddy Kitchen's resignation of the Chair of the Society was reported in the *Times* on Saturday 16th September 1978: she had resigned 'not because of any new internal dissension' but because 'she had too much work to do, having been commissioned to write three books'.

Post-Mortem and New Plans

On 23rd August, 1977, Mottram was in correspondence with Allen Fisher, seeking to make overall sense of what had happened at the Poetry Society. He writes:

> The difficulty for socialists is not going to blow away: how to survive in a capitalist society and a basically capitalist world. Defeat is a defeat for any alternative—we try to form the new within the shell of the old (the familiar words still have good meaning). Monteverdi worked for Church and

State. I teach in a number of capitalist structures—University of London, Polytechnic of Central London, the Council for National Academic Awards, and all the universities and colleges I work in in the world. But I don't think I finally say less than I would otherwise. Strategy is where action is—i.e. praxis is at least one third strategy, one third tactics, and one third nerve: considered as method, that is.

Mottram doesn't go on to analyse the Poetry Society years in the light of these pronouncements, though he shows a very clear sense that those events were a small part of a larger social and cultural struggle, seeing them as part of an on-going dialectic in which the attempt is made to 'build the new in the shell of the old.' He is mainly using his own example of contriving to work within the opposing structures (and—which he doesn't say—to receive salaries and grants from it) in order to counter Fisher's plan of refusing any future contact at all with any organisation in receipt of Arts Council money. For instance, Fisher proposed to ask, before allowing his work to appear in a magazine, whether that magazine was in receipt of any such subsidies. Mottram can see that such a policy is pretty well impossible to maintain—the shell of the old has to be accepted. Hence, his own boycott was more targeted—it was a specific boycott of the Poetry Society which he maintained to the end. I will come back to this, but will first quote from earlier correspondence with Roger Guedalla in which the latter too tries to place the events in a wider political context. The letter to Mottram of 20th April 1977 (which is mainly about payments for the last Mottram issues of *Poetry Review*) ends with these reflections:

I am also very depressed at what has happened at the Society . . . We have handed the Society back to the most reactionary elements and it seems that all the efforts of the past five or eight years have come to nothing and Osborne and his friends have achieved exactly what they wanted. I did think, and I continue to think that we had a great chance to break their stranglehold but I never thought it would be easily or quickly achieved. I thought it was a serious and continuing struggle and I never thought we would give in so easily. . . . I have read a great deal and thought a great deal about the role of the radical artist in a capitalist society struggling in just the ways we have been doing. I have discussed the problems at length, in particular with friends in the I.M.G. [the International Marxist Group], the I.S. [the International Socialists] and the W.R.P. [Workers' Revolutionary Party] as well as with Tribunite members of the Labour Party and associates of the Militant Faction. I have always seen it as a political struggle, and thus as a question of tactics and organisation. I have taken it all very seriously but have been constantly reduced to being forced to make puerile gestures to prove that I am more radical than somebody else. This sort of thing has more to do with psychology than politics.

The organisations mentioned here would be prominent in the politics of the next decade, when the 'Militant Faction' attempted to build the new within the shell of the old Labour Party. Tactics and discipline were the tools, and especially the take-over of local branches of the Labour Party, in more-or-less the same way as the Poetry Society was taken over. But Guedalla's point (which is a strong one) is that the dominant radical group at the Poetry Society in the 1970s was often anarchic and provocative, rather than Socialistic and disciplined, or, at least, tactics were not co-ordinated, and wavered in an erratic way between the two extremes, particularly in the crucial 1975-76 period.

Allen Fisher, in August 1977, was on a similar wave-length, but with the difference that he was looking for a reconciliation, or at least some degree of consistency, between cultural and political practice. Fisher had been reading Mottram's essay 'The wild good and the heart ultimately: Ginsberg's art of persuasion', later published in Fisher's magazine *Spanner* 15 (London, 1979 for 1978). Fisher writes 'The new emphasis you give Ginsberg's reading manner and public stance is important to me, so much so that it begins to terrify me quite deeply.' He goes on to identify a distinction between 'American anarchy and uncollective action', on the one hand, and an 'England' in which there is 'more chance of socialism': in America, people are only 'collectively *against* the establishment' (my italics), but they are not collectively *for* anything, 'not collectively making that action on any kind of agreed-upon principles short of that negative.' He goes on, while stressing his admiration for Bob Cobbing, to point to the inconsistency of Cobbing's call at the Poets Conference meeting the week before for (on the one hand) solidarity of boycott against the Poetry Society, and at the same time, for continued acceptance by individuals of the National Poetry Secretariat's money, even though the latter was *part* of the Poetry Society and received its grant from the same Arts Council source. Fisher insists that his own position is to 'reject entirely': he adds (after taking in related matters) 'more and more I want to say "No"—"No more halfway houses". And by that meaning to say that these many individual stands must become collective stands if they are to be effective.' This stance of 'no involvement', he says, might seem like 'passivism towards the art aggressors and holders of money': it is not opposition to the principle of subsidy (on the contrary, that is 'money that IS ours by RIGHT'), but opposition to corrupt subsidy, that is 'the system that gives money to its own friends only to the deliberate exclusion of all else'.

It is striking in all of this how intensely the social and political conscience is wrestled with in an effort to come up with consistent principles and then live with them. The language is reminiscent of that of the religious Dissenters of earlier centuries, and the search for an untainted praxis gives no quarter to the individual, so that Fisher is driven towards his plan of making a 'Declaration' of his stance which will be sent out with his poetry when he sends it for publication— indeed, he tells himself, 'include declarations of stance wherever opportunity allows.' Mottram doesn't attempt to meet him head-on and dissuade him, but puts forward his own more lenient and humane tactic of building the new within the old. The failure of the Poetry Society venture, then, brings all these issues of cultural politics to a head.

Fisher also puts forward a plan for a replacement journal for radical poetry, following the appearance of the final Mottram *Poetry Review.* Taking up the theme of Mottram's notion of the British Poetry Revival, he proposes the title *Renaissance Information.* An initial committee will be set up, consisting mainly of CoLP members (The Consortium of London Presses), these being 'London-based printers' formerly associated with the Poetry Society print-shop, namely Cobbing, Upton, Griffiths, cheek, and Fisher himself. The first two issues would be edited by Mottram, 'to show continuity from Eric's editorship of the old *Poetry Review*'. There would be twenty pages (forty sides), printing 400–800 copies, appearing three times a year, and the five presses to 'undertake to do the work equally, eight sides each', and 'collective collation', with each press collating its own section of the magazine. Subscriptions would be £2 or £3 for three issues. It is, in many ways, a rather bizarre plan, with organisational requirements which would (surely) defeat a military requisitioner with unrestricted powers, let alone a group determined to 'cut out administration' by using 'oral communication' whenever possible. Clearly, the perception that the Poetry Society venture lacked consistency of collective action has produced a plan which envisages rather too much of it.

Mottram's reply to the plan on 23rd August is understandably doubtful about the proposed name. He would add Simon Pettet to the list of printers: he feels that there should be articles as well as poetry, so the journal should be 'at least quarterly and sixty pages', He says, 'by articles

I mean pieces which really extend information' (rather a different stance from the one taken in *Poetry Review*). He then comes back to the broader cultural issues discussed in Fisher's lengthy letter:

> I agree: it is a matter of the powerful poets of American anarchy whom we admire and have used for our take-off. They are not socialists and—politically—doomed to fine forms of protest and esoteric information collection—or the appalling anthropologistics of the Milwaukees. (I'm doing an article on this for *Margins* at the moment.)

These are shrewd comments, indicating that Mottram is far from being uncritically admiring of his favoured American poets. On the contrary, he is well aware of the limits and limitations of their cultural stance. Here the intertwining of poetic practice and political practice is again striking, but Mottram goes back to what he had said at Poets Conference a few weeks before in support of the boycott of the Poetry Society:

> As for the money issues, you know how I think on this and I said as much as I could at the Poets Conference meeting. But maybe I didn't make one thing clear—once a poet/publisher allows himself to be a token permitted rebel and takes Osborne's money, he is finished. He has become a permitted avant-gardist—i.e. a freak or jester. He has perpetuated the idea that there is a mainstream and that the Arts Council/Poetry Society clique represent it and that he is willing to be an appendage to that kind of activity.

This is clear enough, but it is difficult to see how being a 'token permitted rebel' in relation to the Arts Council is fundamentally different from Mottram's own position, working within all those capitalist structures (the University of London, the CNAA, and so on), not 'saying less than I would otherwise'. Why isn't Mottram himself also a 'freak or a jester' in circumstances that seem very similar, except that one group takes a grant and the other a salary? Why can't building the new in the shell of the old be done with the help of a grant if it is OK to do it with the help of a salary? This contradiction is at the heart of a most meticulous and tutelary correspondence, and Mottram seems to tell Fisher two different and contradictory things, perhaps deliberately leaving Fisher to work out a reconciliation between them for himself. Many of the poets and publishers seeking grant-aid did not, of course, hold a salaried post of any kind, much less one which afforded the kind of leeway then allowed to a university lecturer.

The same issues and contradictions are present in Mottram's more antagonistic correspondence with Robert Vas Dias. In his letters to Vas

Dias, Mottram has clearly asked him why he colluded with the Arts Council's imposition of control on the Poetry Society instead of resigning in protest, and Vas Dias replies that he couldn't resign because he needed the job. Mottram, I think, would himself have resigned his post if he felt himself morally compromised by keeping it, but on the other hand, adhering to the 'building the new within the shell of the old' formula is a good rationale for never seeing any need to do so. It is, then, something of a blind spot. In many ways he had more in common (as regards his personal situation and privileges) with the arts administrators he so much disliked than with the poets whose livelihoods were much more precarious than his own, but he never recognised that or made any (so to speak) ideological allowances for it.

The Boycott of the Poetry Society

In line with the views discussed by Allen Fisher, Eric Mottram and others in the summer and autumn of 1977, Poets Conference met on 25th November and approved a motion calling for a complete boycott of the Poetry Society. The press statement issued on 26th March (on the occasion of the radicals' walk-out from the General Council of the Poetry Society) was re-issued, and the Manifesto originally drawn up by Jeff Nuttall for the Poetry Society was adopted by Poets Conference. In spite of this, a state of total boycott (as envisaged by Allen Fisher) of all initiatives or enterprises associated with the Poetry Society or the Arts Council was extremely difficult to maintain in practice. For instance, an Anglo/French Poetry Translation Conference had taken place in the autumn, and a book of work by the participating poets and speakers was published. The published work included Mottram's 'Descents of love: songs of recognition' (which had also appeared in Mike Dobbie's 'Mugshots' series in 1977, for which the series format was a single, longer piece of work on a folded sheet of A4 card with passport-size photographs of the poet on the front, and with all copies signed by the author, the print-run being around 200). Mottram had written to Robert Vas Dias complaining about what he saw as 'highhanded' treatment of the poets, that is, not paying them a fee and requiring their 'handing over copyright to the Poetry Society.' Poets included in it received a free copy of the book, and Vas Dias offers Mottram another one 'in lieu of a fee' and quotes the printed copyright declaration ('copyright 1977 by Eric Mottram'). The rights or wrongs of this particular case are not the point here, and I use the example simply to show that in practice the totality of the boycott of the Poetry Society had (so to speak) an inevitable element of flexibility, and did not prevent Mottram's own appearance in print in a publication by 'Poetry Society Productions Ltd'. On the other hand, the same section of the Mottram archive (Mottram, 4/3/64–76) also contains a flier for the 'Poets in Person' programme at the Poetry Society for January–March 1978 in which he has underlined the names Elaine Feinstein, Roy Fisher, Colin Simms, Geoffrey Wainwright and Edwin Morgan, presumably because he regarded these as radical supporters who ought to be operating the total boycott of the Poetry Society.

Mottram's friends saw the contradictions, and were frank and honest enough to say so. Back in May 1977, when Mottram was giving radical sympathising poets a hard time if they read at the Poetry Society, MacSweeney wrote to him 'I don't see it as a compromise to read there, any more than it is to print *Poetry Review* (if it happens) on the premises or Bill, Bob, cris getting loot for [doing] it.'[2] In another letter later in the year MacSweeney takes up the theme again, in response to comments in Mottram's letters, pointing out, in effect, that poets are freelance operators who are not in position to turn down such offers, as salaried persons might be:

> I do think you're being a bit harsh on Chris and Jim for reading [at the Poetry Society]. Look, I know the fierce principles involved, and I support them, I am part of the fight. BUT: both poets read out of sheer necessity. Neither of them has a plush job like you and me with regular salary.[3]

But for Mottram, the boycott of the Poetry Society, and the bitterness engendered by the whole episode, could never end. In May 1985 London University's Department of Extra-Mural Studies had the idea of putting on a lecture series on modern American poets at the Poetry Society, and wrote to Mottram (in all innocence, presumably) inviting him—as one of the University's most prominent Americanists—to contribute a lecture. Eric must have written back a pretty stiff letter, putting them in the picture about the Poetry Society, though he did give them his views on the kind of American poets who ought to be covered. They took his

[2] Letter of 19th May 1977, EM5/151/1 in the Mottram Archive.

[3] Mottram Archive, letter of 29th October 1977, EM5/151/1.

advice, at least to the extent of including a lecture on John Ashbery. The letter to Mottram continues:

> I was of course surprised and unhappy to read your comments on the Poetry Society, and I felt I had to take the matter up with them. I understand that the senior staff and the Council of the Society are now substantially different from those of the years of your contact with the organisation.... We are of course sorry that you do not feel able to give a lecture. (Mottram, 4/3/87–93)

What may well have been the final communication between the Poetry Society and the poets of the 'BPR' was a typed request to Bob Cobbing, dated 7th July 1988 concerning a planned exhibition of little press material at the Poetry Society, to be assembled by Geoff Soar. The letter goes on to express sentiments which seem well-meant, but somewhat naïve:

> We see this exhibition as emphasising the vital role played by small presses and little magazines in contemporary poetry. I could also begin to heal the unfortunate breach between the ALP [The Association of Little Presses] and the Society. We at the Society regret that it ever took place: it is time it was put behind us. We hope that you and the ALP can agree with that sentiment. We would not want this exhibition to be the cause of further ill-feeling. (Mottram, 4/3/87–93)

Cobbing forwarded the letter to Mottram with a scrawled note: 'Dear Eric, Any comments, or suggestions as to how I should answer the above?' Eric may well have made a few suggestions, but they were probably not printable, and none are recorded in the archive.

Diaspora and Becoming 'the Re-Forgotten'

'In hell, the [post]moderns are punished by awarding them a huge, sensitive and critically informed general readership. I wish them *sales,* I wish them the *book group* . . . ' (Don Paterson, from 'Aphorisms', *London Review of Books,* 3rd February, 2005, p. 24)

I will end the 'Chronology' section by considering, and re-imagining, the consequences of the March 1977 walk-out, which led directly to the June 1977 AGM that restored the Poetry Society to its traditional form. We might begin by asking what they would have talked about, those ousted avant-gardists, if they had gathered in the 'White House' bar next-door to the Poetry Society in the long light of that midsummer Saturday evening in June 1977 after the AGM. Topics for discussion

would surely have included such questions as whether the defeat could
have been avoided. They might have asked themselves whether a more
flexible response a year or so before would have saved the day, and
whether they should have protected that bridge-head into the cultural
Establishment, so painfully built up over a six or seven year period. And,
they must have asked themselves 'What Now?' Did they already sense
the shadow of the long years that lay ahead in which they would play
the role of the culturally re-forgotten (Iain Sinclair's phrase)? In *The
Failure of Conservatism in Modern British Poetry* Andrew Duncan describes
the mood which set in during the late 1970s:

> The expansiveness of the 1960s was replaced by a siege mentality . . .
> [which] had three results: fetishization of the elements of style which
> signalled 'marginality'; crimped loyalty (so that reviewing and theorisa-
> tion in the little magazines was cliquey and intellectually dead); psycho-
> logical withdrawal from the stage, so that this poetry became invisible to
> younger poets (p. 176).

For what came next for these poets was at least a decade and a half of
total cultural exclusion—no profiles in Sunday papers, no studio lights,
no platform appearances at Summer Festivals. Not for them the Faber-
style poetry promotions of the mid-eighties, 'poets touring in helicop-
ters, bankrolled by ticket sales from *Cats*, and the Madison Avenue-style
promotional schemes, photo-shoots in costume, and television appearances used to promote the twenty poets of the so-called New Generation
in the spring of 1994'.[4] Instead, they had chosen something like the
'elected silence' of the Cistercian,[5] a desire not be heard that conse-
crated their incorruptibility, their determination to remain above the
snares of the commercial 'Spectacle'. Hence, their work became hard to
find: you wouldn't come across it unless you were part of 'the samizdat
circuit' yourself, 'or unfortunate enough to drink at one of the pubs
where they still have readings in a back room.'[6] So when the tide began

---

[4] Keith Tuma in *Fishing by Obstinate Isles: Modern and Postmodern British Poetry and
American Readers,* Northwestern University Press, 1998, p. 57. *Cats* is the successful
Andrew Lloyd Webber musical based on T.S. Eliot's *Old Possum's Book of Practical
Cats,* of which Faber holds the copyright.

[5] The phrase 'elected silence' is from the opening of the poem 'The Habit of
Perfection', by G. M. Hopkins, another poet who 'chose' the poetic twilight of
obscurity ('Elected Silence, sing to me/ And beat upon my whorled ear').

[6] Iain Sinclair, preface to *Conductors of Chaos: a Poetry Anthology* Picador, 1996, p. xiv.

to turn towards 'experimentation' (of a kind) in the early 1990s, most of them would be exactly where they had been in the 70s, which is to say, on the outside (or on 'The Margins', as they flattered themselves by calling it). Ahead of them, that Saturday in June 1977, lay years of self-financing, of getting by, of temping, or supply-teaching at GLC social-priority schools, of gardening or grave-digging for the Borough Council, of getting up at five to hump barrels in the 'Anchor Brewery' on Bankside, or just signing on to pick up unemployment benefit. And at the weekends, distributing their work would mean literally and exactly that—getting on the bus to *Compendium* in Camden Town and *Turrett* in Kensington Church Walk with a dozen copies in a shoulder bag, and touting them sale-or-return, with one third off, and a promise to re-visit in a month's time. And meanwhile, other people's books—real books with proper covers and ink that stayed on the pages—were commissioned, and published, and reviewed, and acclaimed—books by people who wouldn't know them and their small-press kind from Adam (or, in a few cases, Eve). The action was somewhere else, and they were tasting the bitter fruits of defeat. Peter Robinson, a poet and one-time 'Cambridge poet' who has written a thesis on the work of Roy Fisher (one of the few figures admired by both 'Cambridge' and 'London' avant-gardists) writes, 'I remember feeling much worse when, in the late Seventies, it became clear that a loose affiliation of Oxford-based writers had taken over the metropolitan power base.'[7]

The lot of the 'BPR' poets, then, was 'The Scene'—a sequence of *déja-vu* poetry readings that stretched to the crack of doom—with their steady-state audiences of belated Dadaists, proto-modernists, hopelessly addicted word-junkies—always the same faces, just a little bit older each time. If nothing else, those audiences were faithful—the trouble was, they never quite reached double figures. Usually the poet giving the reading was on first-name terms with every member of the audience, and had shared flats, or squats, or cleaning rosters over the years with most of them. Again and again poet and audience faced each other for the ritual of phatic communion in the 'function rooms' found up twisty stair-cases above pubs in Camden Town, Chalk Farm, or Tottenham Court Road, rooms that seemed to have been left over from the 1930s and were otherwise more-or-less disused—musty curtains, buffalo-horns, bedroomy wallpaper, brown-marmalade panelling, murky lighting,

---

7 (Peter Robinson, http://jacketmagazine.com/20/pbi.html).

unspeakable carpets.[8] There might have been functions you could comfortably perform in these rooms, but reading poetry wasn't one of them. An unfamiliar face at these gatherings would cause puzzled glances, and the suspicion that the faithful might be in the presence of an Arts Council spy, enviably picking up 40p copies of Mottram-era *Poetry Reviews* at public expense. Endless such evenings lay ahead in the Poetry Gulag at 'The Margins'. It was always November or February, rain or sleet spattering the window panes, the walk to the Tube station still to come. Such were the consequences of that fatal day in June—that midsummer Saturday in Jubilee Year when normal service was resumed at the Poetry Society, the year of Johnny Rotten, and Virginia Wade, and the chain of 'Coastal Beacons'—when the Battle of Earls Court was fought and lost, and the long after-life of British avant-garde poetry began.

The foregoing paragraphs represent a pessimistic view of the 1977 *débacle*, one which sees the remnants of this avant-garde grouping as trapped in a cycle of compulsive, ultimately directionless repetition (the kind of cycle which is hauntingly called, in Roy Fisher's *City*, 'a cemetery of performance'). Surveyed with a less drooping and more auspicious eye, however, the picture looks rather different, for the radical impulse was not snuffed out by the Poetry Society debacle, but *displaced*—it simply migrated elsewhere. For instance, in the late 1970s, 'The Orpington Talks' were organised by Robert Hampson, Erik Vonna-Michel and Ken Edwards. These were a series of three all-day Saturday seminars led in turn by Eric Mottram, Allen Fisher, and Bob Cobbing, at Lower Green Farm, Orpington, where the three organizers were then living. As I recall them, these events filled the substantial wood-panelled living room of the old farmhouse—a building left-over from a former age, bizarrely surviving in the midst of modern suburbia.[9] These events took something like the role of the Poetry Information evenings at the Poetry Society during the Mottram era. They involved a substantial commitment of time by the participants, and were part of the process of educating an audience in the procedures and varieties of the new poetries. They were advertised in *Time Out*, although most of the faces there were

---

[8] This draws on Roy Fisher's description (in *News for the Ear*, Stride, 2000, p. 18) of the rooms in which jazz is usually performed.

[9] The Bob Cobbing day, 8th July 1978, was recorded on three cassette tapes which are now in the Mottram Archive at King's College (Mottram, 14/1/30).

familiar.[10] Also already underway by late 1977 was the King's Poetry
Series, run by Eric Mottram at King's College London: Roy Fisher read on
6th December 1977, and the series ended with another Roy Fisher reading in 1984. Later came the 'Sub Voicive' poetry readings, chaired by
Lawrence Upton since 1994, and the Sub Voicive 'colloquia', which are
all-day talks and seminars on aspects of radical poetics. The fifth of these
took place at Birkbeck College in September 2001, on the theme of 'How
do we perform that?', while the sixth was in March 2004 at the Camden
Peoples' Theatre with the theme 'Perhaps Trespass', concerning cross-
overs between poetry, painting, dance, and performance.

Cris cheek gives a broader list of 'what came after', in this dispersal or
diaspora phase of the 'BPR', emphasising the general lack of any sustaining academic infrastructure or affiliations of the 'London' poets (in
contrast to the 'Cambridge' poets):

> places and events (Kings College readings, Rasp workshops, Goldsmith's
> meetings, Orpington day lecture events, Sub Voicive readings, Association
> of Little Presses Book Fairs, Robert Sheppard and Patricia Farrell's
> Peckham evenings, Virginia Firnberg's weekend at the International
> Students House and such like). It's also worth pointing out that although
> dozens traipsed in and out of Kings for readings and semi-open sessions
> there was no institutional/ educational basis in London other than
> E(ric).M(ottram). Academic contexts simply didn't figure heavily, at least
> not in comparison to each other's short-life houses, the *Rainbow Cafe*, pubs
> such as *The Moon, The Archers, The White Swan*, shops (*Camerawork* and *Four
> Corners* and *The Laundry* in Lambeth Walk), converted derelict industrial
> premises (LMC, LFMC, X6, Chisenhale), galleries (ACME, House) and work-
> shops (such as JGJGJGJGJGJG . . . . . .'s in Covent Garden). Certainly a differ-
> ence from the Cambridge set up i reckon.[11]

Here again is that 'London'/'Cambridge' dichotomy; the edgy friction
between them kept them apart, but it increasingly seems to me that
these two avant-gardes needed each other, and that their separation in
the 1970s was a key factor in the outcome of events, for each had qualities the other lacked, and they would have been a more effective force
for permanent change if they had been able to find a way of working
together. Indeed, the 'Cambridge'/'London' divide is in some ways a
version of the divide between what I earlier called 'conservative radicals'

10   Basic data from Ken Edwards on the British Poets Archive at http://www.
     jiscmail.ac.uk/cgi-bin/webadmin?A2=ind0002&L=british-poets&P=R13841&I=-1

11   cris cheek on British Poets Archive, http://www.jiscmail.ac.uk/cgi-bin/
     webadmin?A2=ind9711&L=british-poets&P=R11943&I=-1

and 'radical radicals': each, to repeat, needed at least a little bit of what the other had. The 'London' group, as the present account makes only too evident, was always looser and more anarchic, and it paid the price for that, so that members who eventually achieved fame usually did so for something other than poetry—perhaps Iain Sinclair is the best example—or else found success in academic spheres alongside their poetry, examples being Brian Catling, Allen Fisher, and Robert Hampson, Professors, respectively, of Fine Art, at the Ruskin School in Oxford, of Poetry and Art at Manchester Metropolitan University, and of English at Royal Holloway, London University. 'Cambridge', in comparison, was closely-focused, with a well-defined institutional affiliation. Though making quite a thing about its disdain for publication and publicity, it has in fact always been very astute and canny about protecting and promoting its identity (often by denying it has one). No 'London' avant-garde poet has become as well-known as J. H. Prynne—paradoxically famous for shunning publicity—or achieved anything like his status as a distinct cultural 'brand', which is known about even by those who have never read him.

Themes

6

The 'British Poetry Revival'—Some Characteristics

So far no attempt has been made to describe the kind of poetry (or poetries) hitherto simply designated as 'radical' or 'BPR' poetry, leaving a kind of vacuum at the heart of this account. The task of filling this gap can be approached in two different ways: the first way is to posit a central division in British poetry and then describe that division in broadly 'institutional' or 'generic' terms, rather than in terms of specific aspects of practice, so that on one side we have poets associated— however loosely—with a particular journal, or press, or poetry-workshop, or poetry-anthology, or with a particular set of forebears, or a particular location, educational institution, or set of intellectual, social, and political attitudes. On the opposing side we would have poets associated with *other* journals, poetry workshops, etc. Doing it this way slightly removes the emphasis from the strictly *writerly* consequences of sharing a particular set of cultural affiliations, and emphasises instead the cultural or intellectual formation as such. The other approach is to begin with the writing itself, and try to identify recurrent tropes and features which the members of the alleged grouping are statistically more likely to manifest than those who do not belong to that group. This second approach is chiefly the method I follow in the later sections of the present chapter, whereas the first approach provides the basis for most of the remainder of the book. Crudely expressed, the first method places the primary emphasis on the writer, and the second on the writing. Of course, neither method can ever entirely exclude the other, but each has a recognisable *predominant* emphasis. Predictably, the usual reaction from poets themselves to any attempt to identify affiliative groupings is to say that the members of the alleged group have little or nothing in common, or that no such group exists. In fact, one might argue that a sure sign of the existence of a group is an upsurge in the issuing of denials that there is one. Thus, Andrew Duncan proclaims (in *The Failure of Conservatism in Modern British Poetry*) that 'Recent good resolutions have made me renounce the "Cambridge experimental axis" as an analytical tool. Formal analysis suggests that there is no resemblance between the usual suspects' (p. 132). It is true, of course, that the 'writerly' approach to groupings can exaggerate affinities of content, style, and technique; it is also the case that it is conceivable that a number of poets could share attitudes, outlets, and locale without there being any perceived affinities of writing practice at all. But that seems, on the whole, unlikely. In any case, the aim of using the 'writerly' approach to groupings is to suggest the *repertoire* of practices on which a given set of writers draw, even though the actual mix and emphasis will vary from one to another. In the same way, all chess players use the same repertoire of moves, but the 'mix' is different and distinctive in the case of every player of talent. In another mood, I should add, Andrew Duncan *does* write about the Cambridge 'School' collectively— see below—that is, about the 'Cambridge' writers featured in the anthology *A Various Art*, the very title of which draws attention to the diversity within the notional unity of the grouping.

It seems to me, then, that there is a recognisable affinity between 'BPR' poets, at both the 'institutional' and the 'writerly' level, and that it is possible to begin to describe some of the elements which contribute towards this recognisable affinity. But let me begin with a recent authoritative account of the major divide in recent British poetry, Peter Middleton's essay 'Poetry after 1970' in *The Cambridge History of Twentieth Century Literature* (ed. Laura Marcus and Peter Nicholls, Cambridge University Press, 2004).

The 'BPR'—an 'Institutional' Account

Middleton first discusses in a general way the sense that there is such a division, and writes that 'the main reason why there appears to be "no coherence on the poetry scene" is a division between two kinds of poetry, neither of which has an accepted name, that could with considerable cause be called Postmodernist and Modernist' (p. 769). The Postmodernist kind of poetry was 'ascendant for most of the [post 1970] period and is represented in such anthologies as Blake Morrison and Andrew Motion's *The Penguin Book of Contemporary British Poetry*, 1982; *The*

New Poetry, edited by Michael Hulse, David Kennedy and David Morley, (Bloodaxe) 1993, and Sean O'Brien's *The firebox: poetry from Britain and Ireland after 1945*, (Picador) 1998. But this kind of Postmodernism was 'less radical Postmodernism than in fiction or the visual arts and often looks less modern than the Modernists' (p. 770), for it is 'Postmodernism as play, as withdrawal from political ideologies and commitment, and of the treatment of identity and history as style' (p. 770).[1] By contrast, the Modernists are 'much harder to find': they 'write in a continuous tradition that includes Surrealism, High Modernist writers like Gertrude Stein, James Joyce, Mina Loy, Hilda Doolittle, and both European and American modernists' (p. 770). Their work can be found in anthologies which tend not to stay in print so long, such as: Andrew Crozier and Tim Longville's *A Various Art*, (Carcanet) 1987; *The New British Poetry*, edited by Gillian Allnutt, Fred D'Aguiar, Ken Edwards, and Eric Mottram, (Paladin) 1988; Iain Sinclair's *Conductors of Chaos: a Poetry Anthology* (Paladin) 1996; *Other British and Irish Poetry since 1970*, edited by Ric Caddel and Peter Quartermain, (Wesleyan University Press) 1999; the elaborately titled *Foil: An Anthology—Poetry, 1985–2000, Defining New Poetry and Performance Writing from England Scotland and Wales, 1985–2000*, edited by Nicholas Johnson, (Etruscan Books), 2000, and Keith Tuma's *Anthology of Twentieth-Century British and Irish Poetry*, (Oxford University Press), 2001. Work of the kind represented in these anthologies, says Middleton:

> retains the Modernist belief that the poem is capable of challenging the public sphere, investigating history and science, making discoveries, and is alert to the insights of literary theorists, and identity politics. It recognises that language is already in play as the scene of desire and the field of the 'other', that it can be fragmented, neologistic, philosophical, and can show subjectivity in the process of emergence and deconstruction. They don't think experimentation is an itch. (pp. 770–1)

This usefully indicates a range of (neo-)Modernist attitudes and beliefs, though without indicating how any of these poets seek to embody or express such attitudes in poetic practice. Middleton then describes the 'Cambridge' and 'London' sub-groups of [late] modernism in institutional terms, the former being 'a group of poets, whose connections were routed through Cambridge as both place and university, [who]

---

[1] For the purposes of discussing recent and contemporary poetry, it would be helpful to insert the word 'late' before 'modernism', which I will do from this point onwards.

began publishing in earnest during the seventies with several independent presses—Ferry Press, Grosseteste, and Street Editions—and were
eventually represented by the anthology *A Various Art'* (p. 782). In this
kind of Cambridge work, 'words carry their full weight of variant meanings and etymological connections' and 'syntax retains a haunting
awareness of what authoritative statement and authorial sincerity
sound like, yet the fragmentation of sense compels this communicative
bond to question itself repeatedly' (p. 783). This is a very useful and
expressive formulation of the characteristic tone and feel of 'Cambridge'
writing, though, again, there remains the further step of showing what
exactly syntax does—*syntactically*—when it is 'retain[ing] a haunting
awareness of what authoritative statement and authorial sincerity
sound like.' The 'London' branch of the late modernist avant-garde, by
contrast, is seen as more heterogeneous, as 'linked by the belief in the
value of radical innovation and diversity, as well as cross-overs into other
media'. Some of the major 'London' figures had little formal higher
education ('and therefore freed themselves of the anti-intellectualism
which had bedevilled British culture in the twentieth century', p. 783).
They were 'often committed to projects rather than single poems', and
their work often made 'large intellectual, emotional, and aesthetic
demands on readers' (p. 783). The figures mentioned include Allen
Fisher, Lee Harwood, Bob Cobbing, cris cheek, Maggie O'Sullivan, and
Bill Griffiths. This broad descriptive mapping of the field into the two
major 'camps' (that is, postmodernist and [late] modernist), and into two
major regional sub-divisions of the second camp (that is, 'Cambridge'
and 'London'), provides an extremely useful basis: the fine detail can
then be provided by an essay such as Robert Hampson's on cris cheek,
which details the range and extent of the 'London' group's 'cross-overs
into other media'[2], and Andrew Duncan's essay on the 'Cambridge'
group, 'Such that commonly each: *A Various Art* and the Cambridge
Leisure Centre' (in *Jacket 20*, December 2002)[3], which explores the provenance and affiliations of this group.

Another 'institutional' account, though with the emphasis on a
rather longer provenance, would identify a kind of long-standing
'dissenting tradition' in poetry into which the radical poetry of the
1970s fits. This is the approach taken by Ric Caddel and Peter
Quartermain in their introduction to the anthology *Other British and Irish*

[2]   http://www.pores.bbk.ac.uk/1/index.html

[3]   http://jacketmagazine.com/20/dunc-camb.html

Poetry since 1970. An expanded version of this introduction appeared in the on-line journal *Jacket 4,* 1998:[4] the two editors see a 'buried' experimental tradition, 'dissenting and largely neglected if not indeed suppressed':

> Its history has yet to be written, and stretches back to Clare, Blake, Smart, and the two Vaughans, Henry and Thomas. It is a tradition which in this century has not been ashamed to borrow from overseas models (such as [the tenth century Iranian poet] Rudaki, Horace, Whitman or Apollinaire), and which runs counter to the mainstreams of British verse.

In twentieth century British poetry, Basil Bunting is seen as a bridge to the American branch of this dissenting tradition:

> Basil Bunting used to say of the thirty years 1920–1950 that they were 'the American years,' and would talk of the great American poets, Niedecker, Pound, William Carlos Williams, and Zukofsky, limiting his esteem for Eliot, and only excepting from what he called the doldrums of English poetry in those decades the work of David Jones, Hugh MacDiarmid, and (with some diffidence) himself.

Here the view of the dissenting tradition is highly specific: it holds its distance from the most prestigious form of 'high' modernism in poetry—T. S. Eliot's early work—and seems to feel that although literary Modernism first flowered in Europe, it took deeper root in America and sustained its momentum for longer. In this sense, the strong American influence, and the international affiliations generally, which opponents of the radicals at the Poetry Society in the 1970s so much resented, had a compelling rationale.

The 'BPR'—a 'Writerly' Account

Another very useful essay which performs a similar task to Middleton's, but from a 'writerly' rather than an 'institutional' perspective, is Ken Edwards's 'The Two Poetries', in *Angelaki,* 3/1, April 2000, pp. 25–36. To understand poetry, says Edwards, you must understand 'the paradigm within which it is made: that is to say, its cultural history, its overall aesthetic purpose, the expectations it assumes in its community of readers' (p. 25). He argues that 'the schism between modernist-derived,

---

4   (http://jacketmagazine.com/04/otherbrit.html)

or avant-garde work, on the one hand, and other poetries in English is a major rift or fault line running through contemporary British poetry' (p. 25). Much of the essay discusses notions of 'paradigms' and ways of *theorising* the difference, but the core of it is an *illustration* of some of the characteristics of the 'two poetries' based on a comparative examination of a poem by Matthew Sweeney which had appeared in the *New Statesman* in 1984, and was selected by Michael Hofmann for the annual prize for the year's best poem in that journal; this poem is used to represent the 'non-modernist paradigm', while representing the modernist paradigm is the first stanza of Allen Fisher's poem 'Atkins Stomp', which is the first of four 32-line stanzas in the poem, the poem itself being the sixth of fourteen related poems in Fisher's book *Brixton Fractals*, 1985.

I will not quote from either poem, since I am more interested here in sketching the range of contrasting 'Postmodernist' and 'Modernist' features which Edwards identifies. He concedes the modest worth of Sweeney's poem: 'it eschews the flashy smart-aleckry of the then fashionable "Martian" school. As descriptive writing, it succeeds in "painting a picture" with an economy of means, and it doesn't belabour its point' (p. 30). Typically of a competition-winning poem, he says, it has 'autobiographical content, preferably harking back to a middle-class childhood . . . the frequent use of the simple past tense in descriptive/narrative mode, and a moment of sex or death tastefully handled. . . . [and] the final line . . . serves as closure or epiphany' (p. 30). In Fisher's poem, by contrast, we don't have 'normative language of description and narrative': there *is* both description and narrative, but 'the discourse is discontinuous, jagged; . . . the techniques include collage and montage'. As with the Sweeney poem, there is a strong sense of place, 'yet the reality of that place is rendered as in a Cubist painting rather than a snapshot: there are fragments of (overheard?) conversation . . . but no speaker is named' (p. 31). Other 'curiosities' include 'typographical irregularities', for example 'opening quotation marks not balanced out, creating uncertainty about where a fragment ends', and 'the poem is peppered with single words in a non-serif typeface': these words are from 'a word list provided by the poet Richard Miller, and clearly function as an irruption of the aleatory, or chance, which Fisher has chosen to incorporate into his textual weave' (p. 32). There is an author's endnote to Fisher's poem which cites '"resources" used—*Investor's Chronicle, Hansard,* Janson, Mandlebrot (the inventor of the term "fractal")', giving a sense of the range of reference in the poem, 'from the fields of finance, politics, art history, and mathematics'. Overall, then, 'the materiality of language as the substance of the poem—what it is made of—is constantly foregrounded by the rapid shifts in register and other discontinuities, even as the language carries forward the argument. The poem subverts itself again and again with humour and parody of its own language' (p. 32). Generally, its methodology is comparable to that of 'visual artists such as Beuys, or with the music of Berio or Stockhausen. In other words, it is not out of place in the great current of twentieth-century modernism.' A final summarising contrast between the two poems is drawn in terms of how they differ as energy structures: Fisher's demands active participation from the reader, it requires 'continuous creative input of the reader to constellate its energy, driven by the material rush of its language', whereas the Sweeney piece seems to need only a spectator, for 'with its pared-down language . . . [it] seems to tend to wind down into a low-energy equilibrium state' (p.33). Edwards ends with a useful summarising table listing important characteristics of the two poetries (re-christened 'The Mainstream' and 'The Parallel Tradition'), and I reproduce his table here:

THE MAINSTREAM	THE PARALLEL TRADITION
'Clarity of expression'— normative language use	Non-normative language use: extended vocabulary and/or broken syntax, parataxis Foregrounding of modes or registers, language as material or sound, constructivism
Coherent narrative, transparency reference, functionalism	Multiple viewpoints or foci, lack of authorial 'presence' Politics of poetic form
Single point of view, the lyric voice	Open form, use of indeterminacy
Rhetoric or argument Closure—epiphany	Metonymy—material/metaphor overdetermination
Foregrounded use of metaphor and simile	

Middleton and Edwards together give a useful alignment of views on the nature of the major divide in contemporary British poetry, and in particular on the character of the 'Modernist' side: Middleton's is predominantly an 'institutional' description; the Modernist poetry of 1970 onwards is (especially on the 'London' side) politically and intellectually engaged 'challenging the public sphere, investigating history and science, making discoveries, and is alert to the insights of literary theorists, and identity politics', while also (especially on the 'Cambridge' side) highly conscious of the language medium itself, so that 'words carry their full weight of variant meanings and etymological connections.' Edwards supplements this with a closer account of the specific qualities of the Modernist writing—typographical irregularities, mixtures of register, lack of 'authorial presence', and so on. Both also emphasise the affinities of this kind of Modernist writing with radicalism in the other arts—music and painting, for instance—and the article by Robert Hampson supplements these two pieces further by showing in detail the range of links and affiliations between the modernist poets of the 1970s and experimental or counter-cultural work in London especially.

'BPR' Poetry Exemplified—Carlyle Reedy

These overview accounts by Middleton, Caddel and Quartermain, and Edwards, give a general sense of what 'BPR' poetry can be like: I will supplement these by looking closely at one piece of work published in a Mottram issue of *Poetry Review* to show how initially daunting and unfamiliar such work could seem at its most uncompromising. The piece in question, by Carlyle Reedy, is listed in the *Poetry Information* summary of Mottram issues of *Poetry Review* as '(isle of sheppey)', and it appeared on two facing pages, 86 and 87, in *Poetry Review* 66:2 (the second of the large-format Mottram issues) in 1976. It could also be described, though, as a sequence of three short 'place' pieces, respectively entitled: '(isle of sheppey)', '(Arizona desert)', and 'written at wivenhoe', but for convenience I will follow *Poetry Information* and refer to it as '(isle of sheppey)': the two pages are reproduced below exactly as printed, and readers can judge this point (three pieces or one?) for themselves. I have chosen Carlyle Reedy as my 'worked' example because her work features in the highly successful anthology *Out of Everywhere: linguistically innovative poetry by women in North America and the UK* (ed. Maggie O'Sullivan, Reality Street Editions, 1996), and because Reedy gives an extremely illuminating account of her aims and methods as Chapter 34, 'Working Processes of a Woman Poet', in *Poets on Writing: Britain 1970–1991*, (ed. Denise Riley, Macmillan, 1992). The two pages of '(isle of sheppey)' are reproduced on the following pages as originally printed:

Carlyle Reedy

(isle of sheppey)

     the wind
   dragging
a hand bronze
  turns in the furrows

    open
    the palm

  bottle on stone
the healer shucks
wheat
the seed in

our body
  shining

Sun far on interminable
  Sheaves the worshipping
    ancestor
    dreams
going slowly
  slow we
  sow the lines

  now dredge song from

    . . .

(Arizona desert)

  grains of
    sand
       grind the wheel

  to stop

  here Seurat

     in silence
     heat is
     steady on

an old highway. the peat fine
petrified bone. A light shone
on the car. It hit broadside. One roan
horse split as by laser
                              Quick
                    flesh incident.
                                   negative
                                   ionized
                    night fallen over it.

rag & bone man
at world's end

               scrap
          iron
               icon years, the end

     a cornea. Uncertain

     the cornice, passing

     "in age man seeks"

treeless   asphalt
          what lie could teach
               position in this landscape?

     "less diversion . . ."
                              Pain
Knots   like rock
          In bone amassing

     ". . & no more collecting."

          in the gutter,
          Rain.
               . . .
written at
wivenhoe

          wind at an angle
               clean
          the crane

framing bones. a strained music
               silence

               man is

Sun
at twilight
catching small

worms in the viscous bay meanwhile

   g u l l s
          the inheritors
   c a l l
   c a l l

the skeleton hull
    open   to sand

mist   the ghost
on barren land

                 a mast. A mark/
                    now dark

          the waters

∽

Getting a purchase on such material is not by any means easy: I've
suggested already that the three sections are all meditative impressions
of places, but the three don't make an obvious set: the first and third
'match' each other—two English coastal places, the Isle of Sheppey, on
the Kent side of the Thames Estuary, and Wivenhoe, on the Essex side,
but in between, incongruously, is the Arizona Desert. There are incon-
gruities, too, in the titling of the sections, the first two bracketed, the
third not; 'Arizona' with a capital initial letter but 'wivenhoe' not; the
first two titles merely designating the places, but the third ('written at
wivenhoe') highlighting the act of writing and recording. All three highlight natural processes—the wind furrowing a tidal race, petrification
and fossilisation of organic materials, the gradual stripping down of a
wrecked boat by wind and tides, and so on. The piece is interested, too,
in the effect of natural forces on human objects—the car disabled by
sand in the machinery, and the wrecked boat, beginning their passage
to scrap iron or beach wrack. The natural forces are at first viewed or
imagined as if seen by 'worshipping ancestors' but, then the sensibility
seems to reverse its polarisation, so that the natural forces seem merely
the equivalents of forces made by humans, so that the dead horse is

seen 'as [if] split by laser'. The un-attributed and fragmented quotation in the 'Arizona' section seems to hint at human evolutionary development, a movement away from merely seeking novelty—('in age man seeks . . . less diversion'). The ending, though, is stark, almost a returning of the landscape to natural forces (gulls the inheritors, the skeleton hull, the ghost on barren land, and the dark waters).

In addition to this kind of 'overview-reading', the contextualisation provided by the poet's own general comments on her work and procedures is certainly helpful, even though the procedural comments in Riley's book were made many years after the writing of this particular piece, and without any specific reference to it. Especially relevant to broad-scale, panoramic, visionary writing like this *Poetry Review* piece is the fact that the role envisaged for the poet is an extremely elevated one: she cites Mayakovsky's example as demonstrating 'the imperative of identifying with a large social body as its representative' (Riley, p. 261). For her, the poet must be experimental, taking a stance of 'cornered high risk with lunatic daring', and the woman poet must take the additional risk of 'presuming to challenge Apollo' (p. 261). She describes various forms this daring may take, offering six distinct procedural approaches. She begins with the 'poetry of image . . . based in the contemplation of things seen, in the material of the world and in the mind that looked upon them' (p. 262). But here the high rhetoric is brought down to earth, for 'To find "hidden musics" and "things unseen" no particular mystification was necessary. One merely looked at ordinary reality, thought through the image in the mind, and refined out of the work any extraneous or unnecessary data.' (p. 262). This gives a useful lead-in to the '(isle of sheppey)' set. She goes on to commend, 'a poetry of image with no event', and refers to Wallace Stevens's 'Thirteen ways [of looking at a blackbird]', as well as to her own attempt 'to get as near as possible to a condensed, satisfying observation in which emotion or awareness of temporality may come through image alone' (p. 262). All these phrases seem useful in relation to '(isle of sheppey)', which seems, as indicated above, like a succession of landscape 'stills'.

This is in contrast to her second mode or procedure, 'the visual cinematic experience', which approximates in its effect to a series of film clips. Her third type contains elements of the first two, 'mixing cinematic visual factors with preoccupation with the sound of language, the fragmentation of language by some outside influence, such as influx of data and timing changes or breaks in speech patterns happening while walking down the street having a talk' (p. 264). Maintaining the cinema metaphor, this third type suggests something like snatches of sound-track. The first three procedural types, then, work through a cinematic analogy—the first is like a still image, the second like a film-clip, and the third like extracts from a soundtrack. The second type, especially, seems to emphasise *perception* of the environment and its representation, hence, I think, the mention of Seurat in the second piece, where the heat-glare on the desert highway seems to break up the scene into intense points of light. Although I am not claiming a tight correspondence of the three linked 'sheppey' pieces to these first three procedures, as outlined in the much later article, there are some suggestive overlaps, and the crescendo of emphasis on sound in the third (wivenhoe) piece is very marked: the low-lying shore and the skeleton of the wrecked boat in the sand are set in a *sound*-scape (the wind, the gulls, strained music, silence) rather than a *land*-scape.

Her fourth procedural type is a kind of collage of 'found' items, intermixed, juxtaposed, fragmentary, and again, there are strong elements of this in the *Poetry Review* piece. This type seems a little less easy to assimilate to the cinema metaphor, unless we think of the most disjointed and teasing kind of avant-garde cinema practice. She does link this fourth type, though, with things seen 'from the window of a train or moving in a car past signs and symbols of our civilisation', perhaps calling to mind the 2004 film *London Orbital* by Chris Petit and Iain Sinclair (Illuminations Films for Channel 4 Television), which mainly consists of filmed 'traffic runs' on the M25 motorway around London. The two remaining types seem less immediately relevant to the earlier *Poetry Review* piece, but I will add them here for completeness: Type five, 'poetry as event and as performance', sees the poem as a 'score' for performance, with the poet-as-producer now sidelined, and the poet-as-performer brought to the fore, and following a set schema (or series of such) to perform the poem in different ways (or, to be more specific, as different poems). This type seems especially relevant to 'The Slave Ship', which is reproduced in both the *Out of Everywhere* anthology (pp. 145–148) and the OUP anthology of British and Irish Poetry edited by Keith Tuma (pp. 630–632), in which, as Tuma writes, 'the two fonts . . . suggest two voices, or personal narrative and a more impersonal commentary, but the relationship between the two is more fluid and complex than that' (p. 629). Here (with the fifth procedural type) the notions of acting, producing, and performance perhaps keep the cinematic metaphor residually present, as does type six, which is another blend, where 'what is developmental is in relationship to what is often arbitrarily fixed, in mixes and traces' (p. 267). So the text has a fixed part (the *names* of composers, in the example given), and a *composed* part, and the two are interwoven. This (to offer a final filmic link) is suggestive of the kind of film which incorporates both scripted and improvised elements. My slightly 'tightened' version of Reedy's six-part aesthetic is offered to show the high degree of thought-out emphasis on procedural options and constellations of possibility seen in the work of poets and performers of this kind.[5] Clearly (in my view) the poets and their sympathetic critics of the 1970s needed to do more than they actually did at the time to provide their potential audiences with some *ab initio* insight into the aesthetics, the politics, the history, and the poetics of this kind of performance practice.

The 'BPR'—Six further 'Writerly' Characteristics

I want, finally, to add a supplementary annotated catalogue of some frequently occurring writerly characteristics of post-1970 Modernist or 'BPR' poetry, taking examples from other writers. Firstly, there is a frequent use of *extreme* minimalism or implicitness: I say 'extreme', because nearly all poetry has a degree of brevity and compression—few poems are as long as novels—and because poetry is always to some extent (as Auden said) a *laconic* art. A simple example can be seen in Lawrence Upton's *Wire Sculptures* (Reality Street Editions, 2003), described by Allen Fisher as 'a broken raft of narratives', 'written from the moving boundaries of South London and at the boundary of his being', they offer (among other things) 'degraded urban landscapes, politicised critiques, mundane violence, perplexities of perception' (Alison Croggan). Most of these features are seen in the poem, 'Sutton', which reads complete:

feet in the face
blood on the wall

ball lightning

ha-ha ha-ha-ha

---

[5] For further relevant discussion see Harriet Tarlo, 'Provisional pleasures: the challenge of contemporary experimental women poets' in *Feminist Review* , vol. 62, no. 1, 1999, pp. 94–112.

gut into the knife

he fell that way
honest

Compression here reduces an image, an impression, to little more than a word or a pair of words, and it is this succession of such 'residual images' which constitutes the body of the poem, so that the words left on the page seem just a trace of a verbal structure which has all but vanished. The word 'image', of course, is misleadingly re-assuring, because it implies something realised and complete, very much as in the traditional currency of poetry. Some other word is needed which would convey the effect of a series of fragmentary impressions which are 'strobed' onto the intellectual retina in a way that is contrived to seem mechanised rather than 'hand-crafted'. These 1970s Modernist poets always want to escape that self-conscious air of creating bespoke, 'hand-stitched' language which will be appreciated by readers for its workmanship, or (to change the metaphor) savoured, sip by sip, like a rare vintage, by readers who are verbal connoisseurs and appreciate the precision and 'just-so-ness' of each metaphor and turn of phrase. It often seems to me that the complete absence of this particular aesthetic dimension in 'BPR' poetry is one of its most distinctive (and, to many, most offensive) characteristics. The 'look' of Upton's lines is also characteristic of these poets—no capitals, no punctuation, brief, phrasal lines, spacing varied expressively, and so on.

Yet in Upton's example here, the fragments *cohere*—they are all recognisably glimpses of the same incident. By contrast, a second frequently found technique is when each phrase constitutes, so to speak, a separate 'verbal capsule', and the text is made up of a succession of these capsules, each embodying a single percept, but with no apparent containing structure of logic or cohesion. The term 'hard-edged imagery' was sometimes used for this feature in the 1970s. The definitive characteristic of this technique is the use of a rapid succession of fragmented and disparate images, in sharp contrast to the more orthodox poetic practice of building a much smaller number of images in a much more sustained way, around an identifiable 'containing' concept. This rapid montage of disparate, fleeting images or concepts can also be called 'flick imagery': this example is from Robert Sheppard's 'Letter from the Blackstock Road' in *The New British Poetry*, ed. Gillian Allnutt, etc:

A lazy supermarket cockroach comes out to die. Robin mugs old ladies in Stoke Newington. An inferno lights up the quadrangle in high wind: paraffin paroxysms flare the height of a tree and we can feel the heat indoors. Exit Pearl. Hood is remanded. The anger of politics subverts the tenderness of love. Vice versa.

The surreal effect achieved here goes beyond any notion of a 'broken raft of narratives': there are bizarre impressions of a latter-day Robin Hood in Stoke Newington, a blazing quadrangle, blazing wrecks (at Pearl Harbor?), the destruction of *HMS Hood* in World War Two (?), an anticipation of the television images of the Windsor Castle fire of 1992, and so on. Here the 'fracturedness' of the material is emphasised by the contrast with the completely normal prose punctuation. Each sentence unit is a complete brief-exposure impression—a scene briefly illuminated as if by a lightning flash—and the reader animates them as they spark against existing images in his/her mind (as in my reading, above). As Edwards noted in his 'Two poetries' article, such poems need this corresponding flare of energy from the reader's mind to bring them to life, since the poet is deliberately *not* filling out the images so that they can sustain their own presence.

The general effect of flick imagery of this kind is the disruption of all possible viewpoints from which the material might cohere. Another way of expressing this is to say that poetry of this kind is often characterised by 'unstable chronotopes', the 'Chronotope' being Bakhtin's word for the space-time continuum in which a depicted event is located. The projected locale of a poem is not usually a single event in a singular place in the realist sense, but a 'meta-space/time intersection', which may be a hybrid of the real, the imagined, the remembered, the possible, constituting the playgrounds of the 'deconstructed subject', that is, the speaker who is not a singular 'I', but may combine 'you' and 'us', or animate and inanimate. In practice, of course, a great deal of poetry in general resists the establishment of stable chronotopes, poising ambivalently between the moment enacted and the moment recalled. But, again, what is often evident in 'BPR' poetry is a more extreme version of this instability and ambivalence. Another word for it is 'polyphonic subjectivity', which is Felix Guattari's term for the situation in which there is no stable 'I' in the poem, but a shifting across 'I', 'we', 'you' positions, or else a series of utterances emanating from a variety of sources, in such a way that, though we may have a definable *voice*, we cannot link that voice to any conceivable fixed *speaker* or fixed situation.

A third common characteristic exists in paradoxical contrast to the minimalism already discussed: it is a trait which might be called 'Maximalism', which is definable as the tendency to create elaborately structured sequences of poems on a Poundian scale of ambition. But whereas *The Cantos* is a simple linear sequence, these poets are often engaged on huge works, conceived, like *The Cantos,* like *Finnegans Wake,* to occupy a lifetime, but often immensely complicated in internal structure. As cris cheek recalls of the 1970s:

> There was a serious, commitment to 'poetry'. Readings were often long (one reader for 80-90 minutes or more). Many writers were working on extended sequences or series of interconnected works. I remember a significant percentage of readings involving the use, either for punctuation or ambience or accompaniment or interruption or juxtaposition, of pre-recorded cassette tapes.[6]

And the liking for ambitious scale and complex structures continued well beyond the 1970s. See, for example, the 'Resources and Notes' at the end of Robert Sheppard's impressive book *The Lores* (Reality Street Editions, 2003), which has the following explanation of the overall structure of which *The Lores* is part:

> *The Lores* is part of *Twentieth Century Blues,* the core as I like to think of it, but it is not the whole of Twentieth Century Blues 30. *Jungle Nights in Pimlico,* (a footnote to Book Two of The Lores [sic] and also IM 5; Empty Diary 1943, Number Two; and Duocatalysis 12) was published by Ship of Fools in 1995. The previous *Flashlight Sonatas* are *The Flashlight Sonata,* Stride, 1993, and *Empty Diaries,* Stride, 1998.

So the projected totality (as I read it) is a mega-work called *Twentieth Century Blues* which has at least thirty parts, of a single part of which the book-length *The Lores* is not the whole. *The Lores* itself is divided into Part One and Part Two: Part One has six sections called 'books', most of which are divided into sub-sections which have their own sub-titles and are designated by roman numerals. Some of these sub-titles seem to indicate further sub-sub-sections and other interlocking sequences— thus Part One, Book 6 has the sub-headings 'Time Capsule 2' and 'Torn Elegy 2'. The Borgesian complexity of this kind of thing seems designed to posit labyrinthine mega-structures whose complexity can never be

---

6   British Poets Archive, http://www.jiscmail.ac.uk/cgi-bin/webadmin?A2=ind9711& L=british-poets&P=R11943&I=-1

grasped or completed. What such devices above all express is ambition and undauntedness, much disliked and perhaps too easily ridiculed by the kind of poet happy to turn in short lyrics which give impressions of (for example) a misty morning on Wimbledon Common. Such complexity of scale and ambition is not, of course, limited to Sheppard, but sometimes seems almost the norm in 'BPR' circles: in their *Jacket 4* version of the *Other British and Irish Poetry* introduction, for instance, Caddel and Quartermain note that 'In 1975 by his own count [Allen] Fisher was involved in thirty-four projects, including collages, found texts, mail art, dream poems, experiments in music and art, as well as performance; by 1995 his published works (pamphlets, books, tapes and records) numbered over one hundred'.

A fourth common 'BPR' feature is that in terms of the structure of individual pages, these poets often make use of 'open forms' or 'field composition', ultimately derived from Charles Olson's 'Projective Verse' essay, whereby the arrangement of the words on the page is not one-dimensionally linear, but seeks to allow 'variable' readings—juxtaposing one block of text with another that is opposite to it on the page, for instance. The aim is to give the page a structure of contiguity, juxtaposition, parataxis (literally 'side-by-sideness'), rather than sequentiality, linearity, or familiar kinds of combinatory logic. This technique of arranging pages 'spatially' rather than 'sequentially' (viz, *not* simply in left-to-right, top-to-bottom chronological sequence): is designed to allow 'crossing': this is when a text is readable in different ways: for example, a text arranged in parallel columns may allow readings across the columns working from top to bottom, as well down each column in turn. A concomitant part of open field methods is the disuse of standard punctuation (already commented upon): representing a pause, or marking a sense-unit, by extra spacing, or by breaks in lineation, is a more flexible method than the use of punctuation. The removal of punctuation often allows a variety of possible interactions between groups of phrases, in the way that open field methods favour. However, residual elements of punctuation are seen: the colon and semi-colon, for instance, remain popular, perhaps because of the inherent ambivalence involved in points which are neither full-stops nor commas, but combinations of both. Sometimes poets (again, it's a way of signalling an allegiance to major modernists like James Joyce) re-invent punctuation, using dashes or oblique strokes between phrases, often to introduce an air of improvisation or impressionism. These devices are usually accompanied by the elimination of initial capitalisation and of the straight left-hand margin.

On the 'open field' page, furthermore, the language often has an element of 'liminalism', often seeming to be poised on a conceptual threshold or interface, so that the words may seem to poise the reader mid-way between signifier and signified, making us experience sound patterns and the 'rustle' of the signifying process itself, while the world signified by the words becomes in some way subordinated to the words themselves, as if 'mere' referentiality is being to some degree held in abeyance. This is like saying that we are involved as readers in watching language being (re)-invented, rather than language being used (terms used by Robert Sheppard about Maggie O'Sullivan's poetry). Thus, words are sometimes selected and juxtaposed in poems because of aspects of their form and sound, rather than (just) their meaning—the signifier rather than the signified is what counts. Thus, in the Carlyle Reedy piece just looked at we have near the end the lines:

a mast. A mark/
　　　now dark

Here the word 'mast' seems to generate or produce 'mark', a word of similar shape and appearance, and 'mark' in turn seems to generate 'dark', a word of similar sound. There is a repeated pattern of two-syllable phrases, and the oblique stroke after 'mark' seems like a visual equivalent to the projecting mast of the 'skeleton hull'. Hence, the signifiers themselves seem to be the generating feature, rather than (or as well as) the signifieds, so that pattern becomes as important as sense, or in the terms of Roman Jakobson and Claude Levi-Strauss, this poetry 'projects the principle of equivalence from the axis of selection into the axis of combination'[7]

As with the Carlyle Reedy poem, poetry which has been reduced to the radically minimalist, residual state discussed earlier often relies quite heavily on the signals given by a title, and these subtle uses of titling effects constitute a fifth common feature of 'BPR' poetry: some titles are specific or denotative, of course, but more often they are allusive, open, teasing, ironic: the titling techniques are similar to those used in contemporary art; that is, they often seem to have a quasi-independence from the piece they are attached to, pointing in a different direction, for instance, or having an impact or a hermeneutics of

---

[7] 'Describing Poetic Structures: Two Approaches to Baudelaire's "Les Chats"'(1966), in J. Tompkins, ed., *Reader-Response Criticism.*

their own, *not* like the titles of, say, 19th century novels, which usually designate a character (*Emma*), a place (*Middlemarch*), or a theme (*Persuasion*) in a straightforward way. The effect is to (deliberately) make 'recuperation' difficult, where the notion of recuperation designates our tendency to re-incorporate the strange, the innovative, the challenging as quickly as possible back into the patterns of the known. We may recuperate 'random image' poetry, for instance, by 'narrativisation', by constructing a naturalistic story from the fragments on the page. 'Oblique' titling is one element which deliberately sets obstacles in the way of recuperation, as do the lack of connectives between different elements of a piece, the lack of cohesive, 'motivated', or 'mimetic' flow.

Finally, the texts of 'BPR' poets often contain many disparate or 'disjunctive' elements, such as bizarrely mixed linguistic registers (as already discussed)—slang and street-talk juxtaposed with highly technical, abstract or 'learnéd' language. The disparate elements may be residual traces culled from other texts, such as fragments from advertisements, paragraphs or phrases from newspapers, from government statements, and so on. The effect of committing such disruptive acts of 'civil disobedience at the level of the sentence' (critic Keith Jebb's phrase of Robert Sheppard) is analogous to techniques used in painting by modernists like Braque and Juan Gris, so again there is a sense of writers interested in continuing the unfinished business of modernism. If adopted as a formal process of composition, this incorporating of other texts in fragmented form produces the 'cut-up' or 'fold-in' text, which may consist of several partial texts, usually with some random or 'aleatory' formula to pre-determine the exact form of the splicing. These techniques, of course, date back to the Dadaists, and in recent usage, the provenance can be traced to the 'anti-rationalism' of the Beat poets of the 1950s, and to similar forces in a range of arts in the 1960s, for example, in the music and theorising of John Cage. A further step along the road of dislocating linguistic registers involves the 'vernacular transcription' of regional dialects or languages, like the 'Lallans' of Hugh MacDiarmid or the Glaswegian dialect of much of Tom Leonard's work. In Leonard's case, the sounds and grammatical patterns of Glasgow speech are represented by modifying standard spelling, as in his 'Unrelated Incidents', in which he quotes MacDiarmid's opinion of the Glasgow dialect—'its thi lang-/wij a thi/guhtr thaht hi/said its thi/langwij a/thi guhtr.' Many British-Caribbean poets, by contrast, prefer 'interlingualism', in which Black British or Caribbean speech forms are used as well as Standard English. The effect of both techniques is to foreground issues of cultural discontinuity and social difference.

This section has provided a very rudimentary set of descriptions of some of the common features of 'BPR' writing. It is very much broadly 'indicative' in spirit rather than comprehensive, and it does not deal at all with sound and visual poetries. But it will, I hope, highlight some of the elements of the new poetries which seemed nihilistic, destructive, or deliberately provocative to more traditional poets, thus contributing to the vehemence of the Poetry Society clashes of the 1970s. Contact with more actual poems, of course, will extend any such attempt to summarise the procedural repertoire of innovative poetries—typically, what had seemed a single category will come to seem in practice to be part of a constellation of related, but subtly different, sub-techniques. But that is inevitable, since all taxonomies are simplifications of the complexities of practice.

7

Eric Mottram as Critic, Teacher, and Editor

The driving force for change at the Poetry Society was Eric Mottram, the man who took over the editorship of *Poetry Review* in late 1971. The published interviews with Mottram (see under 'Secondary Sources' in the list of sources, below) give a strong sense of his dynamic, forceful, yet ultimately elusive personality, and his own extensive writings vividly illustrate the breadth and depth of his intellectual interests, and his voracious erudition. This immense body of work is listed in Bill Griffiths' bibliography of Mottram's writing,[1] but it is nearly all in fugitive publications which not even a major university library would possess: *Blood on the Nash Ambassador* of 1989—out of print, but obtainable—is the only collection of Mottram essays a serious enquirer has any chance of gaining access to outside special collections and archives. There is a need, then, for a substantial new *Selected Essays* to bring his work to wider public attention than it enjoys at present. His own difficult and allusive poetry has only once received the kind of sustained explication it requires (in Clive Bush's *Out of Dissent*, Talus, 1997), and this kind of enterprise would really need to be continued on an almost Olsonian or industrial scale if serious hopes were entertained of facilitating general access to the poetry.[2] But Mottram's influence was predominantly as a critic, teacher, and editor, rather than as a poet, and many of those who sought out his published essays were prompted by some kind of previous direct contact, such as attendance at lectures, seminars, or readings.

---

[1] Available on-line at http://www.kcl.ac.uk/kis/archives/mottram/mottbib.htm

[2] Mottram's poetry can most conveniently be sampled in Caddel and Quartermain's *Other British and Irish Poetry* anthology, pp. 158–162.

Mottram as critic—beyond linearity

Eric Mottram's critical writing is of three basic kinds: firstly, there is material of broad scope and ambition which lists, catalogues, and comments upon the significant writers, influences, and ideas in a particular field. With this kind of work, the reader has a sense of being offered a new world of writing, an immense new quarry to explore, and of being provided with a helpful map with which to do so, as well as an indication of some of the major landmarks. The seminal essay on the British Poetry Revival[3] is of this type. The Mottramesque trope of 'rapid notation or summary' dominates this kind of work, so a typical paragraph begins:

> But the stimulus of American poetry is a constant factor in the new [British] poetry . . . the presence of Zukofsky for Pickard; of Jack Spicer and Barbara Guest for Chris Torrance (and also for Allen Fisher); of Thoreau and Robert Duncan for Jeremy Hilton; of certain New York poets (particularly John Ashbery) for Lee Harwood, and of other American poets for Colin Simms, Ken Smith, Paul Evans (among others). Bob Cobbing, Peter Mayer, Peter Finch, Dom Sylvester Houédard, and other British soundtext poets (then more usually called visual poets or concrete poets) were already part of an international scene stretching from Latin America to Germany. (p. 39)

The sense of what I mean by annotative 'mapping' will be evident here—nineteen names are mentioned in less than a dozen lines, and there are many paragraphs in the essay like this; so the passage also has the limitations of maps: it doesn't illustrate or exemplify what exactly is meant by the 'presence' of one poet in the work of another, nor hint at how these presences differ in at least some of the cases cited. It also conveys the impression of one-way traffic, of British poets passively absorbing the influence of Americans, an impression which later commentators (like Keith Tuma and Robert Hampson) have been at some pains to eradicate, or at least complicate. Whereas the British sound poets are equal members of an international 'scene', the rest almost seem to be just spreading the American poetic word in Europe.

Because an ambitious, comprehensive 'cataloguing' aim predominates in this kind of work, terms of praise are enthusiastic and suggestive, but often a little vague and un-illustrated: thus, another paragraph begins:

---

[3] Re-printed in Hampson and Barry's *New British Poetries,* MUP, 1993.

> Precision and logic in poets such as Prynne and Riley moved towards the
> surreal, but was always deftly conscious and never relied entirely on the
> formulations of Breton and Freud. (Hampson and Barry, p. 38)

What exactly is suggested by 'precision and logic . . . mov[ing] towards
the surreal'? Nothing precise, surely, unless the statement were to be
made concrete with illustrations from the works in question. Nor is it
clear what the quality of being 'deftly conscious' actually entails, or how
this would (or could) be manifested in a poem. This strand of Mottram's
critical work, then, opens new ground, provides a reading list, makes
suggestive links and connections between different writers, and often
indicates intellectual and cultural resources which will be helpful in
reading it further—but it doesn't usually provide any close explication,
simply trusting to the reader's intelligent application and development
of the broad principles it lays down.

A second format found in Mottram's writing is the collage or 'mosaic'
of key quoted fragments from a wide range of 'resources', such as the
booklet 'Entrances to the Americas: Poetry, Ecology, Translation'
provided for a Polytechnic of Central London conference in 1975. This
substantial document (about fifty sides of A4) is startling in the way it so
frequently anticipates present-day concerns and attitudes ('Ecology', the
concept of 'The Americas', rather than the USA and 'South America',
and so on), and amazing in its range of concerns. It consists of a series of
block paragraphs, substantially made up of quotation from various
sources, with an explicit thread of linking commentary. It begins:

> The issue is translation. Octavio Paz believes that 'In writing an original
> poem we are translating the world, transmuting it. Everything we do is
> translation, and all translations are in a way creations.'

The crucial importance of notions of translation (crossing and dissolv-
ing boundaries, and therefore creating new syntheses) is something
Mottram felt very keenly, and he several times said that the relative lack
of poetry in translation was one of the weaknesses of his period as editor
of *Poetry Review*. But the essay has a density which is considerably beyond
what any reader—*any* reader—could be expected to absorb. There is an
indigestible quality to this compendium, and a certain lack of any sense
of proportion or indeed of any discernible strategy of composition in the
writing. The only way to use it is as an encyclopaedia to dip into or
quarry: every dip will produce something striking and useful, but cumu-
latively, the strikes just cannot work together. This kind of writing, then,

is a development or intensification of the first; it dissolves any residual notion of writing continuous prose, and seeks to escape from the hated and constantly denounced 'linearity' of our cultural norms and habits. It is non-linear in the sense that it simply presents a mass of evidence rather than an ordered argument: the paragraph-blocks could be shuffled into a different order and it would still, in the main, be the same essay and have the same effect.

This kind of work suggests that Mottram was really a pioneer of American Cultural Studies who was never content to be just a literature specialist: for him, literature was always part of a cultural continuum, and the ramifications of the continuum were vast. An impression of its vastness is given in a letter of March 1977 to Barry MacSweeney in which he gives an account of what he is currently working on:

> 'The R[ed] B[ank]' is a piece on the image of the [Native American] Indian in white lives—from Columbus and Vespucci to the present day. The other paper at Vienna was on the bestselling fiction read on US campuses in the sixties showing the degree of revolution among the so-called riotous and rebellious students was minimal in their reading as well as their action physically and politically. I've been working on a series of compendious resource papers—these will be the first books of the PCL's American Resources Centre which I opened with a paper on 'Technology and Culture in America 1850–1900' which I'm delivering again at Nottingham University next weekend. It tries to handle the cultural field by looking at interactions of literary culture, machines and inventors, clocks and trains, factories and theories of nature. . . . Then I have a fourth appearing called 'The Location of Dangerous Shoals', on the figure of the scientist in American culture: that's in a book due out in early summer. And I'm now working on 'Underground, Outasight, but not Out of Mind', with which I have been asked to open the British Association of American Studies conference at Oxford in April. This is part of my huge file on the term 'underground' which I may have told you about. The idea is to trace American fears of invasion from within and without, underground and UFOs and so on, from 1776 to 1976—my little contribution to the centenary celebration! These will all go with the 'Guns in America' piece, and the 'Dionysos in America' article, and 'Living Mythically', and [the] hope is that there will be a coherence called a book![4]

In later years this kind of 'joined-up', broad-scale approach to cultural phenomena came to be called 'New Historicism', but Mottram was practising it—especially in what he called his 'resource papers'—before it had a name.

[4] Letter of 14th March 1977 in the Barry MacSweeney Collection, Newcastle University, BM15/1/8.

The third kind of essay takes the work of an individual writer, providing, not exactly explication, but (again) a kind of 'informed orientation' towards that writer. Generally, Mottram's preference is to write about the whole of a poet's output, rather than about individual books or poems, so that typical titles are 'The poetry of . . .' or just the poet's name, followed by a quoted thematic pointer, as in 'John Ashbery: "All, in the refined, assimilable state"'. This Ashbery essay (*Poetry Information*, 20 & 21, pp. 31–49) seems to me typical of Mottram in this mode: quite large blocks of text are quoted, but the commentary always then moves away from the text rather than towards it, never picking out words or phrases for closer analysis, but always moving immediately to one of the general principles which Mottram constantly extols; thus, at one point eight lines of text are quoted, followed by the comment:

> Characteristically here, the sentence explodes linear logic and the insurance of apparent coherence, replacing them with sheer plasticity: a typical twentieth-century procedure of the arts and sciences—process and mobility excite by their flair and elevation rather than by any movement towards stasis and imposed order. (p.33)

Mottram doesn't attempt to show in detail (or even at all) *how* the sentence 'explodes linear logic and the insurance of apparent coherence, replacing them with sheer plasticity', and the reader wanting such explication, explanation, and demonstration will have to look somewhere else for it. Instead, we move immediately from the solidity of the quotation to the abstraction of the general principles, without any transition through the vital intermediate realm which brings the two together. The principles cohere round a familiar dichotomy: on one side are the rejected negative categories—'linear logic', 'apparent coherence', 'stasis', and 'imposed order'—and on the other the positive terms—'sheer plasticity', 'process and mobility', 'flair and elevation'. Many of Mottram's close single-author critiques are reducible to recurrent conceptual dichotomies of this kind; all 'inter' concepts are good— 'interface', 'interaction', 'interpenetration' (a much favoured word) and so on—anything, in fact, which suggests flexibility and merging, while whatever is fixed and separate is denigrated. Mottram's own response, I think, to the kind of critique I am offering here would be to say that his work seeks to provide the 'training' which is required by the kind of contemporary poetry and art he favours (see later for the notion of 'training'), but that he stops short—on principle—of actually trying to do the reading for the reader. Thus, the readers of this Mottram essay on

Ashbery have to grasp the principles he offers and then seek to apply them to their own reading of the text—there is simply no point (I can hear him saying, with that impatient snort) in his trying to *show* the reader, phrase by phrase, how a particular passage 'explodes linear logic and the insurance of apparent coherence'. If you can't begin to see this for yourself, then perhaps you should be doing something simpler in life than trying to read contemporary poetry, something like running a political party, or designing garden furniture.

Mottram as Teacher—Imagining Synthesis

As a critical writer, then, Mottram's methods and forms are somewhat unusual, but his broad-sweep work does vital path-finding for readers and constantly seeks to build a trained and informed audience for his poets. However, he often worked in a closer and more nuanced way on texts in the teaching situation. It may be of interest to attempt to convey the atmosphere of these sessions, and I will take as an example a teaching session from Eric's course 'The American Imagination of Synthesis', part of the MA in United States Studies, taught at the old Tavistock Square premises of London University's Institute of United States Studies. The Seminar Room was right at the top of this elegant but impractical (from the academic point of view) Georgian town house. The room had sloping ceilings and occupied the most of the top floor, having being knocked into a single space from what had presumably been servants' attic bedrooms. Hence, the room needed a series of columns which supported the roof and blocked the view from several points. The central space was occupied by a large seminar table (made up by pushing smaller tables together in the manner of seminar rooms world-wide). These seminars had a distinct air of occasion, and were very crowded—perhaps forty people, probably exceeding the building's restricted and always troublesome recommended floor loadings—when Allen Ginsberg read at the Institute around the same period, half the audience (including me) had to stay on the street outside, shouting up at the window until he appeared on the narrow balcony and read a few of the poems from there. The sessions were scheduled to run from ten o'clock till lunchtime, with a break half way through, so that people could go downstairs to the basement and get plastic cups of coffee.

Eric's style was to read the material from pages of notes, mostly typed, but often with inserted hand-written sheets. He read, not with a flat 'reading out' monotone, but in a forceful way, with appropriate vigour and indignation. He would pause from time to time, scanning a sheet, then discarding several in succession: he was mostly using, I think, the typescripts of articles or invited formal lectures. He would tell us that what he was using was due to appear in (say) the *International Times*, and this would increase the sense of attending an event in some way special, since it was by no means common then (in pre-RAE days) for academics to be frequently publishing books and articles. As a teacher he was intensely 'subject-centred': he always conveyed a powerful sense that he was dealing with matters that were urgent and important, and that the enemies of culture and their thought-police might clatter up the stairs at any moment and try to put a stop to the proceedings. For him, the enemies of culture were often within the University itself, and he was constantly keyed up ready to repulse them. I remember an undergraduate session in his room at King's College (in the old Chesham Hotel in Surrey Street) when a porter opened the door and glanced round the room, realised it was occupied, said 'Oh, sorry, Sir, just checking', and closed the door again. Eric bounded out of his chair and chased after the man in a fury demanding 'Checking *what?*'

The notion of student-centred or discussion-based teaching provoked much derisive snorting: he once told me disdainfully of a seminar he'd been to at which the students were discussing the material, and 'the person who was being paid to teach wasn't teaching.' This could never be said of him: when he was being paid to teach he was teaching, and usually he had to be reminded of the desirability of a coffee-break. When I saw a film-clip, many years later, of one of Jacques Lacan's 'seminars' I recognised the charged atmosphere and the pervasive sense of occasion, except that Mottram did not have a group of favoured hearers to whom insider remarks and in-jokes were addressed: rather, every member of the audience was treated with the same detached coolness. He neither implicitly encouraged nor explicitly invited discussion. When somebody ventured a contribution he would listen and nod with quite vigorous apparent assent, but often without looking at the speaker—he would be looking down at his notes for the next point he wanted to make, sometimes turning pages, or he might glance at his watch, or stare thoughtfully out of the window while still nodding. It wasn't deliberate bad manners—it was just part of that intensity of focus on the material; he had calculated his time, and knew how long it would take him to get through what he planned to deliver. His view was that discussion could happen after the class instead of taking up time during it—he was a man whom a friend reports as serving a mushroom omelette with the mushrooms *alongside* the omelette rather than *in* it, and he seemed to serve up the ingredients of his teaching in the same sequential way.[5]

On this occasion, (and I am now reconstructing an MA session on American poetry from my early 1970s notes, and adding hypothetical retrospective reconstructions in square brackets), Mottram began with an emphasis on the perceived need, in the United States of the late nineteenth century, for national union;

> After the Civil War there was no union—the cohesive myth-making about America [of the kind seen in Hart Crane's 'The Bridge'] was necessary because the country is so big; a myth seeks to make a *single* statement, encompassing *all* that has happened. By contrast, William Carlos Williams is the 'self projected', that is, he offers [for example in *Paterson*] an epic structure without [such defining] absolutes [as are seen in Crane]. His basic project is 'no ideas but in things', that is, a total secularisation [of values]. The ambition was to do away with symbols, and to be 'objective'. See [Williams's] 'For Elsie'—complex, but not with metaphor—simply description of things which *are*: each stanza, almost, and each line being an object, hence the separation between lines—nouns and verbs—which are really objects. [It is] more descriptive than a set of metaphors (see Dewey, 'Art and Description'). Note: Williams's 'Wheelbarrow' poem also, as simply an object, without trimmings. Also '[The] Yachts', in which case the whole thing is a metaphor. Also 'Spring'—objects defined, but not analogies of anything else—no anthropomorphism. The language simply carries the perception—[It's] simply a series of pieces of evidence. Later [he] called the poem 'a field of action' [in his essay 'The poem as a field of action', *Selected Essays*, New Directions, 1969, pp. 280–91]—spatial not linear. [It's] simply a true statement of language—movement in mutual understanding. [It] applies [too] to Olson, Duncan, Zukofsky. [The poem] is not a linear sentence [sequence?]: there are often several ways of reading— better to simply *see* it. See *New American Poetry 1945–1960* (ed. Donald Allen): pragmatism—act first, define later, by poetics. Form never more than an extension of content.

Here the contrastive linking of Crane's 'The Bridge' and Williams's 'For Elsie', as two poems which try to 'say America' is a highly suggestive one: Elsie is the Williams's maid, and the poem begins 'The pure products of America go crazy'; in this sense, Elsie is '*indicative*' of America, but not *symbolic* of it, as Crane's bridge is. Mottram's opposition to notions of symbolism was a frequent motif of his teaching; he sided with Williams and the Objectivists because 'nothing can stand for anything else', and this leads to the rejection of metaphor, the trope in which something stands for something else. This distrust of what others would see as an innocent verbal figure anticipates key aspects of Derrida's work in the following decade, just as the rejection of experiential empiricism and 'low-key realism' anticipated the Althusserian phase of British criticism in the 1980s (as epitomised in Catherine Belsey's *Critical Practice*). Another of his catch-phrases, 'The linear novel is dead' (the first thing Ken Edwards, as a student at King's, remembers Mottram saying), encapsulates exactly that rejection of realism. Indeed, several times in recent years I have heard announced as new discoveries things which Eric told us about in the early 1970s (such as the fact that high-voltage power cables generate an electro-magnetic field which can have harmful effects on humans). As a teacher, then, he supplied the persistent key-notes which are needed to give back-bone to what is being taught (which his writing also did), while in addition the teaching situation enabled him to engage with text-specifics in ways that he seemed inhibited about doing in print.

Mottram as Editor—'Act First, Define Later'

When he took on the editorship of *Poetry Review* in 1971 he came into contact with a general audience almost for the first time, not exactly a mass audience, of course, but one to which he was unable to present the kind of 'training' which he thought essential for the appreciation of the kind of poetry he believed in. The decision (as editor of *Poetry Review*) not to explain, not to editorialise—to hive off that function to elsewhere ('Act first, define later')—meant that puzzlement, outrage, and eventual rejection by the readership were pretty well inevitable. There is a letter in the Mottram archive (Mottram, 4/3/77-79) from Anthony Rudolf, founder of the Menard Press (which specialised in poetry in translation) gently criticising the decision not to editorialise in the journal, and not to defend his editorial policy at one of the AGMs of the Poetry Society:

> Yes, the AGM was nasty, but not half as nasty as the general Council on Saturday. . . . . I feel—and I know you won't mind my saying so as you know that I support your work—that you were mistaken in not saying something at the AGM and I still feel that an editorial would be a good idea with those daft members having letters published in the newsletter . . . the pressure would be off you and on the ideas. But you have the absolute right to edit as you see fit.

The last point is a very telling one: in the absence of any editorial statement or public rationale, the accusation that the editing was governed
merely by personal whim was a difficult one to refute. It may be that the
force of this point made Mottram change his mind and issue the editorial statement which appeared in 66/1 in 1975: according to the
Mottram catalogue this undated letter is referring to the 1977 AGM, but
this cannot be so, since the struggle was over by then, and it is clearly
the 1975 annual meeting, when a motion was put forward challenging
the editing of *Poetry Review* and calling for a poll of the membership:
Rudolf was on the General Council then, but not in 1977. In any case, it
would not make sense to say that an editorial would be a good idea if
Mottram had already published one, as he had, of course, by 1977.

Whatever else, there is no getting away from the fact that editing a
poetry magazine entails extensive correspondence with poets and readers. The editors of *Poetry Review* have always complained about the daunting volume of letters and submissions, and indeed, about the daunting
volumes of manuscript work which some poets submit.[6] At its highpoint,
there were 500 submissions a week, an impossible number for an editor
who has a full-time job elsewhere to cope with, and arrangements were
eventually made for initial weeding out to take place at Earls Court before
the material was sent on to Mottram at King's College.

In the early period, at least, the Poetry Society Secretary forwarded to
Mottram letters of complaint about the journal. The Mottram files, for
instance, contain an annotated copy of 63:1 (spring 1972) returned by a
disgruntled member. The reader's objections were mainly to minor
infringements of grammar or of linguistic etiquette: in the case of
Jeremy Hilton's 'Flimby Pit', he is irritated by the opening 'a solitary
man on a vast waste/ of slag'—and wants to know why it's a lower-case
'a', and so on. Another item is a card forwarded from the poet Dannie
Abse renewing his Poetry Society subscription, 'though with some hesi-
tation . . . In my view the magazine over the last few issues has been
insultingly boring and silly for any adult readers'. Mottram didn't forget
such insults, and returned them when he could. A few years later, when

---

6   In the Poetry Society *Newsletter* in 1970, Derek Parker, then Editor of *Poetry Review*,
    disclosed that in the past 12 months he had received over 21,000 poems for
    consideration for the magazine (ACGB/62/103, folder 'Correspondence April 71–
    November 73'). In the same period he had actually published 121 poems (across
    four issues of the journal). Often in his own editorship of *Poetry Review*, says Eric
    Mottram, '200 envelopes a week' were being received ('Editing *Poetry Review*'.
    pp. 154–5, Poetry Information, 20+21, winter 1979–80).

Abse succeeded Basil Bunting and Hugh MacDiarmid as President of the Poetry Society, that very fact, in his view, epitomised the Society's lapse back into mediocrity. Abse, he says in *Prospect into Breath* (p. 39), 'was the person I always think of as Dr Abscess. I mean, one of the dreariest poets the world's ever seen.' Often the complainants parade their tender sensibilities and testify to an amazingly-sheltered upbringing. Writing of the first Mottram issue, with the line 'I fuck you' on the first page, a correspondent says (17th November 1971):

> I find in this copy of the *Review* many words which I have seen written on lavatory walls since I was a child. I am in my middle fifties and have only recently become aware of the meaning of such words. (Mottram, 2/11/04)

Letters of this kind seem to come from all over suburban Britain— Edgeware, Surbiton, New Quay, Dorking, Guildford, Leigh-on-Sea—and from addresses which seem redolent of a vanished tea-and-crumpets world—Bobbs Hill, Woodlands Road, Whitechurch Lane, 'Pathways', Woodland Place, 'April Cottage', Elmsleigh Drive, 'Hall Lodge', South Avenue. In the later years this kind of correspondence either drops off, or is no longer forwarded to Mottram, or if forwarded, then no longer kept by him.

Correspondence with the poets themselves didn't always end when the material was published, and poets sometimes had quite complex and time-consuming follow-up queries. For instance, after the publication of *Poetry Review* 62:3 in 1971 with his cover design, Dom Sylvester Houédard (the Dominican monk and concrete poet known as 'dsh') sent, not a postcard, but what might be called a home-made postal-slip in his characteristic typography:

> what happens to blocks from wh the cover was done? cld it be used by Newcastle [where the Laing Gallery was doing a dsh retrospective exhibition] with acknowledgements for the catalog? indeed cld i even use it for a 71 christmas card???? (Mottram, 4/2/1–2)

Letters from strangers who wanted to be in the journal sometimes contained bizarre forms of emotional blackmail, and the Mottram Collection has several letters and submissions from the early period which later on would have been filtered out, such as this from December 1971: 'This poetry belongs to a relative of mine who is blind in both eyes and bringing up five small children on a very small income without a wife.' The letter (sent in the 1970s) is accompanied by more

than thirty pages of poems, all dated between 1943 and 1956. Other
correspondents sound amiable enough, but seem to want the editor to
make sense of their lives for them:

> dear eric,
>
> i'm a bit nervous about sending you this—but i'm chancing my arm. no-
> one whose read it (admittedly in incomplete and longer versions) under-
> stands what the fuck its about. and me—i only wanted to be simple.

At the beginning, like most editors, Mottram makes the mistake of
discussing material he has rejected, sometimes resulting in return
letters which give glimpses into oddly-complicated lives:

> i'd like to meet you. . . from now on i'm a hospital porter/we live in sepa-
> rate worlds. i love my publisher's wife. we both understand we are in
> competition for his favour. a big book is coming out this year.

When the desired meetings actually happen, the gratitude expressed is
not always without barbed cross-currents:

> It was nice to meet you the other evening . . . Having written to you three
> times and never having received a reply, I pictured you as a reserved,
> almost surly character. (I had also, incidentally, imagined you to be quite
> a lot younger). (Mottram, 4/2/50)

Another letter is from a potential contributor whose dissatisfaction with
the Poetry Society has evidently been mollified by actually visiting it:

> I enjoyed the evening you gave with Jeff Nuttall at the Poetry Society, and
> my mother-in-law, whom I brought as a guest, liked your poems particu-
> larly. I can't remember what my complaint was about the Poetry Society,
> but if you ever can think of a person who I could have a good complain to
> about it I'd appreciate it. (Mottram, 4/2/14)

Poets whose work had been accepted were sometimes touchingly
grateful: one writes 'Thank you for reading me. You're the second
person I know who does. I married the other one' (Mottram, 4/2/14).
Sometimes there is unintentional humour which seems little likely to
inspire confidence in the poetry being submitted: 'I have been writing
poetry since the fifteenth year of my life. I am now eighteen': and
'Enclosed is a selection of my work entitled 'Give me back my hat, you

old scoundrel'. Sometimes there are uncomfortable undertones: 'Years ago', says one correspondent, 'I was on the short list for the American job which fell to you.' That expression 'fell to you' has the subtle implication that it was really just a matter of chance that Mottram was appointed rather than the writer of the letter. As here, it is quite often difficult to understand what correspondents really want: one asks 'Did you ever hear anything about the UCL job I mentioned? I've not, not so much as a dickey bird.' Often correspondents adopt a bullying tone which seems the least likely route to securing the favour of publication:

> The last time I had cause to write to you was to complain that a manuscript poem of mine had not been returned to me. You replied that it had. Three months (or thereabouts) later I received this poem back from you with a rejection slip. Looking at it closely I would say that it had never been read by anyone at your end. (Mottram, 4/2/15)

All the same, more poems are sent with the complaining letter, along with the comment 'I must apologise for the rather scruffy appearance of the poems'. This typed letter has a hand-written endorsement from Poetry Society Secretary Michael Mackenzie: 'this sort of paranoia is irritating, but if you *could* enclose some sort of encouraging noises with the rejection slip there would be no harm done'. But Mottram was not capable of making encouraging noises—the noise he made would certainly have been his characteristic snort of derision.

In the first year or so (especially 1971 and 72) Mottram's editorial practice was to make detailed points on work he had solicited and accepted, often making very specific comments on particular poems and pointing out what he saw as variations in quality. For instance, on 22nd May 1971 Paul Evans writes:

> When you wrote me about *Current Affairs* (from Kent [State]) you said re. no. 5 that it was original in 'thought and deed'. Then that the last two lines were perhaps not needed—what did you mean? (I can see why the two last might be overstating, but the other remark...?) (Mottram, 4/2/14)

Of course, the correspondent does not ask what is meant by 'original in thought and deed'! Clearly, engaging at this detailed level, especially in the days before e-mail, could become a time-consuming business, paving the way, if the editor wasn't careful, to an open-ended postal seminar of close-critique and discussion. Less demanding poets were simply grateful for the honesty and closeness of the response, like Tom Clark, who writes,

'It's good to come across an editor discerning enough to realise when one falls short. I am very pleased, of course, about the ones you've accepted' (Mottram 4/2/25–26), and another poet writes 'Thank you for your letter: I was pleased to hear that you are going to use those poems. I expect you are right about their less risky syntax and delineation, which was not intentional' (Mottram, 4/2/25–26). Sometimes a poet—in the last resort, as it were—would even give a simple answer to a simple question, like Bill Butler: 'The title for the hotel poems is "The Hotel Poems."'

Beyond Editing—'Tuitional Correspondence'

But on some occasions Mottram seemed willing to enter an open-ended dialogue, so that a kind of tuitional-correspondence began. Practitioners like Lee Harwood would take up Mottram's 'further reading' suggestions and 'do the knowledge' in a systematic way, as indicated in a letter written from Greece on 25th July 1972:

> As must be obvious to you from 'The Long Black Veil' [the sequence featured in the opening pages of Mottram's first *Poetry Review*], I've been working through the knowledge or information side of my work. And I guess my six months of Pound and Olson reading are obvious, for better or worse, (a bit of both really). (Mottram, 4/2/25–26)

Another such quasi-teaching correspondence relationship was with the poet Ulli McCarthy (later Ulli Freer) who writes on 4th January 1973, giving a very interesting mimetic rationale for the kind of typographical dislocations which were characteristic of the work of 'BPR' poets:

> After 'Horsetalk' I did not write for a while, just took to the land walking up and down mountains through bracken and bogs and so on, and then started work: felt that the layout was important—footpaths of words on the page, lost quarry tracks, space rolled in, and I used capitals in the middle of words so that the page was like a field and the words the obstacles one came across—you could not say where your feet would stumble, but the words try to show it. (Mottram, 4/2/37–39)

These 'tuitional' relationships sometimes developed with younger poets whose work he had solicited, but the requests for work from established poets didn't always produce the desired result: on 27th October 1972, for instance, he had received a brief typed note from Ted Hughes (Mottram, 4/2/51) in response to a request for work for *Poetry Review* ('not able to find a suitable piece at present'). It is difficult to imagine Mottram approaching Hughes in this way even a couple of years later, when 'Ted Gunn and Tom Hughes', aka 'the dreaded "Raven" Hughes' were despised for being the only contemporary poets his badly-taught students arrived at university having heard of (pp. 36 and 39, 'Prospect into Breath' interview). Another typed note in the file, dated 22nd June 1976, is from J. H. Prynne, responding to a similar request for material (possibly seen at this stage as being a trifle belated). It reads:

> At the moment I do not have anything suitable, so that I cannot respond very positively; and I must admit that there are times when I do not feel altogether enthusiastic about publishing work in magazines. (Mottram, 4/2/52)

It is tempting to read between the lines here and sense, again, that oft-noted tension between the 'Cambridge' and 'London' wings of the poetic avant-garde of the period, and to see, perhaps, a (subliminal?) desire to demarcate spheres of influence. Also, the odd reluctance to put poems in magazines (where else can they be put?) hints at that ambivalence about publication which is always a strand in the avant-garde outlook. It is perhaps particularly a characteristic of the 'Cambridge School', Iain Sinclair implies, in the introduction to his Picador anthology *Conductors of Chaos,* seeing these poets as a group as 'indifferent to fame', as 'the ones that have been locked away, those who rather enjoy it' (pp. xvi, xvii). If so, they probably learned their 'clinically modest' stance from Prynne, who was their senior member. Prynne refused to be included in Keith Tuma's Oxford University Press anthology of British and Irish poetry. By definition, an avant-garde looks to a future in which tastes will be transformed, and tends to despise the tastes of the present in which publication takes place.

Those who submitted unsolicited poems to *Poetry Review* because it had now been reborn, often accompanied the submission with praise of recent issues, which was a useful signal that they might be on the right poetic wave-length: 'I've been most impressed by recent issues of *Poetry Review*', says one: there is praise from a Belgian writer who had seen *Poetry Review* at the British Council Library in Brussels, and from an American poet who had seen it in the library of Dartmouth College. But eminent poets could sometimes be grouchy: Cid Corman, one of the American invitees published in 63:2, summer 1972, takes the opportunity of complaining that Mottram's entry on 'Little Magazines' in the *Penguin*

Encyclopedia of American and Commonwealth Literature doesn't mention his magazine *Origin*. As with several of the letters from Mottram's American poet correspondents, there is a good deal of stereotyping comment on 'England', seen as a place characterised by the old school tie and the class system, but Mottram seemed to elicit this kind of thing by projecting that 'little England' stereotype in his own letters to Americans and others. Anselm Hollo, for instance, 15th July 1973, responds to Mottram's accounts of his precarious position at the Poetry Society: 'It's pretty damn incredible, the way that old mob's still hanging on to their tired little notion of England and English and the world; seems to me they missed not only the 20th, but a number of preceding centuries' (Mottram, 4/2/32-33). Such sentiments were the rather monotonous small change of the regular small talk of avant-garde groupings at the time. Then, as the end approached, poets tried to squeeze a last few poems into *Poetry Review* before the door closed for ever: 'I understand you might be editing one more issue of the *Poetry Review*', writes one poet (2nd January 1975), and another writes 'Enclosed a set of six poems I'd like considered for *Poetry Review* before it finally eludes your grasp' (1st June 1976).

An important final strand of editorial correspondence, especially to a beleaguered editor such as Mottram increasingly was, were the letters of specific praise and support from those who are committed to the same cause. For instance, the poet John Hall writes (4th January 1974, from a Cambridge that he somehow makes seem very distant) urging him to hold fast: 'I had heard something indistinct about rumblings at the Poetry Society. I am pleased to hear that you have come though it all with the mag still under your arm. We can't afford any recessions at this stage.' Another poet, Chris Torrance, writes from Wales, 14th August 1975:

> The new issue sounds really great. The names really ring though. What a platform *Poetry Review* has been for the *real* new poetry this last few years. And Sinclair's book *Lud Heat,* due any moment, to do for London again, from a different but essentially linked angle, what [Allen] Fisher's book is doing. For years London has been crying out for an 'open field' work, and now two of our best men are at it . . . I do feel more and more, especially after the conferences, [at Central London Polytechnic, when Mottram has presented his defining 'British Poetry Revival' essay] that something is really happening here and that a force is emerging. (Mottram, 4/2/51)

That exhilarating sense that 'a force is emerging', and that his journal helped to provide the vehicle for it, was obviously sustaining and inspiring to an editor subjected to constant criticism, and even abuse, from within the Poetry Society.

8

The Poetry Society Transformed

By the mid 1970s the Poetry Society had effectively been transformed into a completely different organisation from what it had been before. Various accounts and reminiscences of this period give a vivid sense of what this new Poetry Society was like. Robert Hampson, for instance, (in an article on the work of cris cheek), describes the range of activities which had now developed at the Poetry Society:

> This was the period when the Poetry Society was briefly a centre for the work of what Gilbert Adair later called linguistically innovative poets. During this period cheek was print-shop manager at the Society, and a regular attendee of the experimental poetry workshop there; and, through the Society's regular readings and Eric Mottram's 'Poetry Information' lecture series, had access to the work of English poets such as Allen Fisher and Lee Harwood as well as that of an older generation of American poets, Jerry Rothenberg, Robert Duncan, John Giorno, Ed Dorn.[1]

Cheek himself (in an obituary tribute to Bob Cobbing) describes the situation which led to his becoming manager of the print-shop at the Poetry Society in the mid 1970s:

> Bob [Cobbing] was 55 and i was a young punk turning 20. One day an offset litho was delivered to Earls Court Square and Bob, together with others of the regular staff there were stood around it in the wide corridors. "Lovely machine", or some such he said, very excited, then turning sort of in the direction of anyone who'd listen followed with something along the lines of "pity nobody knows how to use it". "I do" i said,

[1]   http://www.pores.bbk.ac.uk/1/Robert%20Hampson,%20'cris%20cheek% 20in%20manhattan'.htm

blagging with brashness. Bob took a long look at me and smiled a little. The result was that i spent the upcoming weekend downstairs with manuals trying to get ink to stay on a page. Bill Griffiths was certainly in on this act and together with Bob we set about producing an issue of *Poetry Review*. We were very much learning as we went. The issue has its own charm. We got better at it and had a lot of practice as that open print-shop was launching about 40 books each month at its height of activity in 1976–77.[2]

Not everyone would agree that the issues of *Poetry Review* produced by the enthusiastic amateur printers on the Poetry Society premises had 'charm', but readers can judge for themselves in their local university or central library by consulting *Poetry Review* issues 65:4 (1975) to 67:1/2 (1977).

'Beer-Sipping, Anarcho-Syndicalist Poets'

Another significant activity at the Poetry Society during this period was the fortnightly experimental poetry workshops run by Bob Cobbing, which Bill Griffiths described much later:

Bob also ran a weekly 'concrete poetry' workshop at The Poetry Society in the 1970s: visual poetry, sound poetry, almost any poetry that was willing to experiment with performance. It was an active not a discursive session and brought me into contact with many new approaches to writing and performance—not least the multi-voice techniques Sean O'Huigin brought over from Canada. (The workshops continued later elsewhere—I last met Bob at one in the summer of 2002.)[3]

Another major associate with Cobbing's activities at the Poetry Society was Lawrence Upton:

I've known Bob Cobbing for over three decades . . . I was one of those he encouraged to join The Poetry Society and stand for election to the council, so that we could change its policy—there was a time when Cobbing was Treasurer, Jeff Nuttall was Chair and I was Deputy Chair; and that's a conceptual work of art in itself. We've made poems together and co-edited. We've performed together. For some years, we didn't speak to each other.
  He's all right. A bit contrary sometimes. Frequently casually brilliant. Has a very good taste in whiskey. Sometimes slightly curmudgeonly.

[2] http://www.indigogroup.co.uk/llpp/tributes.html

[3] http://www.indigogroup.co.uk/llpp/tributes.html

Always generous. Full of energy, physical and mental. Immensely creative. . . . *Writers Forum* alone would be a considerable achievement. At the time of writing, June 2002, it has published about 1100 items over at least 40 years, or roughly one every two weeks; and it is still active despite Cobbing's age and growing infirmity. There is still a need for it.[4]

The atmosphere at the Poetry Society, then, had radically changed: it had become part of a wholly different cultural formation, and was now linked to a network of experimental writers and artists flourishing in London at that time, and adumbrated by Robert Hampson as 'a set of interlocking/intersecting institutions in London in the early 70s: the Association of Little Presses; the London Musicians Cooperative; the London Film Makers Cooperative; the West Square Studio; the Acme Gallery; the Polytechnic of Central London Poetry Conferences; the Sound and Concrete Poetry Conferences; the Poetry Society; and, later, Camerawork; Four Corners; Chisenhale Studios; the X6 dance space.'[5]

Socially, it was male-dominated, anarchic and chaotic, as suggested by Peter Finch in a cameo of the White House bar (in the hotel next-door to the Poetry Society):

> We're sitting the White House, the hotel bar next to the Poetry Society in Earls Court Square. Criton Tomazos is standing on the mantle piece ripping bits out of a book and chanting. Bob has drunk almost half a bottle of whiskey and is still standing, or leaning. Jennifer [Jennifer Pike, Cobbing's wife] arrives in her small car to take us home. The vehicle is full of boxes, papers and bits of equipment. We push Bob into the front seat but there's no room for me in the back. I climb onto the roof rack. We drive. Somehow we get back.[6]

A retrospective attempt to characterise the 'London' atmosphere (by poet Ira Lightman, in discussion with Robert Hampson on the British Poets e-mail list) suggests some of the transitional and eclectic elements which the London poets were part of, and this more impressionistic kind of summing up can usefully supplement the eye-witness accounts which centre on particular events, occasions, and places:

> I'd characterise the London 'scenes' as a broadly cheerful, informally constituted, beer-sipping anarcho-syndicalist tendency with scattered

---

4 http://www.indigogroup.co.uk/llpp/tributes.html#upton

5 Hampson, as before

6 http://www.indigogroup.co.uk/llpp/tributes.html#peter

residual Marxist undertones. A disaffected avant-garde trace element, neither leading with sense of direction nor sharing any articulated sense of who and what it might be 'in the front' of. . . . . Residues of liberal hippy idealisms blurring into punk and Goth. Singular 'outsider' or 'indifferenter' projections. Verging on arch romantic at times.[7]

'A Distressing and Disgusting Experience'

Inevitably, the new Poetry Society was not to everybody's taste, and tensions and antagonisms began to develop. In October 1972, for instance, publishers Abelard-Schuman arranged a reading at the Poetry Society by their poet David Jaffin (in no sense a stereotypical 'conservative' figure), and the following account of the evening was written by an irate attendee who sent copies of it to Michael Mackenzie, Secretary of the Poetry Society, to the Chair of the Arts Council, and even to the Prime Minister:

> It was a 'distressing and disgusting experience' for all those present ('13, including the poet'): The smell of beer pervaded everything, the hallway was dirty and the noise from the bar made one think of a back alley public house. After ten minutes of struggling to hear David Jaffin, the door flew open and a long-haired lout screamed 'Bomb'—it was dirty paper which fell all over the disillusioned audience. We cleared up the mess, only shortly after to have the same fool plus half a dozen more come shoving [?] into the room shouting 'Litter Bomb'—my husband gave them three seconds to leave, and they ran up and down the corridor shouting—we left, and wrote suitable comments in the Visitors' Book in the hallway'.

This is the earliest allegation (1972) I have seen that the two sides in the poetry disputes at the Poetry Society sometimes disturbed or disrupted each other's meetings—there would be more in the years that followed. Readings by the radicals sometimes contained an element of 'self-disruption' anyway, especially when they were on the borderline between a reading and a 'happening', as was the case with Jeff Nuttall's anarchic performances. Part of the response to the Witt Panel by a Poetry Society staff member in 1976 read:

> She said she did not know Jeff Nuttall very well, but when he had given a reading at the Society she had found broken eggs on the rostrum next morning, a tin of golden syrup underneath the piano, with a doll stuck in

---

7   http://www.jiscmail.ac.uk/cgi-bin/webadmin?A2=ind97&L=british-poets&
P=R69815&D=0&H=0&I=-1&O=T&T=0

the syrup and there was talcum powder everywhere. Mr Nuttall had also run round in his underwear. There were only twelve people at the reading.

In the summer, some of these events took place *en plein air* across the road from the Poetry Society in Earls Court Square:

> She reported that when the Poets Conference organized a reading in the Square, only 29 people were present (not 50 as stated in the newsletter) and the rostrum, loaned from the Society for the occasion, then lay in the square for two weeks or more. When it was finally brought back it was dumped in the entrance hall.

Events at the Poetry Society could be boozy and prolonged, especially at the weekend, and 'on Saturday mornings she often found people had stayed all night, particularly during the winter, when the electric fires were also left on all night because the people were so drunk.' Another respondent to the Witt Panel recalled that:

> Seeing intoxicated members of the Council urinating against the wall of the adjacent church cottages after a particularly stormy general meeting of the Society might lead one to wonder how the future of our great national heritage should have come to rest in such hands.

Another vivid description at a specific Poetry Society event is given by poet Kathleen Raine (1908–2003) in her written contribution to the Witt Panel. She gave a joint reading at the Poetry Society in the spring of 1976 with Robert Gittings, and found the event, the surroundings, and the ethos not at all to her liking:

> I went to read poems in the company of Robert Gittings. I was frankly disgusted at the dirty state of the premises (a beautiful house and formerly well cared for), and by the nameless boors who hung around the bar until they deigned to come upstairs (late) bringing their beer with them. One vomited over the floor during Mr Gittings' reading. I left as soon as possible, courteously escorted to a cab by Mr Cotterell.

One can sense in a number of these comments the remnants of an era when 'beer' had distinctly lower-class connotations—would it have been a little bit better if people had brought their glasses of wine upstairs, rather than pints of beer? At least, there are elements of a bewildered sense that poetry has somehow got into the hands of the wrong kind of people, and the regrets about the 'beautiful house formerly well cared for' seem to have this same air (though I write as one of the 'nameless boors' hanging round the bar that day and eventually coming upstairs late with my beer).

The atmosphere at the Poetry Society in the mid-seventies, then, was lively and unpredictable, but also edgy, macho, and confrontational, with very uneasy relations between many Council members and the paid staff of the Society, who tended to be distrusted and suspected as would-be subverters of the radical motions which were being carried at the General Council meetings. There are many accounts of stormy meetings, and their effect upon the atmosphere of the building. Another staff member responding to the Witt Panel writes:

> I indicated in speaking to you that Council and Executive meetings were not orderly. I should, I think, have been less reticent. Not only are the rules for order not observed, but drunkenness, shouting, personal abuse and obscenity are common. Since such behaviour is tolerated at meetings, it is natural enough that it carries over to day-to-day encounters between Council members and staff. I must stress that not all Council members are at fault; the Chairman, Treasurer and their party bear the responsibility.

The staff felt harassed and beleaguered, especially as the conflicts came to a head in mid decade: 'the Treasurer and Deputy Chairman constantly used the [office] phone to discuss their personal bickerings and sat on the desks, which made it difficult to work.' A constant theme for comment by staff and visitors was the shabby condition of the premises, and fears were even expressed about the dangers posed by the conditions, of which a staff member gives a graphic account:

> When the print-shop opened in the basement, poets making copies of their own work were allowed to come into the general office during working hours, evenings and weekends to duplicate their work. They constantly left empty boxes, inky stencils, the pages of their books and waste paper lying around our office. (One manuscript was once retrieved from the dustbin after several hours' panic and a complete disruption of a morning's work). This was quite intolerable at one stage when a poet spent a whole day running the machine and coming to me at frequent intervals to ask for advice on its operation. He was not being supervised by anyone from the print-shop. When I complained the office machine was taken down to the print-shop, and I fear that has made matters worse. The room is a chaotic mess with absolutely no flat surface free to lay work out on as it is being copied—particularly difficult for double-sided pages. Everything is inky and our clothes regularly suffer. The floor

is piled high with empty cartons, old inky stencils and shavings. It is frightening to think that people are allowed to smoke in this room which contains much highly inflammable printing liquid. This should be looked into as a matter of urgency.

The key element here is the way the customary demarcations between different areas are not respected, so that staff are left without any dedicated work space to call their own. The kitchen area is described in similarly vivid terms, and with the same implication that these spaces act almost as a metaphor for the chaotic or anarchic element which was now a regular element in the Society's workings:

> The lack of hygiene in the kitchen is disgusting. The housekeeper does her best to keep it clean, but it is an impossible task for her. On Monday mornings the kitchen is full of unwashed beer glasses. The counters by the sink are used to store pages of *Poetry Review* and other publications. Beer crates and empty cans are left in the middle of the floor. On occasions I have gone to use a dishcloth and found it has been used to mop up printing liquid, and coloured inks are left in the sink. Frying pans are left for about a week at a time with fat in them (after having been used to fry sausages and onions—sometimes for use in the bar). Broken glass is regularly left lying about. Dirty crockery is left piled up in the sink.

Of course, various cultural clashes, as they might be called, are implicit in these descriptions. A clean and well-ordered environment, characterised by good manners and meticulous habits, connoted middle-class conformity, which was essentially what the poets who frequented the Society at this time wished to escape from. Alternative Arts venues had a kind of trade-mark surface tattiness which was read as almost a mark of authenticity (the Roundhouse was typical in this respect), and the Poetry Society looked and felt re-assuringly un-plush—it didn't *feel* like part of the Establishment, whereas the Arts Council, up at 105 Piccadilly, certainly did. The shift which had taken place at the Poetry Society was shrewdly described by one of the staff members in her deposition to the Witt Panel when she said that it had changed from a *poetry* society to a *poets'* society. The struggle which came to a head in the mid 1970s could be summed up as an attempt to take it back to being a society for poetry rather than a society for poets.

The 'Purges' (1): Poetry Round

One of the effects of the transformation of the atmosphere and balance of power at the Poetry Society in the mid 1970s, particularly after the radicals achieved a strong majority on the Council at the AGM in June 1975, was a series of alleged attempts to discourage non-radical groups from holding readings and workshops on the Society's premises. Indeed, the accusation that non-radical groups had been 'purged' from Poetry Society premises was frequently made as the conflict between conservatives and radicals reached its climax in 1976–7. Was there in fact any such 'purge'? The main 'non-radical' groups meeting regularly at the Poetry Society were 'Poetry Round' and 'Poets' Workshop.' 'Poetry Round' met on Wednesday nights and was for 'amateur' poets, using an 'open forum' format, in which participants turned up and each read out a poem, followed by commentary and discussion. 'Poets' Workshop', by contrast, was a 'closed' (invitation-only) group for quasi-professional poets, and its meetings critiqued the content and technique of poems which had been circulated to members beforehand. It had been founded by a group of published poets in the mid 1960s (George Wightman, Phillip Hobsbaum, Peter Porter, George MacBeth, and Alan Brownjohn) and had met at the Poetry Society at 7.30 on alternate Fridays since 1966. It was the successor to a Writers' Workshop associated with 'The Group' poets, which had been 'managed by a committee consisting of Peter Porter, Martin Bell, George MacBeth, Keith Harrison and George Wightman,[8] so it represents the residual 'Group' element—an important strand in post-war British poetry—within the Poetry Society. In order to make the sequence of events as clear as possible I will give a brief 'diary' or 'timeline' showing what happened to each of these two groups, beginning with 'Poetry Round'.

6th July 1974

Minutes of the General Council meeting held on this day record that 'Mr Cobbing showed some concern about the current state of 'Poetry Round' (the Wednesday workshop), which appeared to have become rather acrimonious and counter-productive. It was agreed that it would be closed down for several weeks during the summer.

---

[8] Archive of Kevin Crossley-Holland, Leeds University

Autumn 1974

Bob Cobbing and Lawrence Upton phone Laurence Cotterell (Poetry Society Chair), about a row they had in the bar with 'Poetry Round' people, and convey 'allegations of a "fascist" conspiracy to impose an extreme rightist complexion on the Round.' Cotterell himself had seen no evidence for the allegations when he attended 'Poetry Round' shortly after hearing about them, but he felt that the 'open house' format was a bit amateurish for a National Poetry Society, and that the [radicals' own] 'Poets Forum' series, which subsequently replaced it, was more 'professional and fulfilling', 'all of which does not alter the impression that the leading Activists were determined to get rid of events . . . which were not under their direct control' (Laurence Cotterell, in his evidence to the Witt Panel).

6ᵗʰ July 1975

At Executive and Management Committee, it was reported that 'in view of the unsatisfactory situation which had developed, it was agreed that the self-styled Chairman of "Poetry Round" [David Lovibond] should be given notice to cease using the premises of the Society for meetings of that group and should find other accommodation, while being invited to take the name elsewhere, in view of the fact that the Society would be organising its own "Open House" poetry function in the future as an integral part of the Society's activities'. It was later decided that the resolution passed at this meeting was something that needed ratification or rejection by the Council in the first place, and because of the opportunity the Chairman had given to Lovibond to put his case to the Council via the Chairman.

13ᵗʰ September 1975

Following a meeting of the General Council on this date, a letter was sent to 'Poetry Round' (dated 17ᵗʰ September) informing it of the refusal of permission for its meetings to be held on the Poetry Society's premises. No reasons were given, and the group wrote to ask what the reasons were, receiving a reply dated . . .

11ᵗʰ December 1975

. . . which gave the following explanation:

> From all available evidence the Council came to the conclusion that the atmosphere and the reception accorded to newcomers was discouraging

and there tended to be a narrow outlook displayed. The Society endeav-
ours to run an integrated programme of events at the N.P.C., covering as
wide a range of poetry interest as possible; we have therefore decided to
broaden the perspective of the 'open house' venture by organising our
own Poets Forum in the coming season, with rotating Chairmen drawn
from Council members and other poet-members of the Society, who will
have widely differing methods and approaches. ('Poetry Round' evidence
to the Witt Panel)

Unsurprisingly, the group did not find this a satisfactory explanation,
and they stated in evidence to the Panel that:

Not only was the evidence scanty, but, worse, there was never an opportunity to discuss the subject with the Council. Poetry Round was stopped
without any explanation being given to the many members who had
found it a fruitful group to work in—particularly recently. We believe we
can justify the way it was run, we were never given the chance.

The 'Purges' (2): Poets' Workshop

The sequence of events in the case of the 'Poets' Workshop' manifested
a similar pattern, as follows:

6th July 1974

Concern was expressed at the General Council meeting, about the noise
made by 'Poets' Workshop' on Friday nights: 'It always disturbed the
reading being held at the same time. It was agreed to ask them to be
more careful in future, and it was further suggested they might
consider moving to the downstairs library'.

September 1974

'Poets' Workshop' were asked to begin their meetings at 8.00 rather
than 7.30 to avoid disturbing the reading which began at that time.

15th January 1975

At the Executive & Management Committee, under AOB, Item C, it is
recorded that 'Mr Upton asked that Poets' Workshop meet in the downstairs library, while their meetings on Fridays started at 8pm. They
always interrupted Society meetings on Fridays with the noise on the
stairs.'

6th July 1975

At Executive and Management Committee, 'it was confirmed that the organisers of Workshop had been given a definite fiat [diktat?] concerning the absolute necessity of switching from Friday evening to some other time for their meetings.'

15th August 1975

Poets' Workshop received a letter from the General Council asking them to change their meetings night to Thursday. They acknowledged the letter, saying that their membership would have to be consulted, as the autumn programme had already been printed.

26th August 1975

A reply told them that the change had already been 'decided upon' and was now a 'fiat'. They asked the Executive to reconsider, or at least allow three months' notice, and were able to lobby Laurence Cotterell on the night of the Executive meeting. He undertook to raise their points but phoned later to tell them that the Committee had declined to reconsider the matter. Since they felt that they could easily be deprived of Thursdays too if the Executive decided to stage one of its own series of events on that evening too, they felt obliged to leave the Poetry Society and made the move to the 'Black Bull' in Fulham. Accordingly (and this brings the two separate timelines back together), the fate of the two groups had been determined by 22nd September 1975, when the minutes of the Executive & Management committee note that 'it was agreed that the informally arranged monthly workshop [Poetry Round] . . . was to cease', and that 'the Chair reported that Poets' Workshop had now moved to the "Black Bull" in Fulham'.

It is, of course, difficult at this distance from the events to be at all sure about what was really happening. The fact that these two non-radical groups were excluded at around the same time for such different reasons does suggest that something like a 'purge' of non-radical groups from the Poetry Society was taking place. 'Poetry Round' was excluded for 'intrinsic' reasons (because of alleged shortcomings in the content or conduct of its meetings), and 'Poets' Workshop' for 'extrinsic' reasons (because of alleged problems caused by meeting at the same time as another group).

The follow-up document to the Reformers' 1975 Manifesto was its 'Explanation of the movement for a reformed Poetry Society', issued for the January 1976 EGM, which cites these exclusions as the other incident (along with the rejection of the vote on *Poetry Review* at the 1975 AGM) which had sparked the Reform Committee into being. According to this document:

> During an argument between three members of the Executive Committee and two members of 'Poetry Round', a group which used to meet as a function of the Society [sic], it was revealed that 'Poetry Round' was in danger of expulsion from the Society's premises. Also, during the weekend preceding the argument, the Secretary of 'Poets' Workshop' had received a letter requesting him to change the date of meetings from Fridays to Thursdays or to take the Workshop elsewhere. It was felt that the Society's reasons for the request were inadequate and that such a change would result in irredeemable inconvenience for the Workshop's members. Negotiations on the matter were refused by the Executive Committee, and the Workshop now meets elsewhere. Finally, a discussion group derived from 'Poetry Round' was refused meeting space for its alleged connection with the Manifesto of the movement for reform. (Mottram, 4/3/13-14)

When the Witt Panel was convened, it took particular pains to gather evidence concerning the exclusion of non-radical groups, and while a general invitation was sent out to members asking for written responses, some individuals were specifically invited to write, and were prompted on what to write about. Laurence Cotterell, for instance, was asked by Robert Vas Dias (who was presumably responding to a request from the Panel) to supply him with a list of cases in which the facilities of the Centre had been refused, 'and I take this to mean the eviction of "Poetry Round" and "Poets'Workshop"', but Cotterell preferred to send this data directly and in confidence to the Panel, indicating the extent to which relationships of trust within the Poetry Society had broken down.

The radicals' own view on this matter was put by Roger Guedalla, who had been a member of the Executive Committee, and was still a member of various Poetry Society sub-committees; in his letter to the Witt Panel he writes:

> I was away in France when the argument first broke out last August/ September concerning the use of our premises by a group of people later

to be called the 'Reforming Committee' . . . As I understand the situation these people had been allowed to use the Society's premises at a very nominal rent, which I understand was never paid. Not one of them was a member of the Society, and when it was found that their activities caused problems in our attempts to tape the Friday evening readings, they were asked to move to another night. Their activity had long clashed with our own 'Poet in Person' readings, and the noise of their footsteps and their habit of dropping in for a brief listen before their own event started was always rather a nuisance. (Mottram, 4/3/36–46)

If one were making a list of strategic errors made by the radicals in the whole Poetry Society affair, it would be difficult to avoid the conclusion that the exclusion of unsympathetic groups was very significant. Other errors would include: the decision not to have reviews and discussion in *Poetry Review*; the decision to print the magazine on the premises when inadequate technical facilities and experience meant that a shabby-looking product was inevitable; the alienating of the paid staff of the Society; and the reluctance, in practice, to make the print-shop facilities available to poets beyond a narrow circle of like-minded radicals. Ranking these factors would not be easy, but the 'purges' would surely come pretty high up however any such ranking was done.

9

Taking a Long View

As we have seen, in spite of the Arts Council's hopes, matters did not improve at the Poetry Society after the departure of the radicals, because the underlying issues could not be solved by the departure of a handful of people of whom the Arts Council did not approve. It was therefore inevitable that the conflicts of the 1970s would continue to recur. It may be that many of them are inevitable anyway, because the whole concept of a National Poetry Society is a non-starter, since poetry-writing is just not a 'socialisable' activity, and the kind of consensus needed to 'nationalise' it is neither desirable, nor, probably, obtainable. Beyond these broad issues, however, a whole set of specific practical and ideological difficulties remained untackled. Firstly, the Earls Court premises of the Poetry Society were ill-suited to the role of a National (or even a London) Poetry Centre. Earls Court is too remote from the main cultural nexus of London to play that kind of national or 'show-case' role: audiences *will* go to that part of London, as is proved by the success of the Troubadour Café in near-by Brompton Road (founded in 1961), but that venue has a club atmosphere, hosts jazz, folk, blues, and perform-ance as well as poetry, and has a certain cachet as a place where the greats have performed in the past (Jimi Hendrix, Joni Mitchell, Bob Dylan, Joan Baez, Charlie Watts, and Paul Simon). So it always had cultural standing, and yet wasn't encumbered with the expectations set up by words like 'National' or 'Society'. Currently (2005) the Monday poetry nights at the Troubadour have Arts Council sponsorship, giving the kind of flexibility which the National Poetry Centre always lacked. But even if its building had been somewhere else, it would not have been well suited to its purpose, since the funds were never made avail-able for its basic maintenance, let alone for adapting it properly to its purpose. Not until 1992 was the Society able to disencumber itself of its Earls Court premises, and then only at a knock-down price (so to speak) to a Hong Kong businessman who refurbished it as a family home, naming it 'The Poets House', the missing apostrophe possibly being a nostalgic allusion to the radical days of 'Writers Forum' and 'Poets Conference'. Fund-raising ideas seemed to be in short supply during the radical period of the 1970s, although some appeared in the immediate aftermath. For instance, the first of the National Poetry Competitions was set up by the Society in 1978, with an announced first prize of £1000 and with Ted Hughes, Fleur Adcock, and Gavin Ewart as judges. The following year's competition attracted 27,000 entries at £1 per poem, so this is clearly a way of getting poets to subsidise the Poetry Society, rather than the other way round.

A second unresolved issue is the whole matter of the relationship between literature, especially poetry, and public subsidy. Throughout the period, the Arts Council was deeply ambivalent on this matter: individual poets and presses could apply for grants, and one would expect that whereas the Drama Department might spend most of its allocation in making a small number of large grants to specific companies (such as the National Theatre and the Royal Shakespeare Company), literature grants would mainly be fairly small sums to particular presses, poets, and reading series. In practice, the increasing preference was to follow the lead of the other Arts Council departments, giving most of the available cash to a small number of 'flagship' causes, such as (notoriously) Ian Hamilton's journal the *New Review*. Disputes about Arts Council grants policy came to a head in the 1970s, and led to the commissioning in 1978 of a report into the system of grants to writers, from cultural sociologist Jim McGuigan (now Professor of Cultural Analysis at Loughborough University). This was published in 1981 as *Writers and the Arts Council,* but the Arts Council had pre-empted it by announcing in April 1981 the discontinuation of its grants to writers. These were to be replaced by five bursaries of up to £7,500 each 'for established writers of high literary merit'.[1] McGuigan's *New Statesman* article in response to this event recaps the history of the Arts Council, which had been set up in 1945 on the advice of John Maynard Keynes, chief economic adviser at the Treasury. Keynes advocated subsidising institutions (such as theatres) rather than individuals, assuming that such institutions, 'after the initial injection of money, would become self-supporting'. Of

[1] Jim McGuigan, 'Closed shop, closed minds', *New Statesman*, 29th May 1981, pp. 16–18.

course, they didn't, but McGuigan's belief is that a trace of such views remained in Arts Council thinking. Thus, one might argue, the 'established writers' who would receive the big bursaries had proved their worth by establishing themselves, but, on the other hand, having done so, they were probably not really be in need of subsidy. Awards were made on the joint basis of literary merit and financial need, but the logic of the 'established' criterion is that the former ought to eliminate the latter. The anomaly of subsidising Stephen Spender (a wealthy man) to write his autobiography is the inevitable outcome of the policy. McGuigan's report had advocated a much broader scheme, with greater attention to financial need, a scheme to assist new writers, and some provision for 'community publishing' and non-professional writers, all this as a way of escaping the inevitable allocation of most of the money to 'well-educated middle-class southerners'. In the absence of transparency or appeal, and the inevitable closeness of the connections between Literature Panel members and the London literary establishment, the system is dependent on the questionable assumption that the best writing—the writing most deserving of subsidy—comes from 'established' writers. A solution might be to seek to subsidise readers rather than writers, thereby facilitating the *distribution* rather than the *production* of work of merit. Yet the Literature Department and Panel had been set up in 1966 in response to reports on the low earnings of writers, 'and to Jenny Lee's White Paper *A Policy for the Arts* . . . with the chief aim—albeit a modestly-financed one—of distributing grants to writers'. Not surprisingly, therefore, the 1981 change of policy was interpreted by many as entailing the closure of the Arts Council's Literature Department. Josephine Falk, in her new capacity as Deputy Literature Director, wrote to the *Times* on 25th August 1981 to correct this mistaken impression, and the misreports that it had withdrawn its grant from the Poetry Society ('which is receiving £60,000 this year and a guarantee against loss of £5,000').

The Poetry Society in a New Era

In addition, a series of specific changes affected the Poetry Society and its interests from the mid 1980s onwards, including: in 1986 the library of the Poetry Society (11,000 volumes, mainly twentieth century) was transferred to the University of York on permanent loan: the Poetry Library of the Arts Council (founded in 1953) was moved to the new

Poetry Library on Level Five of the Royal Festival Hall in 1988: the National Poetry Secretariat, formerly a wing of the Poetry Society, ceased operations in 1990: the Poetry Society's Earls Court premises were sold, as we saw, in 1992 and the Society moved to its present prem- ises at 22 Betterton Street in Covent Garden. These changes took place within the context of fundamental alterations in the structures for funding the Arts, for the overall climate and structure within which the Arts Council operated changed considerably from the 1990s, when it came under John Major's new Department for National Heritage in 1992. The start of the National Lottery in 1994 brought a new source of funding, and in 1997 the New Labour government established the Department for Culture, Media and Sport (the DCMS), which became its parent body, funding the arts indirectly through the Arts Councils of England, Wales, and Scotland. Arts Council England is a single develop- ment organisation for the Arts, linking nine regional offices. It published its *Guide to Arts Funding in England* in August 2004, a sixty two page document in which the word 'writer' does not appear. Its five fund- ing programmes comprise: Grants for Individuals, for Organisations, for Touring, for Stabilisation, and for Recovery. The favoured terms are generic designations like 'artists', and 'products', rather than specific ones like 'writers', 'poets', and 'books'. The whole grant-giving structure has the air of being geared to professional fund-raisers working as Local Authority professionals, and it mirrors the complexity of the grant application schemes within higher education administered by bodies like the AHRC (the Arts and Humanities Research Council) and the ESRC (the Economic and Social Research Council).

The changes affecting the subsidising of poetry in the 1990s took place in a context in which there were signs that all was not well with poetry: at the end of 1998 Oxford University Press discontinued its poetry list, on the grounds that it wasn't making any money, attracting much agonised comment (along the lines of 'Minister attacks dons as "barbaric"', *Independent*, 4th February 1999, page 11): the Arts Council itself commissioned a report on the state of poetry (*Rhyme and Reason: Developing Contemporary Poetry*, edited by Ann Bridgwood & John Hampson, Arts Council England, 2000), which reported that sales of contemporary poetry accounted for only 3% of the volume of poetry sales, and that 67% of that was accounted for by a single author (presumably Ted Hughes). This is hardly a healthy state of affairs, and indeed, it would suggest that contemporary poetry—beyond a handful of super-stars—had virtually ceased to exist as a cultural institution.

Evidence from academe around the same time (a 1998 survey by CCUE, the Council for College and University English) showed that contemporary poetry was much less likely to be an element on English degree courses than the contemporary novel.

Another unresolved conflict within the Poetry Society concerns the relationship between the Society's governing Council and its members, and the question of what constitutes 'democratic' practice in this area. Linked to this is the matter of the relationship between the governing Council and the organisation's permanent paid staff. The Council is elected by its members and runs the organisation on the membership's behalf, but the democratic power of the members rests in the democratic principle that in order to take part in the decision-making process you have to turn up at the Annual General meetings and vote. Not going to the meetings is to disenfranchise oneself, handing power to a necessarily 'unrepresentative' group. But the wishes of the members, whether or not they vote, may well be seen as 'amateur' by the 'professionals' whose careers depend on the success of the Society. Reconciling the interests and desires of the three estates—the mass of the membership, the activist members, and the paid professionals—proves impossible in the long term in many organisations like the Poetry Society, and anyone taking a long view of the history of such organisations will see periods of temporary equilibrium alternating with long stretches of open strife. In the case of the Poetry Society, the battles of the 1970s are currently (2005) being replayed: the following is from a member's website in January 2005:

> It may have been in place since its inception in 1923, but the democratic constitution of the Poetry Society could have been a thing of the past by last Easter, if recent Arts Council-sponsored reforms had made it through an entanglement of vigilance, apathy and company law. Members would have lost virtually all their voting rights and been downgraded to "Friends"—with only about a dozen trustees virtually running the whole show. The excuse for this was said to be the Arts Council's insistence that to keep its current level of funding the PS had to improve its governance and treat members as just one group among many that it serves. One assumes this requirement no longer applies in quite the same way, despite the failure to divert members' rights (whether they chose to exercise them or not) into the hands of a tightly-controlled quango.
>
> PS Director Jules Mann said the result of a postal ballot, after the inconclusive March 2004 extraordinary general meeting, made it obvious that members wanted to keep the current membership structure. [The ballot result was 224 in favour of the new memorandum and articles, and

208 against—which like the EGM vote was insufficient under company
law to authorise the change.]

All this seems terribly familiar, especially such elements as the Arts
Council's seeking tighter control over the Society, its crude use of
threats to curtail the grant if this control is not conceded, the desire to
circumvent democratic processes and put the governance of the Society
in 'safe' hands, the pressure to change the emphasis of the Society so
that it serves the perceived interests of 'poetry' rather than poets, the
divided and inconclusive extraordinary meetings, and the recourse to
postal ballots. The new elements concern a rather different social
climate, in which the alleged interests of different 'user-groups' and
'constituencies' which are 'served' by the Poetry Society can be used to
justify the 'streamlining' of governance, with the imposition of a system
of disempowered (but fee-paying) 'Friends' and a small group of empow-
ered 'trustees'. The same member's website takes issue with the
Society's attempt to change its constitution:

> We, the undersigned, attended the Poetry Society EGM on 30th March
> 2004 and feel concerned that the report of that meeting as sent out with
> the letter from the Director dated 2nd April seems to omit a salient
> point.
>   Although there was a narrow majority of votes in favour of the resolu-
> tion [to disenfranchise ordinary members and re-label them as 'friends'],
> Company Law regulations require a majority to be 75% for such a resolu-
> tion to be passed. The resolution was in fact not passed, and the issue on
> which it foundered was the abolition of voting rights of members in the
> proposed new Memorandum and Articles. We urge you therefore to vote
> against adopting the New Memorandum and Articles, otherwise you will
> be voting to abolish your vote. Please write NO on your poll card. . . . We
> believe that the disenfranchisement of the members of the Poetry Society
> is unnecessary, as many other charities have modernised their constitu-
> tions without rescinding members' voting rights.[2]

Occasionally, even some of the signatories' names are familiar from the
1970s, notably that of Alan Brownjohn. The outcome (after an Annual
General meeting in November 2004) remains undecided, but the lines of
the struggle are very clear and very familiar—they are between a
concerted centralising drive (somewhat at odds with the time-hallowed
'arm's length' principle of Arts Council funding), and a push towards a
member-centred Society.

[2]   http://www.martinblyth.co.uk/futureatstake.htm

The Poetry of the 1970s in Retrospect

The foregoing takes a 'long view' of the Poetry Society in the 1970s. To take a similar view of the poetry of the 1970s is necessarily to loosen the basic radicals-versus-conservatives dichotomy, which can seem less absolute in the light of later trends. Till recently, the dominant accounts of later post-war UK poetry saw a conservative, large-press, 'centre' or 'mainstream' implacably at odds with the progressive, small-press radical 'margins'. In this 'two camps' model, each side saw almost nothing of value in the work of the other. This model was partly superseded, from the late 1980s onwards, by a 'new consensus' view which saw evidence of a break-down in the rigid demarcations between the camps. Ian Gregson, in his book *Contemporary Poetry and Postmodernism*, calls this process a 'cross-fertilisation', while Sean O'Brien's word for the same phenomenon, in his *Deregulated Muse: Essays on Contemporary British and Irish Poetry*, is 'deregulation'. During the 1990s, as part of this 'deregulation' process, the avant-garde began to establish an 'above-ground' presence, which is to say, one which was visible beyond the 'parallel infrastructure' of low-tech, small-press publication and distribution networks and regionally-based reading circuits. The result is that the 'parallel tradition' of poetry now has more of a public identity (see, for instance, the reputation of J. H. Prynne, the success of 'Salt Publishing', the prominence of on-line journals like *Jacket,* and the interest in this work from British academics, as evidenced by the British Electronic Poetry Centre at Southampton). So there is some general sense now of the need for sustained advocacy, and a widespread interest in explaining its project to those not already in the know.

There can be no useful going back to an uninflected 'two camps' position, and I have built here on the argument I put forward in *Contemporary British Poetry and the City* (Manchester U. P., 2000) that 'there is a widespread preoccupation by poets of *all* persuasions today with more-or-less "experimental" explorations of such things as: linguistic registers, implied voices, varieties of narrative technique and viewpoint, ways of using metaphor to undermine the "real", and various ways of using myth'. Consequently it is rare today to find the kind of poetry in which 'a straightforwardly autobiographical speaker muses on aspects of his/her love-life, or domesticity or ruminates on relationships with god and nature'. This amounts to saying that the 'defeat' of the avant-garde in 1977 has taken the form of assimilating its lessons and adopting many of its methods. As so often, the indignantly repudiated 'Other' is actually a part of the self with which we were not yet ready to come to terms. This, I would suggest, is the 'hidden history' of contemporary British poetry, using the phrase 'hidden history' to recall Iain Sinclair's remark, in the preface to his *Conductors of Chaos* anthology, that 'the secret history of what Eric Mottram referred to as "The British Poetry Revival of the 1960s and 1970s" is as arcane a field of study as the heresies and schisms of the early Church'.

However, it is the balance of emphasis within ways of reading these events which now seems important, and I want to suggest two possible readings, which (arguably) are quite close together, but differently inflected. The first is a simple 'post-dualist' (that is, post 'two camps') reading, which goes more or less like this: the 1970s struggle at the Poetry Society was a war between two tribes which had *both* been superseded (or were about to be): the conservatives were a prolongation of The Movement and The Group, which were varieties of 'me-speaking', ego-based, 'confessional' poetry which went back to the Georgians and Thomas Hardy round the turn of the 19th/20th century: the radicals, likewise, were a prolongation of 1920s Modernism, with strong elements of Dada and Surrealism and Stein-like linguistic 'experimentation'. The struggle—the dialectic—between these two forces in the early 20th century had never been worked out to a conclusion because it was prematurely cut short by the political crises of the mid century—the global Depression, the Holocaust, the Second World War. The poetic struggle, however, was renewed in the post-war period, firstly in the USA from the 1950s and 60s onwards, where the Beat Poets, the New York Poets, and later the Language Poets were highly prominent, and conspicuously successful in swinging the balance of cultural power in their favour. They did this partly by resourceful use of the media (for instance in the case of the 1957 obscenity trial of Allen Ginsberg's *Howl*—see Appendix III to *Allen Ginsberg: Howl,* ed. Barry Miles, Harper-Collins, 1995), and by developing links with universities and other major cultural institutions. The American model, then, is of a successful avant-garde which seeks (so to speak) to infiltrate the centre, rather than despising and writing off the centre and glorying in its 'marginal' status. Many of the British radicals were strongly influenced (at least for a time) by the poetics of these American groups, *and by their tactics,* and this is reflected in the Poetry Society struggle.

But events overtook both sides, and this is the sense in which the whole 'two camps' struggle has been superseded: what happened, while they were locked in their retro-combat of the 1970s, was the major seismic cultural shift which produced the postmodernism of the 1980s. Essentially, the next hegemony in poetry, represented by the 1982 Penguin anthology *Contemporary British Poetry*, edited by Blake Morrison and Andrew Motion, backed *neither* the retro-Georgians, *nor* the retro-Modernists, and indeed, it (in)famously declared that in 'much of the 1960s and 70s, . . . very little—in England at any rate—seemed to be happening'. The new world represented by that crucial anthology puts the lid on 'candidly personal poetry', announces a general preference for 'metaphor and poetic bizarrerie' which 'represents a radical departure from the empirical mode', and foregrounds poetry like Fenton's which 'draws attention to the artifice and autonomy of [its] text'; in summary, in spite of the unassimilated presence of 'alternative traditions, which are provincial and working-class' (p. 17), the new world may be said 'to exhibit something of the spirit of postmodernism' (p. 20). Though the phrase about nothing happening in the 1970s is often quoted with loathing by the radicals, there is surely much else in the Introduction they would agree with, for they too hate 'candidly personal poetry' (p. 12), exhibit plenty of 'ludic and literary self-consciousness' (p. 12), 'draw attention to the artifice and autonomy' of their texts (p. 19), and use devices which 'emphasise the gap between themselves and their subjects' (p. 12). For the Penguin anthologists, eschewing the 'candidly personal' will take the form of (for instance) the Martianism of Craig Raine and Christopher Reid, the Escher-like, decentred narratives of James Fenton and Andrew Motion, and the baroque whimsicality of Paul Muldoon. Undoubtedly, this seems a diet geared to the moods of the 1980s, a period when poets 'dressed up' for poetry in a succession of ironic roles, just as the pop groups of the day—Adam Ant, the 'New Romantics', and the like—dressed up for the elaborate video fantasies which accompanied the TV presentation of their pop songs. But the point I am emphasising is simply that the new power-centre in British poetry did not, in fact, endorse the conservative side in the 1970s struggle, nor, of course, did it promote the radicals. Instead, it by-passed both—a plague (or plaque) on both your houses (to quote Laurence Cotterell)—and went for something else. In that sense, we are now in a 'post-dualist' poetry world.

The second way of reading the events is to argue that the new dominant regime of the 1980s, and into the 90s, as represented by Andrew Motion, Blake Morrison, Craig Raine, and Christopher Reid in their editorial and reviewing roles, had, when it comes down to it, more in common with the neo-modernists than the neo-conservatives. These four important figures dominated the publication and reception of large-press poetry in the UK in the 1980s: Motion was editor of *Poetry Review*, from 1981 to 1983, and then poetry editor and editorial director at London publishers Chatto & Windus, from 1983 to 1989; Morrison worked for the *Times Literary Supplement* between 1978 and 1981 as poetry and fiction editor and was then literary editor for both *The Observer* and the *Independent on Sunday*; Raine 'was books editor for *New Review*, from 1977 to 1978, editor of the literary magazine *Quarto*, from 1979 to 1980, and poetry editor at the *New Statesman*, in 1981, and then became poetry editor at the London publishers Faber and Faber, from 1981 to 1991: Reid, finally, was Raine's successor as poetry editor at Faber, performing the role from 1991 to 1999. Hence, to get on as a poet in Britain during that period you had to please at least one of them.

In so far as the influential Morrison/Motion Penguin *Contemporary British Poetry* anthology of 1982 was postmodernist, it certainly had more overlap with the Poetry Society radicals' modernist project than with the retro-vision of their conservative opponents. Thus, it could be argued that if the radicals had managed to build something more permanent from their Poetry Society bridgehead in 1976–7 they would have survived into an early 1980s poetry world in which the tide was beginning to move in (at least) something like their direction. The March 1977 walk-out, however, reduced the scope for this kind of 'cross-fertilisation' and ensured that 'BPR' poets continued to lack any mainstream institutional forum right into the 1990s. Consequently, they remained unknown, often, even to academics in British higher education teaching courses on contemporary British Poetry—they were quite simply (to use the Poundian phrase adopted as the sub-title of Hampson and Barry's *New British Poetries*), written out of 'the scope of the possible' in poetry.

Poets competing in the 1980s and beyond for the notice of Morrison, Motion, Raine and Reid were legitimately eager to promote their own interests. Notional groupings (some of which caught on, some of which didn't), like the Martians, the 'New Gen' poets, and the Scottish Informationists, were exploited for their attention-getting potential. It is often said that if several shops are grouped together they generate custom for each other, and in the same way, a poet who is perceived to be part of a group has an increased chance of attracting notice. But, typically, the groupings and affiliations on the avant-garde side do not seem to have such goals in mind at all. Often, the institutions of the 'parallel tradition' have extraordinary longevity—the Writers Forum workshops, for instance, have gone on for fifty years, so that the Sub Voicive reading series, only a quarter of a century into its run, still seems a relative newcomer. But such groupings among the radicals tend to be almost static in size and personnel; the same figures attend them for thirty years or so, and though there is, of course, some 'seepage' of new faces in and old faces out, they remain essentially just what they were at the start, with no dramatic expansion or transformation. Paradoxically, too, they tend to be (literally) *conservative* institutions which keep alive a particular set of possibilities and practices which are unacknowledged or disregarded by the centre. It would seem reasonable for a poet to expect that becoming a member of a grouping of some kind would have some spin-off advantages in terms of what might crudely be called career development, but this was seldom the case in 'BPR' circles. Indeed, Sub Voicive recently advertised one of its star poets as 'one of an almost invisible group of "new" or "subvoicive" [sic] poets whose writings still cannot be found in commercial bookshops'.

In the preface to his section of the *New British Poetries* anthology in the late 1980s, Eric Mottram wrote that most of the contributors to his twenty issues of *Poetry Review* had *chosen* to continue to publish in small presses, but it is perhaps self-deceiving to imagine that they had much choice, or that they had *elected* their small-press quasi-silence as a monk elects the silence of the cloister. At any moment, the implication would be, they might succumb to temptation, drop a collection in the post to Faber or Chatto, and find themselves, within a couple of months, being reviewed in the *TLS,* the *Observer,* or the *Independent on Sunday.* It isn't that the nature of the work they produced placed them beyond the possibility of any such recognition, for work of an even more revolutionary and provocative kind *is* the mainstream in the visual arts. As Andrew Duncan writes:

> The situation of the visual arts, where the avant garde entered the juries, received government patronage, got put on by the British Council, etc., is superior to that of poetry, where the sources of money and information were sealed off by a revanchist conservative group which fought a ruthless war against innovation. There is not a single book on the radical poetry of the 1970s. The discourse around the visual arts is roughly a hundred times more advanced. (http://www.pinko.org/60.html)

Part of the explanation, then, must lie in the specific social formation of avant-garde poets, and to some extent (to return to a point raised earlier) it concerns their attitude to publication, which is often very complex and contradictory, as frequently with avant-garde groups. Some variety of self-publication, in fact, has long been the norm for innovatory writing—it isn't an accident that T. S. Eliot first published *The Waste Land* in a magazine he was editing himself, or that Virginia and Leonard Woolf ran the Hogarth Press. By definition, almost, the quality of something new will not easily be recognised by major publishers, who must cater for an existing set of public tastes. But these existing public tastes are precisely what an avant-garde despises or distrusts, so there is a natural antipathy between established publishing networks and emergent literary groups. The extreme form of this attitude is that not being known, not being published, even, becomes a badge of honour, a mark of quality. In *Liquid City* (Reaktion, 1999), Iain Sinclair, en route to visit Eric Mottram with photographer Marc Atkins, explains to Atkins who Mottram is and what he represents:

> The names don't mean anything to Atkins. This is deleted history—Allen Fisher, Bill Griffiths, Barry MacSweeney, the heroes of the 'British Poetry Revival'—have been expunged from the record. Poetry is back where it belongs: in exile. In the provinces, the bunkers of academe. In madhouses, clinics and fragile sinecures. (p. 38)

This 'off the record' poetry world is the locale of those who, like the poets of the *Various Art* anthology in Sinclair's Re/Active series at Paladin, 'have chosen to work outside the customary institutions of British poetry'. The short-lived Re/Active series, in theory at least, briefly made them 'available to a wider audience', but is that what they want? Iain Sinclair's period as Series Editor of the Re/Active poetry anthologies at Paladin from 1987 to 1992 was the only other instance of radicalism in poetry securing a significant mainstream outlet or institution, and the timescale of about five years for which it lasted is interestingly similar to that of the Mottram regime at the Poetry Society. Five years is roughly the time it takes for the other side to notice that something has happened and launch a counter-strike. The series was scrapped, and existing books pulped or remaindered, on the Rupert Murdoch takeover of the parent Harper-Collins Company.

In reality, then, once you 'choose' to work 'outside the customary institutions' you turn your back on 'a wider audience'. The wider audience is precisely what an avant-garde rejects—its tastes, preferences, addictions, laziness, and so on. The suspicion is, then, that the avant-garde, deep down, is happy when the 'out-reach' projects fail (the Poetry Society take-over, the Paladin breakthrough, etc), confirming their negative convictions about the cultural establishment, so that they can get back to the tight-knit 'experimentalist' community ('ghetto', some would say) and write with and for people they know and trust. This attitude is encapsulated in Mottram's advice to Malaysian writer T. Wignesan, as reported in a footnote to a poem about him in *Radical Poetics* Issue One (London), Spring 1997, edited by Michael Hrebeniak. Wignesan says: 'in the mid-sixties, when I had been published and Eric was then ghosting the American literature columns of the *Times Literary Supplement*, Eric gave me the best advice I've ever listened to in our *métier*. He said very offhand-like one day, and his demeanour meant every word he pronounced ponderously: 'Don't write anything you can get published!'

My point here is that the 'BPR' group possessed the typical avant-garde distrust of publication to an unusually high degree. A certain distrust of easy pleasure, especially the pleasure which readers might derive from their encounter with a work of poetry, often went along with this. Mottram frequently voiced the view that a poem shouldn't be a quick pleasure-fix: the kind of the poetry the Arts Council would support, he said, was 'poetry as a market consumption article like a double scotch or a cigarette': by contrast, the kind of poetry he supported 'did not cater for the middle-class rapid-reader, untrained in contemporary poetics and looking for instant significance and alibis with established, authenticated products'; understanding the 'notations of form, feeling and observation' of the artists he regarded highly 'might take months or years of trained appreciation to understand, with a considerable outlay of time and energy'. This kind of poetry would probably appear without 'the external trappings which signify leisure in consumer-product advertising terms: hard covers with big press signatures' (all quotations from 'The British Poetry Revival', p.18 in Hampson and Barry). Here the distaste for leisure and pleasure, for consumerism and rapid consumption is very marked: instead there is an emphasis on the long-haul, on 'trained' appreciation, on poetry that sounds like hard, sustained work, rather than pleasure. The emphasis on the need for training re-emerges in the *Prospect into Breath* interview:

> I think any activity of value needs training to participate in it. If you go on a rugby field or a climbing expedition and if anybody on it doesn't know what they're doing, isn't skilled, it just drags everybody down. My sense is that one should go into training .... It's quite a scandal that anybody thinks they can take part in the arts without some preparation, in terms of knowledge of what's going on, in terms of forms and how you read and

how you listen, and so on . . . . They have not made the lightest effort to get their literary and poetic bearings. (p. 29)

But who will provide the training? Who will be willing to offer the 'months or years' it takes to begin to understand? In the light of remarks like this we begin, perhaps, to understand the extraordinary longevity of some of those avant-garde groupings, the 'workshops' that seem to go on for ever, every second Tuesday of the month, to infinity and beyond. The distaste for 'product', of course, is also very common in avant-garde circles: the 'work in progress' has greater prestige than the completed work—the labyrinthine, interlinked, open-ended structures of work like Allen Fisher's, for instance, have already been remarked upon. What is valued is process, whatever resists packaging, marketing, commodification, capitalist reification. Since readers, by definition, 'consume' a product, readers are disliked and tend to be seen as parasitical; the only really valued readers are fellow-practitioners, co-members of the workshop, people, in other words, who are worker-producers as well as consumers. At many levels, then, it ceases to be surprising that the Poetry Society ended with a walk-out rather than a counter-coup. As we might always have expected, the inside story is that the radicals weren't pushed—they jumped.

Two Kinds of Avant-Garde, and 'Democracy'

It could be argued, then, in the light of all this, that the decisive factor was not the imbalance of power between the avant-garde and the conservative faction, but the imbalance of power *within the avant-garde itself*. To be successful, an avant-garde needs to have two component groups within itself: the 'drive' is provided by the *radical* radicals, without whom there would be nothing of substance happening (other than the natural desire and ambition of younger artists or writers to supplant their elders). They are the source of the energy, the ideas, the motivating impatience with the past and with the status quo. But the 'steering' is provided by the *conservative* radicals, who are much more pragmatic about how to operate at the interface with the dominant status quo. They have a strategic eye, and ultimately it is their presence and actions which decide whether the avant-garde burns itself out in impotent exclusion, leaving very little changed, or secures the kind of cultural footing which can make the significant inroads which in the end bring about a permanent paradigm change. In the case of the Poetry Society, the conservative radicals came into the picture too late to have a lasting influence, or (if we see 'Cambridge' as performing this role) they remained a separate entity, so that the paradigm shift did not come about, and cultural success moved elsewhere. In the end, people cannot be bullied into adopting progressive cultural attitudes—they have to be persuaded, and that requires a group of conservative radicals with some critical mass. A more ultimately successful radical community—Black Mountain College, North Carolina would be the classic instance—had this vital mixture of different kinds of radicalism within itself.

Yet another way of taking a 'long view' is to look at the 1970s struggle in terms of 'democracy', since both sides accused the other of being 'unrepresentative', of 'packing' meetings, or disregarding constitutional procedures. Implicit in the earlier comments about popular reader-ships, and readerships in general, is a somewhat contradictory stance towards democracy which is evident in both sides of the Poetry Society dispute. Both sides saw the other as 'undemocratic', but neither side is wholly convincing in its claims. Charles Osborne saw the Poetry Society radicals as an 'unrepresentative' clique and sought their removal, even though they had been duly elected by the constitutional processes of that body. His means of bringing about their removal by-passed demo-cratic process, for instance, when he sought to impose three directly-appointed Arts Council members onto the Society's General Council in 1974, and then appointed an investigative panel into the Society's affairs when he couldn't achieve this, apparently selecting its members himself. All this seems anti-democratic, at best, and indeed, Osborne's methods were distinctly autocratic and eccentric—he revelled in his image of being (to quote the sub-title of his memoir) an *un*civil Civil Servant with a barbed wit and a lacerating tongue (or pen) who disdained the diplomatic niceties of Civil Service language. At the same time, however, his cultural tastes are clearly much closer to the norms of his own social class, to which the vast majority of 'users' of poetry belonged, than Eric Mottram's were. The early 'Poetry International' events which Osborne organised feature 'middle-brow' icons like John Betjeman and Dame Edna Everidge, and he admired the light-verse media-satire of Clive James's dreadful and now forgotten 'Peregrine Pyke' saga, which was printed at seemingly interminable-length, and at public expense, in Ian Hamilton's heavily subsidised *New Review*, the sustained financial support of which Osborne sees as one of the major achievements of his period of office as Literature Director. Osborne's own books are on safely-canonised 'high-brow' cultural icons like Kafka and Auden, and the music of Verdi, Mozart, Schubert, and Wagner. Generally, then, he approves, on the one hand, of public, 'democratic' tastes, and enjoys the kind of thing which most educated people are happy to pay money to read, see, or listen to. But, on the other, he is impatient with the democratic process when it elects the 'wrong' representatives and challenges people like himself to contemplate other kinds of cultural product, especially material which is more 'raw' or 'abrasive' or 'offensive' than they are used to.

A similar contradiction, but in reverse, is seen in the case of Eric Mottram: Mottram's much more severely 'high-brow' attitude to ordinary pleasures seems partly generational, pre-dating 1960s hedonism, and embodying a stern imperative that people raise their cultural sights and resist the debasing blandishments of the surrounding commodity culture. His emphasis on 'training' is reminiscent of the Workers' Educational Association ethos of Raymond Williams or Richard Hoggart, but without their positive valuation of working-class culture. Indeed, in that respect the cultural sternness of F. R. Leavis seems a closer parallel, for Leavis has that same undeviating, evangelical conviction of the rightness and moral superiority of the cultural ethos he sought to impose. As editor of *Poetry Review* Mottram could see nothing at all of interest or merit in the poetic scribblings of those who were, from his viewpoint, totally 'out of the loop', and were labouring under the illusion that their personal experience had any potentially wider significance. He found it difficult to contain his contempt for these people (who worked in mental asylums, or had been writing for forty years, or whose work, in the past had 'always been taken' by *Poetry Review*). Eric was as far removed from 'popular culture' as it is possible to be, a man whose classical and jazz record collection and his piano playing were the mainstays of his personal cultural life. When the students at King's College were no longer interested in coming along in the evenings to learn about the jazz greats, he evidently felt that civilisation was ending, and he sounds in interview as bewildered and as impotently indignant as the kind of figure he had spent his whole life opposing. What he despises is the fact that the young nowadays want instant gratification: rather than being fascinated, as he was, by what is difficult, they are just turned off by it. For the first time, listening to Eric, in the autumn of 1994, at what must have been one of his last public lectures, I had the feeling that I was listening to quite an old man.

Culturally, then, Mottram was anything but 'democratic'. At the same time, though, his objections to the Arts Council's treatment of the Poetry Society during the 1970s period are made on the grounds that it was counter to democratic principles, for Charles Osborne, in his view, was acting as a cultural Czar, assuming absolute power to impose his own cultural preferences on the Poetry Society, and refusing to carry out the policy of the organisation in which he held office. The Arts Council's policy was to offer subsidy to individual writers, but Osborne believed that the Literature Panel should only subsidise literary *organisations* (for example, festivals, journals, societies, bookshops, and so on), just as the Drama Panel subsidised theatre companies, rather than individual actors. This is a perfectly defensible position to hold, but it seems less defensible to continue to hold office in an organisation which he had not persuaded to adopt this as its policy. Likewise, grants to organisations (such as the Poetry Society) cannot be conditional upon allowing the grant-giving organisation artistic control: yet, as the Poets Conference document of 1978 pointed out, that is precisely what Osborne tried to do, bringing about a situation where Poetry Society policy was not determined by its elected Council Members. The symmetrical paradox, then, is that the supporter of democratic principles (Mottram) actively disregards democratic tastes, while the sharer of democratic tastes (Osborne) actively disregards democratic principles.

Poetry Review Today

Finally, taking a long view of the events of the 1970s should involve bringing the *Poetry Review* story up to date. The journal was edited by Andrew Motion from 1981 to 1983, by Mick Imlah from 1983 to 1987, and then by Peter Forbes, right through to 2002. It became a much more glossy, commercial product, expressive of the era in which poetry was hyped (notoriously) as 'the new rock n' roll' in the 1994 'New Generation' poetry promotion. It was a highly successful journal—punchy, up-to-date, commercial, and popular. The journal during the Forbes period moved about as far as it is possible to go from the anti-hedonism of the Mottram era, but then the pendulum seemed to swing back again. In 2002 the editorship was taken over by David Herd and Robert Potts, the former a University of Kent academic, and author of a book on the poetry of John Ashbery, the latter a journalist and literary critic much opposed to popularisation and factionalism. Under their editorship, the journal became serious and impressive, though somewhat austere and forbidding in style and presentation. Its political commitment was powerfully left-wing—see, for instance, the article by Andrew Jordan (in Potts and Herd's penultimate issue) on working as writer-in-residence at the Haslar 'holding centre' for asylum-seekers in Portsmouth. The essays published during the Herd/Potts tenureship were distinguished, and the discussion and reproductions of paintings were of self-evident quality, but the mixture may not have been quite what readers expected, and their editorship did not continue beyond the spring of 2005. In early 2005, therefore, the appointment of poet Fiona Sampson as editor was announced, the first individual female editor of *Poetry Review* since the Muriel Spark period in the late 1940s (during part of the Mick Imlah period the editorship had been shared with Tracey Warr). Spark commented: 'I think it wonderful that a woman Editor is taking over again and I hope the new editor will be as successful in attracting good poetry to the Society as I believe I was, way back in 1947'.

Under the brief Herd/Potts regime *Poetry Review* was more sympathetic to radicalism than it had been at any previous time since 1977, although, as the editors say in their valedictory editorial (94:4, winter 2004-5), they took over determined to ignore 'the categories according to which the territory was divided, the short-hand by which British poetry was routinely assessed', because they were convinced that such categories 'had become damaging', and they listed some of the familiar contrastive pairings, 'mainstream/avant-garde, formal/experimental, intellectual/accessible', and several others. I have not avoided such binary terms in the present book, though I am well aware that they can be reductive, and that they can become (as Herd and Potts say) 'an alternative to reading'. I have used such binary terminology mainly because it is impossible to ignore the division such terms designate, and because it would have been impossible to tell the 1970s story without them. But the fact that none of the available terms seem entirely adequate or satisfactory (as discussed in the Introduction) is indicative of the fact that the two sides are now to some degree in dialogue with each other, as they were not in the 1970s. As Peter Middleton puts it, also in a recent issue of *Poetry Review*:

> The very difficulty of naming either tendency is a symptom of this—neither thinks of itself as having such boundaries. The subtleties of the mainstream personal lyric's handling of self-consciousness, or the many ways in which structuring devices are used as part of the generation of

meaning in avant-garde poetry, both require for their full understanding extended immersion in the poetry networks where these modes of writing are dominant. ('Recognition', *Poetry Review*, 94:1, spring 2004)

We have many books which help us to understand 'the subtleties of the mainstream personal lyric's handling of self-consciousness': indeed, that is what the typical 'default' book about contemporary poetry usually does. I hope that the present book can contribute towards helping us to understand the other side of the divide, by telling something of the history of the 'poetry network' in which 'avant-garde' or 'experimental' writing is dominant.

Documents

1. Eric Mottram's 'Editor's Note' (1975)

[Published in *Poetry Review*, 66:1]

EDITOR'S NOTE

With this issue, the fifteenth under the present editor, *Poetry Review* assumes a new format which it is hoped will better accommodate the spatial forms of the wide variety of poems in today's poetry scene. It has never been the policy to spout policy: the poems and their juxtapositions were their own editorial. Criticism and reviews were omitted because the small space in a quarterly magazine had to be given to poets, and because current poetry criticism has little of the standard set by, for example, Hans Keller's analysis of Schoenberg's quartets, or Robert Sherlaw Johnson's book on Messiaen. Reviewing has become an adjunct of the gossip column and those clubs where reviewers try to establish hierarchy. Under Peter Hodgkiss's editorship *Poetry Information* is rapidly rectifying this situation and providing criticism which helps us to read poetry. For this reason, and because of our restricted space, *Poetry Review's* listing of books and magazines has been transferred to the newer contemporary. At one time it was hoped to issue both journals together from the National Poetry Centre, but partly owing to refusals of public money to the Centre, this plan had to be dropped. For *Poetry Review* is edited for the Poetry Society at the Centre, and the editor is elected by the elected General Council. His appointment is regularly reviewed; in fact, during the past four years, it has been difficult to plan for more than one issue ahead, owing to this insecurity, believed to be democratic. But the editor is independent of the Society in all other respects. His real dependence begins with the necessity for *Poetry Review* now to be not only published from the Centre but printed on its premises in the Poetry Society's print-shop, through the Consortium of London Presses. Starting with the previous issue (Vol.65, No.4), *Poetry Review* is independent of money-making presses and their delays and costs, but it is dependent on the improving printing abilities of volunteers whose services are free.

~

Beginning with Vol.62, No.3, Autumn 1971, the editor's guiding idea was to present as much as he could, over a dozen or so issues, of the poetry that has created "The British Poetry Revival 1960–1974"–the title of the summary article in the programme book for the Modern British Poetry Conference. The 32 poets taking part in the two, sections of this conference, held by the Polytechnic of Central London in 1974, together with those included in the Cambridge Poetry Festival of 1975, and the poets included in the weekly readings at the National Poetry Centre during the past three or four years, constitute the core of that revival. We now have a major poetry scene in this country, the first since the 1930s. *Poetry Review* had to represent that achievement and to place it alongside representative poetry from the American scene (which has tended to over-exemplify serious poetry in the English language since 1950–and not without good reason, given its high quality and wide range). In the 15 issues–including the double issue of Vol.65, Nos. 2 and 3–have appeared 94 British poets, 50 Americans, 10 poets in translation, and 6 from other sources. The range in both age and procedure has been correspondingly wide: but it only represents, with perhaps a handful of exceptions which *Poetry Review* pioneered, the achievement of poetry-publishing presses–mostly little presses–in this country and the United States. These poets have been published in scores of other reviews, and their books have appeared from 90 presses in Britain, 69 in America, and 13 in Canada, France, Germany, Holland, Finland and Spain. *Poetry Review* has, therefore, drawn on a healthy scene which it may not have created but which it certainly supports. Given time and space it could be even more representative. For example, it has included comparatively little from the international field of concrete/soundtext work, and not nearly enough poetry in translation.

∾

It simply takes a modest place among many magazines now circulating. (Anyone with an ounce of talent can be published today: being published simply means that someone encourages your work). *Poetry Review* tries to publish new work which shows quality and courage, and hopes to do for poetry a fraction of what, for example, William Glock, did for contemporary music at the BBC. It has registered major changes in British poetry since the 1960s, and it publishes against the false idea that poetry is primarily inherited, imitated and accepted forms in prosody and subject materials. It does not believe that poetry should necessarily communicate with the rapidity expected by the consumer of cigarettes, aspirin, newspaper print, or verses at the bottom of a column in a posh weekly or after the news on BBC2. Poetry is not recognition patterns within a spectator-consumer society, but, rather, language which activates imagination and surprises the reader into new abilities. Therefore *Poetry Review* has not expected to please the casual reader, or the reader who wants something easy to teach with, or the reader who is tempted to identify value with his own tastes. In British poetry today there is no mainstream middle of the road established kind or taste, except in the murderous dreams of censors and government financial controllers. Our best poetry is an international health of poetry which takes forms the artists need.

2. Manifesto for a Reformed Poetry Society (1975)
[Published by the Committee for the Reform of the Poetry Society, the original group opposed to the radicals]

INTRODUCTION

This document represents a consensus of opinion on the condition of The Poetry Society and is not that of a self-appointed pressure group. This opinion was reached after considerable and lengthy discussions by those who have been made aware of the Society's atrophy. We would emphasize that this' awareness has come alike to members of The Poetry Society and to a much larger body of people involved with poetry, but who are non-members.

∾

Any representation of situations that are regarded as needful of reform must be preceded by an explanation of their discovery.

∾

The foundation of concern over the condition of the Society originated with fears that "Poetry Round" might be closed—closed certainly to non-members of The Poetry Society. This incident gave rise to an examination of the whole structure of the Society, particularly the degree to which a small cabal is able to influence or control the direction and nature of functions as vital to the Society as is, for instance, *Poetry Review*.

~

What has been revealed is, at best, a massive indifference to the body and course of poetry and its poets on the part of an all too influential and vindictive group of council members. At worst, there exists an overt hostility, on the part of those persons, towards *any* individual or group that opposes it. Those councillors in this group are closed to representation, their concerns are impacted, they are interested only in sycophancy and nepotism, and they answer *any* genuine criticism with spite and rank vindictiveness.

~

To the detriment of The Poetry Society's original intentions, there is far too little communication between the General Council and the body of the membership, and there is insufficient liaison between the diverse groups currently functioning in the Society. We envisage a Society whose General Council is more directly accountable for its decisions; this means that it must communicate its decisions more promptly and that new channels of communication must be opened so that the process is democratically two way.

~

It is, however, realised that there is a great deal of work undertaken by the Society that is both important to the spread of interest in poetry and that is unaffected by the corruption which is objected to. There is, therefore, an intention to change that area and method of operation.

~

Thus, as we hope has been made plain, this is a movement of reform. We wish to create the kind of Poetry Society envisaged by Norman Hidden in the *Poetry Review* of Winter, 1968/9:

~

There are more aspiring poets today than ever before, and they need the encouragement of an atmosphere that is favourable to their work—the availability of a listening audience, the opportunity of technical discussion, the chance of their poems appearing in print. These are all services that The Poetry Society has provided and will continue to provide to an increasing degree. It is important, however, that the circle in which these activities occur is not an esoteric one. There are many kinds of worthwhile poetry and there is a growing number of young people who wish to experience the entire range that poetry, modern and traditional, has to offer. One envisages as one of the functions of The Poetry Society the creation of an atmosphere at Earls Court Square which is both receptive and stimulating. Receptive in the sense that a poet of eighty might meet a poet of twenty and neither feel out of place; stimulating in that what is new and untried may also have its fling and its fair share of the resources available. Such development would provide a point of equilibrium at which a proper concern for experiment could meet with a proper concern for tradition; and where there would be bridges between the old and the new for those who choose to use them.

≈

In order to achieve this essential openness, we must rid the Society of those who have found a refuge in cliquism, who, without a wide enough audience with whom to connect, turn inwards, writing in the main for themselves. In this they further alienate any potential audience, since an audience postulates a need to connect, that is, to turn outwards. Norman Hidden pointed out that it is this kind of effect which gives much modern British poetry its relatively cynical look, its apparent lack of direction, and an inner quality of negativeness in many cases.

≈

To conclude this introduction, our aim is to create in the Society an atmosphere of sympathy and encouragement for everyone concerned with poetry. We are sure that by opening up the Society there will be brought to it the support and public interest it has for too long lacked.

≈

CONTENTION

The Poetry Society is not establishing the practice of poetry as a vital element in the present British culture. It has failed to do so for several reasons.

∾

Firstly, the philosophical assumptions underlying The Poetry Society's activities are derived from long-held popular notions about the poet being somehow apart from the rest of humanity. Poetry is taken from The Poetry Society on tablets of stone to the people. The people are not encouraged to bring their poetry to the Society, or, at least, only if they pay a membership fee, and even then the opportunities they are offered are extremely limited.

∾

The assumption of the poet's unique position has led to a situation where the few groups surviving to work in the Society's premises are usually specialised, exciting a narrow range of interest and support. Within these groups hierarchies and elites can be perceived where they have no business, and poetry becomes subordinated to the pursuit of status.

∾

This first criticism gives rise to the first two demands. The work of the Society should be organized not merely in presenting the work of a few randomly selected 'established' poets but should seek out, encourage and present the work of the many groups practising in Great Britain. This part of the Society's work should be truly experimental.

∾

The Society should extend its work outside the premises to participate and initiate community events whether centred in a village, a commune, an adventure playground or even where poetry is merely an element in a festival. In this way The Poetry Society would work for poetry, not for a self-seeking minority of its membership.

∾

The philosophical assumptions mentioned earlier condemn poetry to the status of a minority art, and this position is maintained by the structure and membership of the government of The Poetry Society. The present system of elections, requiring only one third of the elected members of the General Council to stand for election each year, results in a continuity of control by an unrepresentative power group. Their position of control is enabled by the limited voting rights of the membership. The third demand, therefore, is that the entire General Council stand for election each year and that members be given the right to choose to vote by postal ballot.

～

These constitutional changes will make the General Council necessarily aware of and responsive to the demands of its membership. The Poetry Society enjoys a unique status by virtue of its national label. Hence it is to be expected that its magazine should be open to all poetry written in the British languages. It is not. Neither will the *Poetry Review* be so, given a policy which allows the appointment of an editor of limited tastes. The fourth demand is thus for an editorial board of five, selected to appreciate the widest range of poetry and to open the *Poetry Review* to its publication. This policy will restore the Review to the status of a magazine from its present position as an anthology of bad verse.

～

With this in mind, the fifth demand is for the Society to support the publication and distribute to its mailing list an alternative review which would be representative of the best poetry in the British languages. It should be obvious that none of the below-named committee members shall seek publication of their poetry in such a magazine.

～

All of these demands are a necessary surgery to remove the canker of self- interest and elitism which dominates the Society at present. None of this would be necessary if the membership of the General Council believed in and worked for the essential life of poetry in the culture and community. A General Council member's campaign for higher fees for poets' readings not only misses the point but yields tacitly to apathy and elitism. Poetry should be written for the people—not for hand-outs. If the General Council cannot perceive this they should get out.

~

In light of our convictions as stated above, we plan to issue this manifesto to the widest possible audience.

Committee for the Reform of The Poetry Society:

Irving Weinman, P.S., Chairman: Denis Doyle, P.S., Secretary: James Sutherland-Smith, Treasurer: Tim Coxe: David Lovibond: Padraic MacAnna, P.S.

3. The Manifesto of the Poetry Society (1976)
[Issued by the radicals at the Poetry Society]

The Poetry Society is an association of poets and enthusiasts whose renewed collective identity is clarified by the situation of emergency in which British literature finds itself. In the face of predominant regressive values it is now useful to say that we are devoted to the practice and propagation of the following convictions:

1. That the creative imagination of each individual is the sole continuing source of new forms, new ideas, and new vocabulary, by which language must be perpetually revitalised.

2. That it is always permissible, and often imperative, to suspend the functioning laws of grammar and syntax when the creative imagination is brought into play.

3. That the day-to-day function of language to communicate rational information is no longer necessarily predominant when the creative imagination is brought into play.

4. That language under creative imagination is called poetry and that poetry no longer has any other useful definition.

5. That literature is passing through a stage of development in which the merit of poetry is most usefully measured by the degree of innovation apparent in its structure.

6. That poetry enjoys a direct social function in the perpetual alteration of the status quo; that it is the source of philosophical, moral, aesthetic, and therefore political change; that in order to function as source it must remain free of existing ideologies and dogma.

7. That the proper study of the creative structures of the past must be guided by a search for those past elements that are useful and appropriate in the present creative situation; that traditional disciplines must be seen as option rather than as law.

8. That poets and critics should not be impeded by their loyalties to various clubs, cliques and groups whose formation and *raison d'etre* have nothing to do with poetry.

9. That the belief in the absolute validity and predominance of traditional forms be granted its rightful place in the Society as the interesting and unique reaction against poetry which it is.

10. That, in a unique Poetry Centre in which printing, bookshop, performance, and library facilities are brought together under the same roof, precedence be given to printing and publication in order to surmount the present exclusion of the best poetry from commercial publications and to inform the Nation of the unprecedentedly large number of poets now working in Britain in the forefront of the creative field.

11. That poets are not concerned exclusively with their native tongue; that poetry is international and trans-lingual, that English poetry should concern itself with poetry and the world, not merely with England and English.

12. That poetry, far from being the mere manipulation of words, is a visionary discipline which informs certain sections of all the arts, and that all media enjoying a poetic character are the concern of the Society.

4. Eric Mottram: 'Editing *Poetry Review*' (1979–80)

[Appended to an index of Mottram issues of *Poetry Review*, in *Poetry Information*, 20 & 21, 1979–80]

EDITING POETRY REVIEW

My election to the editorship of *Poetry Review* was part of internal reforms within the Poetry Society in the early 1970s, instigated by Stuart Montgomery, Bob Cobbing and others, in order to draw the new British poetry into an organization it had rightly considered to be moribund. My mandate was simply to publish a wide range of poetry from this country and America, and for this I had to resign from the Poetry Society's general council, to which I had been elected earlier. Attending general council meetings had prepared me for the virulence and ignorance of the reactionary literary Establishment. I knew what to expect once *Poetry Review* had been projected into the twentieth-century. My only plan was to publish as wide a range as possible of the new British poetry, the best of American poetry, and whatever could be managed from translation. In the event British and American poetry dominated; the weakness in *Poetry Review* was certainly in the relative absence of adequate translations from continental Europe and Latin America. I also believed it necessary to print full lists of current books and magazines of poetry–part of the Society's policy of providing proper information about the poetry scene. Finally the covers were all to be designed by poets themselves. *Poetry Review* would be for poets; judgmental reviewing could take place elsewhere. In *Poetry Review* anyone concerned with literature as a major function in society could find serious work; it was not a review for those who consumed poetry from time to time as a leisure pastime. This meant, of course, that it ran against the grain of contemporary British culture, in which the arts are taken by the rulers and their middle class administrators to be purely the prerogative of the consumer in the marketplace. At first, the new British poets were cautious of an official organ, whoever the editor might be, but the news spread within the year. Even so, the editor relied always on building each issue around work which had been specifically commissioned. Very few completely unknown poets were "discovered" for the obvious reason that, with a thriving small press and little magazine movement, *Poetry Review* could act as a selective focus for what was actually happening: a major British poetry revival. No one who was any good at all remained unpublished somewhere in the scene.

$\approx$

Initially, it was difficult to plan issues ahead, since the Society could sack the editor with short notice, and in any case his appointment was a limited engagement. But once that was cleared up, he could go ahead. The other problem was simply the sheer massive bulk of prospective poetry through the post; at one point it reached 200 envelopes a week. At first, I looked carefully at every poem that came in, but since ninety percent of it was incompetent amateur stuff with the least possible knowledge of twentieth-century poetry methods, this became intolerably time-wasting. The publications committee of the Society took over the job of prior selection, an easy chore, since anyone with the slightest knowledge could detect absence of talent, but a highly tedious one. Many of the contributors accompanied their work with threatening or pleading letters the gist of which was: I am a cripple, I am a night-nurse in an asylum, ninety two, in prison, aged six, writing with my toes only—or simply, I have been writing for many years, or this is my first poem, or *Poetry Review* has always taken my work . . . After six years, the editor had a vision of Britain as a race of poetry-scribbling maniacs whose one aim was to appear in print. Clearly the educational system had convinced them that anyone could and did write verses fit for public distribution. Provided you imitated models accepted by the academic and press Establishment, you were made. Consequently, when it became clear that Poetry Review was a professional journal and not a consumers' magazine, the attacks began, climaxing in the Arts Council demolition of the *Poetry Review* along with the Poetry Society in 1977, the full story of which the public has yet to be told. But in spite of the abuse at each Annual General Meeting of the Society, and the vulgarity of comments in *Agenda* and elsewhere, the editor was in fact re-elected until he had completed 22 issues. On each of these issues he had the inestimable practical assistance of Bob Cobbing, who loyally helped to read proofs and to see the finished product through the printers. Later in the series he was supported by Bill Griffiths, one of the few new major poets *Poetry Review* urged into first print.

$\approx$

The Arts Council, guided by Charles Osborne, killed *Poetry Review* along with the Poetry Society which it represented. The Council's investigatory committee of three, one of whom became the Council's first chairperson at the Poetry Society, were hired to eliminate the reformers and reinstall the reactionaries; and because the Council controls public money for the arts—absolutely and without redress or even reply to enquiry—its victory was complete, aided and abetted by the British Press. Poetry Review dropped back into obscurity. It took an American critic to state clearly what the revolt had been (Abby Arthur Johnson—"The Politics of a Literary Magazine: A study of The *Poetry Review*, 1912–1972", *Journal of Modern Literature*, no. 3, 1973/4): '. . . the journal features writers exploring the possibilities of poetry, both in subject matter and style . . .' It's a fitting epitaph, now that the recognition patterns of consumer-poetry of the literary marketplace reign supreme. But the independent press and magazine world, from which *Poetry Review* drew its strength, is stronger than ever.

[POETRY INFORMATION] EDITOR'S NOTE

Previous to publishing the Index I contacted the General Secretary of the Poetry Society and asked him for information regarding the availability of the Mottram-edited issues of Poetry Review. No reply has been forth-coming but I imagine that copies of most issues are still available from the National Poetry Centre at 21 Earls Court Square, London SW5 9BY. At one time a set of issues was available at a reduced cost but this I may no longer be the case. Maybe those at present in charge at the National Poetry Centre would be quite happy to forget that such a magazine ever existed but it *did* and enquiries about back issues may help to jog their memories.

5. Mottram's Appointment and Extensions as Editor of *Poetry Review*

1st appointment: eight issues: 62:3, Autumn 1971–64:2, Summer 1973: (1)–(8)

9th *December* 1970: letter from Michael Mackenzie, General Secretary of the Poetry Society, invites Mottram to apply for the editorship (two other candidates also approached). 18th *January* 1971: letter from Norman Hidden (Chair of the Society) offers post for two years, i.e., eight issues: editorial fee, £50 per issue (Source: Mottram, 4/3/1–11).

1st Extension: three issues: 64:3, Autumn 1973–65:1, 1974: (9)–(11)
11th *April* 1973: at General Council, George Wightman proposes Gavin Ewart as rival candidate for editorship, but Mottram's re-appointment is confirmed 'for one more year', by twelve votes to one (Minutes). Chair John Cotton informs him of re-appointment in letter of 13th April (Mottram, 4/3/1–11). Owing to financial difficulties, *Poetry Review* is reduced from four issues per year to three, with cheaper production method. Editorial fee per issue raised to £75.

2nd Extension: three issues: 65:2/3, 1975–65:4, 1975: (12)–(14)
27th *March* 1974: General Council re-appoints Mottram for a further year, (ending with the summer 1975 issue), following postal ballot (of the Council) taken because of cancellation of the winter meeting: vote was 12–10 in Mottram's favour (Minutes)

3rd Extension: further year: 66:1, 1975–66:2, 1976: (15)–(16)

14th *June* 1975: Chair's report at AGM announces that General Council has re-appointed Eric Mottram for a further year. 13th *September* 1975: at General Council a motion (proposed by Upton and Cobbing) is accepted, limiting editorship to five years or 20 issues, to apply retrospectively to Mottram.

4th Extension: four issues: 66:3/4, 1976–77–67:1/2, 1977: (17)–(20)
28th *February* 1976: General Council confirms Mottram as editor for next four issues, until spring 1977 (maximum possible extension under new 20 issue rule) and Peter Finch is elected as his long-term successor (Chairman's Report, June 1976 AGM). Voting figures in General Council minutes are: Gavin Ewart 2, Peter Finch 10, Abstentions 3.

6. Data on Mottram Issues of *Poetry Review*

[Augmented version of material published in *Poetry Information*, 20 & 21, 1979–80, compiled by Peter Hodgkiss: for details of Mottram's five successive editorial appointments, see the previous page]

No. Vol.	Date	Pages	Comments	Format	Printers	Method
1ST APPOINTMENT						
(1) 62:3	Autumn 1971	92	listing, 8 pages	Small	Ditchling Press	Letterpress
(2) 62:4*	Winter 1971/2	99	listing, 8 pages	Small	Ditchling Press	Letterpress
(3) 63:1	Spring 1972	99	listing, 12 pages	Small	Ditchling Press	Letterpress
(4) 63:2	Summer 1972	99	listing, 9 pages	Small	Ditchling Press	Letterpress
(5) 63:3	Autumn 1972	96	listing, 6 pages	Small	Ditchling Press	Letterpress
(6) 63:4**	Winter 1972/3	98	listing, 9 pages	Small	Ditchling Press	Letterpress
(7) 64:1	Spring 1973	99	listing, 10 pages	Small	Ditchling Press	Letterpress
(8) 64:2	Summer 1973	99	listing, 13 pages	Small	Ditchling Press	Letterpress
1ST EXTENSION						
(9) 64:3	Autumn 1973	104	listing 13 pages	Small	F.H.Brown,Ltd	Litho
(10) 64:4	1973-4	92	listing 14 pages	Small	F.H.Brown,Ltd	Litho
(11) 65:1	1974	95	listing 12 pages	Small	F.H.Brown,Ltd	Litho
2nd EXTENSION						
(12 & 13)	65:2/3 1975	210	listing 21 pages	Small	F.H.Brown,Ltd	Litho
(14) 65:4	1975	100	No listings	Small	Poetry Society	
3rd EXTENSION						
(15) 66:1	1975	62	No listings	Large	Poetry Society	
(16) 66:2	1976	56	No listings	Large	Poetry Society	)Printed in-house, with
4th EXTENSION						
(17 & 18)	66:3/4 1976/7	86	No listings	Large	Poetry Society	) external
(19 & 20)	67:1/2 1977	136	No listings	Large	Poetry Society	) type-setting

* This issue incorrectly credited as 61:4 on title page.

** This issue incorrectly credited as 64:4 on spine.

All issues litho printed. Nos. 62:3 to 65:4 average size 8.25 × 5.5 inches ('Small'):

Nos. 66:1 to 67:1/2 average size 11.5 × 8.25 inches ('Large').

All contributions (other than poetry information listings) are poetry.

Covers

62:3	Dom Sylvester Houédard	64:4	Pauline Smith
62:4	Jeff Nuttall	65:1	John Furnival
63:1	Jerome Rothenberg/Ian Tyson	65:2/3	Ana Hatherly
63:2	Peter Finch	65:4	Paula Claire
63:3	Jeremy Adler	66:1	Jennifer Pike

63:4	Bob Cobbing		66:2	Kit Wright/ Michael Mackenzie
64: 1	Shoichi Kiyokawa		66: 3/4	Bob Cobbing
64: 2	Ian Hamilton Finlay/ Michael Harvey		67: 1/2	Allen Fisher
64:3	Opal L. Nations			

Place of Publication: London, U.K. (The Poetry Society)

Notes

All issues have bio/bibliographical information on contributors. Nos. 62:3 to 65:2/3 have listing of recent publications compiled with the assistance of Nick Kimberley (then of *Compendium* Books); after that, readers are referred to the listings in *Poetry Information*. All issues contain a list of the members of the Poetry Society General Council and the Poets' Advisory Committee. Issue 66:1 has a page-long 'Editor's Note'—the only editorial comment during Mottram's editorship.

7. The Structure of the Poetry Society

The elected governing body of the Poetry Society was **The General Council**, which consisted of 21 members, until the Extraordinary General Meeting of June 1973, when it was increased to 30, the increase being phased in over three years, with three extra members in 1973, 1974, and 1975. In 1974 the General Council rejected Charles Osborne's demand that three Arts Council's nominees be included in this number. At the 1977 AGM numbers were reduced back to 21 with immediate effect (that is, without a stepped reduction over three years). Council members were elected by members voting in person at the Annual General Meeting, which took place in June each year, but members could be co-opted onto the Council in the case of resignations or other special circumstances. Normally one third of the Council would stand down each year, but out-going members could put themselves forward for re-election. The General Council usually met four times per year.

≈

The day-to-day running of the Poetry Society was in the hands of **The Executive and Management Committee**, which normally met at least six times per year, and was made up of the Chairs of the sub-committees (who were elected by the vote of the General Council). Formal Minutes of the General Council and the Executive and Management were made and kept, but it was not obligatory for sub-committees to do so, and Chairs could make an oral report to one of the major committees.

❧

The range of **Sub-Committees** varied at different periods, but by 1976 (following the changes made after the January Extraordinary General Meeting) the sub-committees were: the Events Committee (which organised the programme of readings at the Society), the Publicity Committee, the Regional Activities Committee, the National Poetry Secretariat Committee, the Publications and Media Committee, the Development and Fundraising Committee, and the Education and Examinations Committee. This was (fairly briefly) the fullest range of committees at any point in the 1970s.

❧

From 1966, when the Poetry Society first received an Arts Council grant, the office of **General Secretary of the Poetry Society** was a salaried appointment, and was combined with the role of **Director of the National Poetry Centre** from 1975. **The Director of the National Poetry Secretariat** was also a salaried post. **The Chair of the General Council** was a non-salaried, elected office, elections taking place at the summer Annual General Meeting. **The President of the Poetry Society** was an honorary post, usually offered to an eminent British poet of the day. **The Editor of *Poetry Review*** was appointed by the General Council, on the basis of a statement of intent and a vote of the General Council if there was more than one candidate. There was also a **Poets' Advisory Committee** for *Poetry Review,* although it was not asked for its advice during the period covered by this book. The Poetry Society also had paid office and house-keeping staff, but much work was done in the 1970s (for instance, in the print-shop set up in 1974, and in the bar) by volunteers. The Witt Panel in 1976 recommended a reduction in the reliance on voluntary labour, and additional paid posts were created, particularly the two posts of **Bookshop and Print-shop Manager** and **Education Officer.**

8. Membership of the General Council of the Poetry Society

[Radicals in bold (where known): Executive members asterisked]

1970–1971 (21 Members)

Robert Armstrong	Oliver Cox	**Eric Mottram**
Alasdair Aston*	Christopher Hampton	F. T. Prince
Asa Benveniste	Norman Hidden* (Chair)	**Anthony Rudolf***
Martin Booth	Frieda Hodgson*	Joan Murray Simpson
Bob Cobbing*	May Ivimy* (Treasurer)	Elizabeth Thomas*
William Cookson	HesterMarsden-Semdley	Denys Thompson
Jeni Couzyn*	**Stuart Montgomery***	George Wightman*

1971–1972 (21 members)

Alasdair Aston*	**Jeni Couzyn***	F. T. Prince
Bob Cobbing*	Christopher Hampton	**Anthony Rudolf***
Greta Colson	Norman Hidden*	Brian Southam
William Cookson	Frieda Hodgson*	Elizabeth Thomas*
Laurence Cotterell	May Ivimy* (Treasurer)	DenysThompson* (Chair)
John Cotton	Laurence Lerner	George Wightman*
Oliver Cox	**Stuart Montgomery***	Vacancy

1972–1973 (21 members)

Alasdair Aston*	Graham Fawcett	Charles Monteith*
Martin Booth	Harry Guest	**Anthony Rudolf**
Bob Cobbing*	Christopher Hampton*	Brian Southam
Mrs Greta Colson	Norman Hidden*	Elizabeth Thomas*
Laurence Cotterell	Mrs Frieda Hodgson	Denys Thompson
John Cotton* (Chair)	Laurence Lerner	Daniel Weissbort
Peter Finch	**Stuart Montgomery*** (Treasurer)	George Wightman*

1973–1974 (24 members)

Alasdair Aston*	Graham Fawcett	**Anthony Rudolf**
Jeremy Adler	**Elaine Feinstein***	Michael Schmidt
Martin Booth*	**Peter Finch**	Brian Southam
Bob Cobbing* (Treasurer)	**Roy Fisher**	Elizabeth Thomas*
Mrs Greta Colson	Harry Guest	Daniel Weissbort
Laurence Cotterell	Christopher Hampton	George Wightman*
John Cotton* (Chair)	Charles Monteith*	
Jeni Couzyn*	Trevor Royle	

1974–1975 (27 members)

Jeremy Adler*
Alasdair Aston*
Martin Booth
Alan Brownjohn
Carol Buckroyd
Bob Cobbing*
(Treasurer)
Laurence Cotterell
John Cotton* (Chair)
Jeni Couzyn*

Gavin Ewart
Elaine Feinstein
Peter Finch
Roy Fisher
Bill Griffiths
Roger Guedalla

Harry Guest
Christopher Hampton
Lee Harwood*

Charles Monteith*
Pete Morgan
Jeff Nuttall
Tom Pickard
Anthony Rudolf
Clifford Simmons*

Elizabeth Thomas
Lawrence Upton*
George Wightman

1975–1976 (30 members)

Jeremy Adler
Alasdair Aston
Alan Brownjohn
Bob Cobbing
  (Treasurer)
Laurence Cotterell
  (Chair)
John Cotton
Elaine Feinstein
Peter Finch
Allen Fisher
Roy Fisher

Roger Guedalla
Lee Harwood
Adrian Henri
Peter Hodgkiss

Eddie Linden

George MacBeth
BarryMacSweeney
Paige Mitchell
Pete Morgan
Angus Nicolson

Jeff Nuttall
Sean O'Huigin
Tom Pickard
Elaine Randell

Ian Robinson

Anthony Rudolf
Clifford Simmons
Lawrence Upton
George Wightman

1976–1977 (30 members)

Jeremy Adler
Vicky Allen

Alasdair Aston
Laurence Baylis
Anne Beresford
Alan Brownjohn

cris cheek
Bob Cobbing
John Cotton
Gavin Ewart

Allen Fisher
Roger Guedalla
  (Treasurer)
Lee Harwood
Peter Hodgkiss
Eddie Linden
Barry MacSweeney
  (Chair)
E. A. Markham
Pete Morgan
Betty Mulcahy
Angus Nicolson
Ian Patterson

Tom Pickard
Elaine Randell

Ian Robinson
Clifford Simmons
Ken Smith
John Stathatos

Lawrence Upton
George Wightman
Marjorie Barton (NPS)
Robert Vas Dias (Sec)

1977–1978 (? Members)

Vicky Allen (Treasurer)	Gavin Ewart	Jon Silkin
Alasdair Aston	Grey Gowrie	Clifford Simmons
Laurence Baylis	Paddy Kitchen (Chair)	**John Stathatos**
Anne Beresford	**Eddie Linden**	**George Tardios**
Bernard Brook-Partridge	Wes Magee	GeorgeWightman
Alan Brownjohn	Betty Mulcahy	
Norman Buchan	**Angus Nicolson**	
John Cotton	Ian Robinson (Dep)	

9. Relevant UK Poetry Organisations in the 1970s

The Association of Little Presses (the ALP)
A self-help organisation for poet-publishers begun in 1966 by Bob Cobbing and surviving until the late 1990s.

The Consortium of London Presses (the CoLP)
A grouping of fifteen small, London-based poet-publishers (including Cobbing and Upton's Writers Forum, Bill Griffiths' Pirate Press, and Allen Fisher's Aloes Books) using the Poetry Society print-shop (set up in June 1974), and printing *Poetry Review* there from 1975 to 1977.

The National Poetry Centre
The Earls Court premises of the Poetry Society were so designated by the Arts Council in 1971, when the Council decided to back this scheme (largely on grounds of cost) rather than a counter-proposal for a National Poetry Centre at the Roundhouse (in Chalk Farm, London) which would have been separate from the Poetry Society.

The National Poetry Secretariat
Set up in 1973, with Arts Council funding, and located at the Poetry Society in Earls Court: its main role was to offer subsidy to the organis-ers of poetry readings outside London. For London, a similar role was performed by the London Poetry Secretariat, which was a joint under-taking between the Greater London Arts Association and 'Poets in Public' and was based at Tavistock Place, WC1.

Poets Conference
An organisation set up in 1970 by Stuart Montgomery, Bob Cobbing, Jeni Couzyn, Asa Benveniste, Adrian Henri, and George MacBeth, to act as a kind of trade union for poets, campaigning for minimum fees for readings and adequate grant aid to poets.

Poets Forum
A fortnightly open workshop for poets set up by the radicals at the Poetry Society in 1976 after the eviction of the rival open workshop (known as 'Poetry Round') run by the conservatives.

Poetry Round
A workshop group for 'amateur' poets, using an 'open forum' format and, in the 1970s, meeting on Wednesday nights at the Poetry Society. Participants turned up and each read out a poem, followed by commentary and discussion. After a series of disagreements with the radicals from 1974 onwards, they were expelled from Poetry Society premises in late 1975.

The Poetry Society
Founded in 1909, and operated without subsidy till 1966 when it began to receive a grant from the Arts Council. From 1971 its Earls Court premises became the National Poetry Centre and received additional subsidy, and from 1973 the National Poetry Secretariat was also based there. In the 1970s members of the Society averaged about 1100, and received *Poetry Review* as part of their membership package.

Poets' Workshop
A workshop group, mainly for published poets, originally set up in the 1960s and meeting fortnightly on Fridays at the Poetry Society since 1966. Duplicated copies of members' poems for discussion were circulated in advance of the meetings and well-known figures such as Phillip Hobsbaum, Peter Porter, George MacBeth, and Alan Brownjohn were involved. In 1975 the group was ousted from the Poetry Society by the radicals.

Writers Forum
The name is used for two distinct but related activities, these being (1) a non-profit-making publisher of innovative poetries founded by Bob Cobbing (with John Rowan and Jeff Nuttall) in 1963, and (2) a series of

open forum workshop meetings for visual poetry, sound poetry, linguistically innovative poetry, performance, etc., set up by Bob Cobbing in 1951 and conducted by him for fifty years until his death in 2002. During the 1970s the meetings took place at the Poetry Society. Writers Forum website: http://pages.britishlibrary.net/writersforum/index.html

10. Alphabetical Who's Who?

This is not intended as a comprehensive listing of everybody involved in the events at the Poetry Society in the 1970s. It is a list of those who are mentioned in the text and on whom information could be found. As indicated in the Introduction, well-known writers like Dannie Abse, Ted Hughes, B. S. Johnson, and Iain Sinclair are omitted.

Gilbert Adair
Founded and ran the Sub Voicive poetry readings in London, 1980–1992, and on his departure from the UK they were taken over by Laurence Upton. (Adair should not be confused with the British film critic of the same name.)

Jeremy Adler
Visual poet of the 1970s and 80s who worked with alphabet shapes and was associated with the Writers Forum group. Professor Emeritus of German at King's College London.

Anthony Barnett (born 1941)
British poet with strong 'Cambridge' links, and also a musician and publisher at Allardyce, Barnett, a small press specialising in poetry, translation, and music.

Marjorie Barton
Director of the National Poetry Secretariat during the 1970s.

Asa Benveniste (1925–1990)
American-born poet who lived and worked in the UK, and was one of the first radical poets to join the General Council of the Poetry Society. His work is included in Keith Tuma's 2001 OUP anthology of British and Irish poetry, pp. 471–474.

Anne Beresford
Most recent collection is *Hearing Things* (Katabasis, 2002). Wife of poet
Michael Hamburger.

Ronald Bottrall
British poet writing from the 1930s, and given high praise by F. R. Leavis
in *New Bearings in English Poetry* (in 1932).

Bernard Brooke-Partridge
GLC Tory Counsellor well-known for his outspoken cultural conservatism, most notably a 'classic rant' against the Sex Pistols; he had said
on TV in August 1977 that 'The Sex Pistols would be vastly improved by
sudden death, they are the antithesis of human kind', etc. Later in 1977
(*Daily Telegraph*, 28th October 1977) he was again in the news, seeking to
explain why the supplier of 'more than 4,000 canes for use in ILEA-
controlled schools' was a Leeds firm which supplied identical items to
the porn trade.

Paul Brown
British small-press poet who ran Actual Size press in the 1980s.

Norman Buchan
He was a radical Labour MP, 'a Marxist who felt the best route to
Socialism lay in the Labour Party.' He was elected as an MP and was
(among other posts he held) Shadow Minister for the Arts. In 1977 he
protested at the decision of the Scottish Football Association to play a
game at the stadium in Santiago, Chile, which had been used as a
torture centre by the Pinochet regime.

Paul Buck
Author of the pamphlet *Time Is,* from Arc Publications, 1975, and editor
of the magazine *Curtains,* a magazine 'combatively interested in the
political implications of an extremist use of language' (Geoff Ward, in
Language Poetry and the American Avant-garde).

Bill Butler
American poet who ran the Unicorn Bookshop and imprint in Brighton:
the shop was raided in 1968 and at the trial in Brighton Mottram was a
defence witness when Butler was charged with stocking obscene
material.

Richard (Ric) Caddel (1949–2003)
Poet and librarian who founded the Basil Bunting Centre at Durham
University and ran Pig Press, with Ann Caddel. He co-edited a significant
anthology of radical British poetry.

Brian Catling (born 1948)
Poet, sculptor, performer. A book about his work, *Tending the Vortex: The
Works of Brian Catling,* edited by Simon Perril, was published by CCCP in
2001.

David Chaloner
Collected Poems published by Salt in 2004.

cris cheek (born 1955)
'Cris cheek is a poet-writer, artist and sound composer interested in
interdisciplinary and hybrid poetic textualities/performances. Born in
London, he now lives in Lowestoft, North Suffolk, where he curates
Sound & Language recordings and publications' (British Electronic
Poetry Centre website).

Adrian Clarke
British poet first published by Mottram in the *Poetry Review.* Long associ-
ation with Bob Cobbing and Writers Forum which included co-editing
AND magazine from 1994. Also co-edited *Floating Capital* with Robert
Sheppard in 1991.

Steve Clews
Currently (2005) Sub-Librarian, Information Systems, University of
London Library.

Bob Cobbing (1920–2002)
Sound poet, visual poet, and performer, and a major figure in the British
'counter-culture' of the 1960s, the Poetry Society in the 1970s, and
founder of poetry organisations such as Writers Forum, the Writers
Forum Workshop of experimental poetries, and Poets Conference. His
work is widely anthologised, including Tuma, pp. 441–444. For obituaries see The *Guardian,* 7 Oct 2002 (Robert Sheppard) and The *Independent,*
2nd October 2002 (Nicholas Johnson).

Laurence Cotterell
Poetry Society Chair in the mid 1970s and editor of First World War poetry.

John Cotton
His collection *Kilroy Was Here* (Chatto & Windus) was a Poetry Book Society Choice. His last collection was *Here's Looking at you Kid,* published by Headland. He was Chairman of The Poetry Society 1972–74 and 1977, and its Treasurer 1986–89. He was editor and printer of The Priapus Press 1967–90 (co-founded with poet Ted Walker). Died in 2003, age 78. His work was included in many anthologies for children.

C. B. Cox
First became well-known as co-originator (with A. E. Dyson) of the education *Black Papers* (a series of pamphlets attacking comprehensive education) from 1969. Cox and Dyson also co-founded the journal *Critical Quarterly* in 1959. In the 1980s Cox chaired national committees establishing the form of the National Curriculum for English.

Jeni Couzyn (born 1942)
Poet, and one of the founder-members of Poets Conference in 1970 and an advocate of a minimum wage for poets. Originally from South Africa, where she was an opponent of Apartheid, and has lived in the UK since 1965. Her Bloodaxe anthology *Contemporary Women Poets* of 1985 has been highly influential.

Ivor Cutler
Cult poet, performer, and songwriter, now (2005) in his eighties.

Andrew Duncan
Critic and poet who was the editor of the magazine *Angel Exhaust,* has written many essays on 'BPR' poetry, and is the author of *The Failure of Conservatism in Contemporary British Poetry* (Salt, 2003)

Ken Edwards (born 1950)
Taught by Mottram at King's College and a member of 'Alembic Poets' and joint editor of *Alembic* magazine in the 1970s. His *Reality Studios* imprint of the 1980s merged with Wendy Mulford's *Street Editions* in 1993 to form the press *Reality Street Editions*. His collection *Good Science: poems 1983–1991* was published by Roof Books, New York, in 1992.

Paul Evans
British small press poet published in *Poetry Review,* in *The New British Poetry,* ed. Gillian Allnutt, et al, and by Arc Publications (*Current Affairs,* 1970).

Gavin Ewart (1916–1995)
Poet who specialised in satirical, comic, and erotic verse—'a sort of minor limerick writer', in Mottram's dismissive phrase (*Prospect into Breath,* p. 39).

Josephine Falk
Examinations Secretary at the Poetry Society in the late 1960s, and from the early 1970s Literature Assistant to Charles Osborne at the Arts Council. By 1981 she was Deputy Literature Director of the Arts Council.

P. C. Fencott (aka Clive Fencott)
Member of the performance group *jgjgjg,* the founder/core members of which were cris cheek, P. C. Fencott and Lawrence Upton; it first performed at the Sound Poetry Festival in London in 1976 and had disbanded by the time of the Toronto Sound Poetry Festival in 1978. Currently (2005) Senior Lecturer in the School of Computing, University of Teesside.

Peter Finch (born 1947)
Cardiff-based poet and performer who edited the journal *Second Aeon* from 1966 to 1975. Currently (2005) Chief Executive of *Yr Academi Gymreig* (The Welsh Academy).

Allen Fisher (born 1944)
Poet, performer, artist, theorist. Major figure associated with the 'British Poetry Revival' (the 'BPR') and initially influenced by the methods of Ezra Pound and Charles Olson. Became widely known in the 1970s for his *Place* sequence (re-published in full by Reality Street Editions in 2005). Is currently (2005) Professor of Poetry and Art at Manchester Metropolitan University and Head of the Department of Contemporary Arts. His work is anthologised in Tuma, pp. 710–720, and he was one of the three poets in Re/active Anthology 1, *future exiles: 3 London poets,* Paladin, 1992. Collection *Gravity* from Salt, 2004.

Roy Fisher (born 1930)
Poet and jazz pianist whose substantial prose and poetry sequence *City of 1961* established his avant-garde reputation. Three different presses (Fulcrum, Oxford University Press, and Bloodaxe) have published Collected or Selected volumes of his poetry—a unique distinction. Anthologised in Tuma, pp. 537–550.

Tim Fletcher
Ran the magazine *First Offence,* beginning in 1986. No. 14 appeared in 2004.

Ulli Freer
Major underground poet and artist, originally from Germany, who formerly used the name Ulli McCarthy. Jeff Nuttall was his art teacher at Alder secondary, where he became involved with Group H (the Hendon Experimental Art Group formed by Bob Cobbing in 1951). His collection *Speakbright Leap Passwood* was published by Salt in 2003.

Lord Gowrie
Alexander Patrick Greysteil Hore-Ruthven ('Lord Gowrie') was born in Dublin in 1939 and educated at Eton, Balliol College, Oxford and Harvard University. Minister for the Arts from 1983 to 1985. He was appointed Chairman of the Arts Council for a five-year term from April 1994 to May 1998.'

Bill Griffiths (born 1948)
First published in Mottram issues of *Poetry Review* in the 1970s; an erudite and always experimental poet who remains a highly individual-istic un-assimilated voice in British poetry. His work is anthologised in Tuma, pp. 760–765, and he was one of the three poets in Re/active Anthology 1, *future exiles: 3 London poets,* Paladin, 1992. *The Mud Fort* from Salt, 2005, is a Selected Poems 1984–2004. For a full-scale, item-by-item commentary on his work see *An Annotated Bibliography of the Works of Bill Griffiths, 1969–2001,* Douglas Jones, MPhil thesis, King's College, London, 2006.

Roger Guedalla
He compiled the first bibliography of Basil Bunting, in 1973, and his own collection of Bunting materials formed the core of the Basil Bunting Collection at the University of Durham.

Robert Hampson (born 1948)
Taught by Mottram at King's College and a member of 'Alembic Poets' and joint editor of *Alembic* magazine in the 1970s. *Assembled Fugitives,* his selected poems, 1973–1998, was published by Stride Press in 2001. He is Professor and Head of English at Royal Holloway College, University of London.

Lee Harwood (born 1939)
Poet, another major 'BPR' figure, but influenced by the New York Poets (especially Ashbery) rather than Pound and Olson. *Selected Poems* published by Paladin in 1998 and *Collected Poems* by Salt, 2004. His work is anthologised in Tuma, pp. 649–655),

Jeremy Hilton
Poet whose work has been well described as standing in succession both to the American modernist and the English pastoral traditions. Now (2005) edits *Fire* magazine and lives in Oxfordshire.

Peter Hodgkiss
In the 1970s he ran the journal *Poetry Information,* which, along with *Second Aeon,* edited by Peter Finch, was a major source of criticism and reviews of 'BPR' material.

Anselm Hollo
Finnish-born poet, academic and translator with a life-long association with Beat poetry, Black Mountain poetry, and the Naropa Poetics Institute, founded by Allen Ginsberg (whose poem *Howl* he translated into Finnish).

Dom Sylvester Houédard (1924–1992)
Known as 'dsh', a Benedictine monk of Prinknash Abbey and a major figure in the international concrete poetry movement: his papers are in the John Rylands Library, Manchester. He was a famous 'networker' whose diary reputedly contained 3000 addresses.

Michael Hrebeniak
Former student of Eric Mottram who went on to lecture at the Royal College of Music, edit a journal called *Radical Poetics,* work on arts documentaries for Channel Four TV, and teach in the English Faculty at Cambridge.

David Jaffin
Author of *Into the Timeless Deep* (Sheersman, 2002). In the 70s his books *Emptied Spaces* (1972) and *In the Glass of Winter* (1975) were published by Abelard-Schuman.

Paddy Kitchen
Biographer (of Gerard Manley Hopkins and Patrick Geddes) and a novelist. She was herself elected to the General Council at the AGM of June 1977, and subsequently became Chair of the Poetry Society, but resigned in September 1978 to devote her time to work on three commissioned books.

Eddie Linden
Founder and editor of *Aquarius* poetry magazine (variously described as 'irregular' and 'very irregular'), which he started in the 1970s on money earned working at Bernard Stone's Turrett bookshop in Kensington—see Stone's obituary in the *Times*, 14th February, 2005.

David Lovibond
Currently (2004) a freelance writer and contributor of articles (mainly deploring 'multi-culturalism', immigration, 'political correctness', etc) to right-wing journals like the *Spectator* and *Right Now!*

Hugh MacDiarmid (1892–1978)
Foremost Scottish poet of the twentieth century, who first became prominent with his long poem 'A Drunk Man Looks at the Thistle' in 1926. He was a founding member of the Nationalist Party of Scotland and a member of the Communist Party.

Barry MacSweeney (1948–2000)
Poet whose debut volume *The Boy from the Green Cabaret* was published by Hutchinson, and the firm 'nominated him for the Chair in Poetry at Oxford; the 19 year old with three 'O' Levels received three votes. It took half a lifetime for his reputation to recover.' Anthologised in Tuma, pp. 755–759.

Wes Magee (born 1939)
Scottish poet, former teacher and head-teacher, specialising in work for children and poetry workshops in schools.

Paige Mitchell
Poet, US-born, UK-resident.

'Eric Noel William Mottram (1924–1995)
Lecturer, Reader, Professor of English and American Literature at King's College London, pioneered American Studies in the United Kingdom, establishing for himself an academic career in this novel field through his own remarkable energy and accessibility as a teacher, his legendary width of reading, and his wit and courage as speaker, interviewer, editor, academic writer and poet. It was not so much the importance of presenting America as of understanding its culture and writing that seemed to him so essential in the modern world—for he rejected that dangerous cultural insularity that would have us ignore wider issues and global responsibilities.' (Eric Mottram Archive, brief biography, King's College, London)

Pete Morgan
A key figure, with Mike Horovitz, in importing the US Beat poets to the UK. Worked with Horovitz on the magazine *New Departures,* and the jazz-and-poetry road show *Live New Departures* (see *Bomb Culture,* p. 181).

Angus Nicolson
'The poet from Uig'. His work featured in *A Poetry Quintet* (Gollancz, 1976).

Jeff Nuttall (1933–2004)
Poet, painter, jazz trumpeter, and anarchist; Chair of the Poetry Society at the height of the wars, and a key figure in the counterculture of the 1960s, whose 1968 book *Bomb Culture* was a defining text of the counter-cultural movement. An obituarist wrote of him: 'with his passing, to join Mottram and Bob Cobbing, the New British Poetry has lost its final most significant proponent. He was a true Dionysian, whose energies—emotional and physical—would brook no compromise.' Eric Mottram had called him 'The only genius I've known.'

Sean O'Huigin
Canadian-Irish sound and performance poet whose work appeared in *Poetry Review* 67:1/2. He later turned to writing for children, picking up a Canadian Children's Fiction award in 1983 for *The Ghost Horse of the Mounties,* and a ban from some schools in Michigan in 1990 because the poems in *Scary Poems for Rotten Kids* were too scary.

Maggie O'Sullivan (born 1951)
Important poet and performer on the 'BPR' scene whose books include
Red Shifts (Etruscan Books, 2000) and *In the House of the Shaman* (Reality
Street, 2003). She edited the influential anthology *Out of Everywhere*
(Reality Street, 1996) and is herself anthologised in Tuma, pp. 795–800.

Joel Oppenheimer (1930–1988)
American poet and academic who studied under Charles Olson at Black
Mountain College in the early 1950s.

Charles Osborne (born 1927)
Literature Director of the Arts Council in the period covered by this
book: he was a journalist, actor, and theatre director for several years
until he became assistant editor of the *London Magazine* and a broad-
caster for the BBC. From 1971 to 1986 he was Literature Director of the
Arts Council of Great Britain, and from 1986 to 1991, chief drama critic
of the *Daily Telegraph*. He published a career memoir entitled *Giving it
Away: Memoirs of an Uncivil Servant* (Secker and Warburg, 1986).

Philip Pacey (born 1946)
His collection *Charged Landscapes* was published by Enitharmon in 1979.
A critical work, *David Jones and Other Wonder Voyagers*, was published by
Seren in 1982.

Derek Parker (born 1932)
Cornish-born, Parker worked extensively in media and journalism: biographer (Nell Gwyn, Byron, Casanova, etc). Edited *Poetry Review*, 1966–1970
(papers and correspondence in the Harry Ransom Humanities Research
Centre, University of Texas at Austin). From 1985 to 2002 he edited *The
Author* for the Society of Authors. Now (2005) resident in Australia and,
with his wife, a writer on astrology.

Ian Patterson (born 1948)
Critic, poet, translator and Fellow of Queens' College, Cambridge, where
he is currently (2005) Director of Studies in English. A selection of his
poetry, *Time to Get Here: Selected Poems 1969–2002* (Salt Publishing)
appeared in 2003.

Simon Pettet
English-born poet now a long-time resident in New York and editor of
New York Poet James Schuyler.

Tom Pickard (born 1946)
In the 70s he founded the Morden Tower readings in Newcastle with his wife Connie Pickard and ran the 'Ultima Thule' bookshop. In the 1990s he moved to London and made a number of documentary films, including 'Birmingham is what I think with' about poet Roy Fisher. Anthologised in Tuma, pp. 721–724.

F. T. Prince (1912–2003)
British poet and Southampton University professor, admired by the New York poets, and author of 'Soldiers Bathing', probably the most famous English poem of World War Two.

Carl Rakosi (1903–2004)
American 'Objectivist poet, social worker, and protégé of Ezra Pound, who died at the age of 100. In the mid 1960s he resumed writing after 30 years at the instigation of Andrew Crozier when the latter was studying with Charles Olson at SUNY-Buffalo. (See *Guardian obituary at http://books.guardian.co.uk/obituaries/story/0,11617,1248964,00.html*)

Elaine Randell (born 1951)
Poet who edited the journal *Amazing Grace* from 1970 to 1972 and later Blacksuede Boot Press with her husband Barry MacSweeney, publishing J. H. Prynne, among others. Her work is anthologised in *Other:British and Irish Poetry since 1970* (Caddel and Quartermain), pp. 190–197, and a collection *Gut Reaction* was published in 1987 by North & South.

Carlyle Reedy (born 1938)
US born, resident in UK since 1964. Poet and performance artist. One of the six women in Mike Horovitz's *Children of Albion* anthology, 1969, and one of the twenty or so to appear in the Mottram issues of *Poetry Review.* Her work also appears in Tuma's OUP anthology of British and Irish Poetry, pp. 629–632.

Peter Riley (Born 1940)
Poet, writer, and book-seller, educated and still based in Cambridge, published by Ferry Press, Grosseteste Press, Carcanet, and Reality Street editions.

Ian Robinson (died 2004)
Editor of Oasis Books and *Oasis* magazine, founded in 1969, and reaching issue 100 in June 2000.

Peter Robinson (born 1953)
Poet and academic who edited the journal *Perfect Bound* in the 1970s

Anthony Rudolf (born 1942)
Literary critic, translator and publisher who in 1971 founded the still
extant Menard Press, which specialises in poetry in translation. He
published an autobiographical memoir, *The Arithmetic of Memory*, in 1999
(Bellew Press) in the experimental form of a categorised inventory of
memories from his childhood and youth.

Robert Sheppard (born 1955)
Poet, critic, and teacher of creative writing. His collection *Tin Pan Arcadia*
(Salt 2004) is the largest published section of his on-going opus *Twentieth
Century Blues*.

Jon Silkin (1930–1997)
Poet and founder of the radical and innovative poetry magazine *Stand*,
which he edited for over forty years.

Christopher Sinclair-Stevenson
Currently (2004) a literary agent, and secretary of the Literary Society;
he previously ran the publishing firm Sinclair-Stevenson (sold to Reed
International in 1995) which published Peter Ackroyd's *Dickens* and was
asked for a one million pound advance for the Dickens and Blake auto-
biographies–£650,000 was eventually agreed.

Clifford Simmons
Deputy Director of the National Book League during the 1970s.
Simmons compiled the anthology *Living Poets* (John Murray), with
current Children's Laureate Michael Morpurgo, in 1974, and wrote the
introductory essay for the catalogue of a National Book League exhibition on the Cuala Press in 1973.

Ken Smith (1938–2003)
Poet, fellow student of Jon Silkin and Tony Harrison at Leeds University.
Co-edited *Stand* with Silkin for nine years. His great work *Fox Running*
was first published as an A4 pamphlet and later re-issued by Bloodaxe in
1981. (from *Guardian* obituary). From 1985 to 1987 he was writer-in-
residence at Wormwood Scrubs Prison, London.

Geoff Soar
Collated the Small Press collection at University College, London.

John Stathatos
Poet and artist, also critic and curator, translator of Greek poetry and commentator on Greek culture. Helped edit the 2nd and 3rd series of *Oasis* during the 1970s.

Glen Storhaug
Edited *The Kilpeck Anthology,* from Five Seasons Press, 1981.

George Tardios
His published work includes (with Dominic Behan), *A Morden Tower Reading* (Newcastle-upon-Tyne: Morden Tower Publications 1976).

Criton Tomazos
Performance artist and poet who edited a journal called *Amaranth* in the mid 1960s, the second issue devoted to his 'cage' project, involving Jeff Nuttall. Tomazos is a recurrent figure in Nuttall's *Bomb Culture*. More recently 'he is opening people's eyes to their surroundings with his Help the Aged 'Citizens' Action' Millennium Award. His 'Wake up to your Environment' project, based in north London, has seen him running lectures, schools visits, events and a newsletter'. (Millennium Awards website)

Chris Torrance (born 1941)
Not Welsh, but long resident in Wales, his epic-length sequence *The Magic Door*, books of which appeared from Albion Village Press, Galloping Dog Press, Stone Lantern Press & Cwm Nedd Press over 30 years, is a major 'BPR' text. He was interviewed by Swansea academic Glyn Pursglove in 1983: see "Interview with Chris Torrance", *Poetry Wales*, 19:2, pp.134–145.

Stan Trevor
One-time co-ordinator of the Association of Little Presses.

Lawrence Upton (born 1949)
Important figure in the 'British Poetry Revival', especially in sound and visual poetics. His most recent work is *Wire Sculptures,* Reality Street Editions, 2003.

Robert Vas Dias
Poet, and editor of the journal *Atlantic Review*, and later of *Oasis*.

Erik Vonna-Michel
Performance poet, linked with the group *jgjgjg*, the founder/core members of which were cris cheek, P. C. Fencott and Lawrence Upton. Vonna-Michel's 'Balsam Flex/Typical Characteristics' published audio tapes of some of their performances.

Diane Wakowski (born 1937)
American poet and academic: her *Emerald Ice: Selected Poems* 1962–1987, published in 1988, won the Poetry Society of America's William Carlos Williams Award.

George (G.B.H.) Wightman
Wightman was 'a member of "The Group" in the 1950s, which died in the mid-sixties and was resurrected as The Workshop at the Poetry Society in Earls Court, steered at various times by George Wightman and others.' The 'Writers' Workshop' section of the Kevin Crossley-Holland Archive at Leeds University includes a one-page biography of Wightman, who was also linked with 'Poets in Public', a group founded in 1963 with readings in London and Edinburgh.

T. Wignesan
Malaysian writer, academic, poet and editor, long-time resident in Paris.

Sir John Witt
Vice-Chairman of the Arts Council of great Britain and Chair of the 'Witt Investigation' into the affairs of the Poetry Society in 1976. He had previously been Chairman of the National Gallery and was later Chair of the Management Committee of the Courtauld Institute of Art.

Sources

A. Primary Sources

(1) **Arts Council of Great Britain records, 1928–1997,** held at the Archive of Art and Design of the Victoria and Albert Museum, which is housed in the Archive Reading Room located at Blythe House, 23 Blythe Road, London W14 0QX (near Olympia).

The relevant sub-section is 'Literature Department: individuals and organisations, 1947–1994' (ACGB/62). The parts especially useful are:

'Poetry Centre, 1968–1976' (ACGB/62/102) [I box file] and
'The Poetry Society, 1966–1994' (ACGB/62/103) [ten boxes]

There is no detailed catalogue which breaks down the material further than this, but the main Arts Council source on the Witt investigation is ACGB/62/103, box three of the ten, which contains the following six folders:

(i) Poetry Society Assessment Committee, Written Evidence, Submissions 1–126 [buff]

(ii) Poetry Society Assessment Committee, Written Evidence, Submissions 127–223 [buff]

(iii) Poetry Society Assessment 1976: Master copies of committee minutes, meetings of 10 June, 16 June, 1 July, 16 July, 26 July, 27 July 1976

(iv) Poetry Society Assessment Committee: Minutes of meetings [blue]

(v) Poetry Society Assessment: miscellaneous papers/press cuttings [pink]

(vi) Poetry Society 'Post-Witt' [green]

[Note: earlier items in this folder are circa Witt; the most recent are 1978, at the top]

The basic catalogue-listing for the Literature Department of the Arts Council is on-line at: http://www.nal.vam.ac.uk/acgb/acgbf.html

(2) The Eric Mottram Collection, King's College, London (Archive Reading Room, Room 302, Strand).

The material is arranged in fifteen sections, of which the most relevant section is Section Four. 'Mottram's editorial role, 1970–1994'. The most useful sub-sections are:

Mottram, 4/2 Material relating to the Mottram editorship of *The Poetry Review*, 1971–1985 and

Mottram, 4/3 Correspondence and papers relating to The Poetry Society as publishers of *The Poetry Review*, 1970–1991

Both sections are sets of boxes, each box containing a number of folders. For example, the box Mottram, 4/2/27-33 contains the folders 27-33, of which folder 27–28 contains material relating to *Poetry Review* 63/4, folder 29 contains the proofs of the same issue, and so on.

A detailed on-line catalogue of the Mottram Collection is available at: http://www.kcl.ac.uk/kis/archives/mottram/moto.htm

(3) The Barry MacSweeney Collection, Special Collections Department, Robinson Library, University of Newcastle upon Tyne.
http://www.ncl.ac.uk/elll/research/literature/macsweeney/

Much of the correspondence about poetry is from the 1990s, while a good deal of the earlier material is personal or domestic, but there are (for instance) several very interesting letters from Eric Mottram written between 1977 and 1982. The material is still being catalogued, but a fairly detailed hand-list is available at the Library (though it needs to be treated with caution, as there are some errors of dating and attribution). The material is recorded in the hand-list by 'boxes', as in the item 'BM15/1/8' (which is a five-page typed letter from Mottram to MacSweeney dated 14th March 1977). But 'box' 15 in the Barry MacSweeney collection ('BM15') is actually one of a number of folders in one of the dozen or so white plastic storage boxes which currently (2005) house the collection.

(4) **The Press Cuttings collection at The Poetry Library, Royal Festival Hall, London**

B. Secondary Sources

These include:

Ric Caddel, ed., *Other British and Irish Poetry Since 1970*, (Wesleyan University Press, 1999), pp. xxiv–v.

Wolfgang Gortschacher, 'Inside the Whale of Britain's Literary Establishment', pp. 51–6 in *Alive in Parts of this Century: Eric Mottram at 70*, ed. Peterjon & Yasmin Skelt (North & South, Twickenham and Wakefield, 1994).

Eric Mottram's own published accounts of the *Poetry Review* period include:

(a) The 'Editor's Note' from *Poetry Review*, 66/1, 1975

(b) 'Editing *Poetry Review*', pp. 154–5 in *Poetry Information*, 20 & 21, winter 1979/80 (pp. 152–154 of this issue is a complete descriptive index for the Mottram issues of *Poetry Review*):

(c) pp. 36–41 of the Mottram interview in *Prospect into Breath: Interviews with North and South Writers,* ed. Peterjon Skelt (North and South, 1991).

(d) Charles Osborne, *Giving it Away: Memoirs of an Uncivil Servant* (Secker and Warburg, 1986), chapter three. 'The Arts Council', pp.149–237, gives a strong sense of the views and personality of Charles Osborne in the period, and pp. 193–206 have specific relevance to these events.

General Bibliography

(1) Books on recent British Poetry

James M. Acheson and Romana Huk, eds., *Contemporary British Poetry Essays in theory and Criticism*, SUNY Press, 1996. Close readings of poets and their contexts from various postmodern perspectives, Donald Davie, Ted Hughes, Geoffrey Hill, and Craig Raine. Approaches range from cultural theory to poststructuralism. 'The book's strength lies in its diversity at every level' (publisher's blurb).

Peter Barry, *Contemporary British Poetry and the City*, Manchester University Press, 2000. Discussion of a number of 'BPR' poets, including Denise Riley, Bill Griffiths, Ken Edwards, Barry MacSweeney, Robert Hampson, Iain Sinclair, and Allen Fisher.

Vicki Bertram, ed., *Kicking daffodils: twentieth-century women poets*, Edinburgh University Press, 1997.

Vicki Bertram, *Gendering Poetry: Contemporary Women and Men Poets*, Pandora, 2005. Sensitive on gender issues, but only discusses securely 'mainstream' poets and has little on 'experimental' poetry.

Martin Booth, *British Poetry, 1964–1984: Driving Through the Barricades*, Routledge and Kegan Paul 1985. A general account of the designated period which tries to cover a wide range of different schools and approaches.

Dennis Brown, *The Poetry of Postmodernity: Anglo-American Encodings*, St
    Martin's/ Macmillan, 1994. The figures considered in this book
    are: Auden, Ginsberg, Plath, Berryman, Hughes, Hill, Ashbery
    and the later R.S.Thomas. It usefully looks back to figures not
    usually considered in this context (Wyndham Lewis, Auden,
    Marshall McLuhan) and takes in some contemporaries who are
    usually placed in other categories (Hill and R.S.Thomas).

Clive Bush, *Out of Dissent: A Study of Five Contemporary British Poets,* Talus
    Editions, King's College London, 1997. This is exclusively about
    the 'BPR', including Eric Mottram, Barry MacSweeney, and Allen
    Fisher. Pages 5-6 comment on the Poetry Society in the 1970s.

Neil Corcoran, *English Poetry Since 1940,* Longman, 1993. Has one page
    on the 'BPR'.

Gary Day and Brian Docherty, eds, *British Poetry from the 1950s to the
    1990s: Politics and Art,* Macmillan, 1996. Chapters on: Poetry &
    Politics; Bunting: Larkin: Harrison & Reading: Ken Smith:
    Redgrove: Heaney: Muldoon, Paulin & McGuckian: MacLean &
    Derrick Thompson: Edwin Morgan: Crichton Smith: Watkins &
    RS Thomas: Women's Poetry: Women Poets: New Voices of
    the 90s.

Andrew Duncan, *The Failure of Conservatism in Contemporary British Poetry*,
    Salt, 2003. A free-wheeling and swash-buckling account of
    British poetry since the 1970s. Pages 175–77 discuss the Poetry
    Society in the 1970s.

Antony Easthope and John O. Thompson, eds. *Contemporary Poetry Meets
    Modern Theory, Harvester*, 1991. The chapter most relevant to 'BPR'
    poets is 'Postmodern Postpoetry: Tom Raworth's tottering state'
    (Peter Brooker).

Wolfgang Gortschacher, *Little Magazine Profiles: the Little Magazines in
    Great Britain 1939–1993*, University of Salzburg Press, 1993. See
    pages 139–141 and 509–511 for the Poetry Society and Poetry
    Review in the 1970s.

Wolfgang Gortschacher, *Contemporary Views on the Little Magazine Scene*, University of Salzburg Press, 2000. Includes interviews and evaluations with/of Eric Mottram and Peter Forbes (one of Mottram's successors as editor of the journal).

Ian Gregson, *Contemporary Poetry and Postmodernism: Dialogue and Estrangement*, Macmillan, 1996. A strong and simple thesis informs the whole book: the 'dialogue' poets of the first half use 'novelistic' techniques—voices, narratives, etc—and constitute the 'mainstream', while the 'estrangement' poets of the second part are the uncanonised, experimental neo-modernists ('retro-modernists' in Gregson's terms), who used to constitute the excluded 'other' of contemporary poetry. The final chapter argues that there has been much cross-fertilisation, since the late 80s, breaking down this dichotomy, and perhaps opening the way to something new.

Robert Hampson and Peter Barry, eds, *New British poetries: the scope of the possible*, Manchester University Press, 1993. See pages 15–45 for Mottram's definitive essay 'The British Poetry Revival, 1960–75', and pages 45–50 for 'Poets and the Arts Council of Great Britain', a 'State of Poetry' supplement issued by Poets Conference in 1978.

Romana Huk, ed., *Assembling alternatives: reading postmodern poetries transnationally*, Wesleyan University Press, 2003.

David Kennedy, *New Relations: the Refashioning of British Poetry, 1980–1994*, Seren, 1996. Kennedy is one of the three editors of the anthology *The New Poetry* (Bloodaxe, 1993), and the book is very much informed by this perspective. This involves a broad eclecticism which resists notions of schools, factions, a mainstream, and so on, and seeks to convey a sense of the 'excitement, energy, diversity, and ambition' [Bloodaxe blurb] of the 1990s generation of poets.

Edward Larrissy, *Reading Twentieth Century: The Language of Gender and Objects,* Basil Blackwell, 1990. This has a chapter called 'Postmodernism: The Return of the Suppressed'. Larrissy sees the rise of Ashbery as symptomatic of the decline of the older American poetic of 'objects' (stemming from slogans like Williams's 'No ideas except in things').

Alison Mark and Deryn Rees-Jones, eds., *Contemporary Women's Poetry: Reading/Writing/Practice,* Macmillan, 2000. A very useful collection: especially relevant to 'BPR' poetry are: Chapter 9 by Maggie O'Sullivan, which both describes and enacts some of her techniques; Chapter 16, by Carol Watts, which is on interpellation and the poetry of Denise Riley; and Chapter 21 by Harriet Tarlo, which is on the contemporary avant-garde and the issue of gender.

David Murray, ed. *Literary Theory and Poetry: Extending the Canon,* Batsford, 1989. Several of these essays contain useful and relevant material.

Sean O'Brien, *Deregulated Muse: Essays on Contemporary British and Irish Poetry,* Bloodaxe, 1997. Takes very much the broadly eclectic view seen in the 1993 Bloodaxe anthology. It deals with 'canonicals' like Larkin, Hughes, Heaney, Harrison, Paulin, Fenton, and Muldoon, as well as 'emergent figures' like Didsbury, Duffy, Jamie, Kay, etc. There is no coverage of 'BPR' orbit poets, to whom O'Brien is usually hostile.

Simon Perril, *Contemporary British Poetry and Modernist Innovation* (Salt Studies in Contemporary Poetry), Salt Publishing, 2005.

Jonathan Raban, *The Society of the Poem,* Harrap, 1971. Reads as if written rapidly and often impatiently, but it is a lively and genuinely enquiring book which takes a look at many different kinds of British poetry at a pivotal moment.

Denise Riley, ed., *Poets on Writing: Britain 1970-1991,* Macmillan, 1992. Much useful and enlightening material by poets in the 'BPR' orbit: see especially the essay by Carlyle Reedy on what might be thought her most extreme forms of avant-garde practice.

Denise Riley, *The Words of Selves: Identification, Solidarity, Irony*, Stanford University Press, 2000. Includes writing on the lyrical 'I' in poetry.

Alan Robinson, *Instabilities in Contemporary British Poetry*, Macmillan, 1988. Chapters are, 1. James Fenton's 'Narratives': Some Reflections on Postmodernism', then chapters on Raine and Reid, Michael Hofmann, Hill, Dunn, Paulin, Heaney, and feminism.

Peter Robinson, *Twentieth Century Poetry: Selves and Situations*, OUP, 2005. Studies of the situatedness of the self in culture, place, and imagination in a range of mainly British poets.

Robert Sheppard, *The Poetry of Saying: British Poetry and its Discontents, 1950–2000*, Liverpool University Press, 2005. 'Unearths a secret history of fifty years of experimental British verse, revealing and illuminating the daring work of poets who have spent half a century rewriting the rules of English poetry.'

Keith Tuma, *Fishing by Obstinate Isles: Modern and Postmodern British Poetry and American Readers*, Northwestern University Press, 1998. See pages 55–58 for an account of the Poetry Society in the 1970s.

(2) Anthologies of recent British poetry

'Postmodernist'

Blake Morrison and Andrew Motion, eds., *The Penguin Book of Contemporary British Poetry*, 1982.

Michael Hulse, David Kennedy and David Morley, eds., *The New Poetry*, Bloodaxe, 1993,

Sean O'Brien, ed., *The firebox: poetry from Britain and Ireland after 1945*, Picador, 1998.

Don Paterson and Charles Simic, eds., *The New Poetry*, Greywolf Press, 2004

'Modernist'

Andrew Crozier and Tim Longville, eds., *A Various Art*, ed. Carcanet, 1987, Paladin, 1990

Gillian Allnutt, Fred D'Aguiar, Ked Edwards, and Eric Mottram, eds., *The New British Poetry*, eds., Paladin 1988

Iain Sinclair, ed., *Conductors of Chaos: a Poetry Anthology*, Paladin, 1996

Ric Caddel and Peter Quartermain, eds., *Other British and Irish Poetry since 1970*, Wesleyan University Press, 1999

Nicholas Johnson, ed., *Foil: An Anthology—Poetry, 1985–2000, Defining New Poetry and Performance Writing from England Scotland and Wales, 1985–2000*, Etruscan Books, 2000

Rod Mengham and John Kinsella, eds., *Vanishing Points: New Modernist Poems*, Salt, 2004.

Keith Tuma, ed., *Anthology of Twentieth-Century British and Irish Poetry*, Oxford University Press New York, 2001

Future Exiles: Three London Poets, Paladin/Re-Active Anthology 1, 1992

Penguin Modern Poets, Volume 10, (Douglas Oliver, Denise Riley, Iain Sinclair) 1996

Maggie O'Sullivan, ed. *Out of Everywhere: Linguistically Innovative Poetry by Women in North America & the UK*, Reality Street, 1996.

(3) Articles and chapters on recent British poetry

Andrew Duncan, 'Such that commonly each: *A Various Art* and the Cambridge Leisure Centre' (in *Jacket 20*, December 2002)

Ken Edwards, 'The Two Poetries', in *Angelaki*, 3/1, April 2000, pp. 25–36

Robert Hampson, 'cris cheek in Manhattan', in the web-magazine *Pores: an Avant-Gardist Journal of Poetics Research,* issue one, October 2001. The journal is published from the Contemporary Poetics Research Centre at Birkbeck College (School of English and Humanities), and edited by Will Rowe. http://www.pores.bbk.ac.uk/1/index.html

Peter Middleton,'Poetry after 1970' in *The Cambridge History of Twentieth Century Literature* (ed. Laura Marcus and Peter Nicholls, Cambridge University Press, 2004).

Robert Sheppard, 'British Poetry and its Discontents' in Bart Moore-Gilbert and John Seed, eds., *Cultural Revolution?* Routledge, 1992.

Robert Sheppard, 'Artifice and the everyday world: Poetry in the 1970s' in Bart Moore-Gilbert, ed., *Cultural Catastrophe*, Routledge, 1994.

Robert Sheppard, "Elsewhere and Everywhere: Other New (British) Poetries", in *Critical Survey* Vol. 10, Number 1: 1998.

Randall Stevenson, *The Last of England?,* Volume 12, 1960–2000 in The Oxford English Literary History, Oxford University Press, 2004. Part II Poetry, pp. 165–270, has four chapters which contain a good deal of useful and relevant material.

Harriet Tarlo, 'Provisional pleasures: the challenge of contemporary experimental women poets' in *Feminist Review* , vol. 62, no. 1, 1999, pp. 94–112.

(4) Studies of Eric Mottram (chronologically ordered and taken from the Mottram bibliography compiled by Bill Griffiths)

'Eric Mottram' by Pierre Joris *Poetry Information* 15 (London, 1976) 23–25

Clive Bush '"Magnificent organization": beyond the nature of authority and the authority of Nature in the poetry of Eric Mottram' in feature 'The authority of Eric Mottram' *Angel Exhaust* 6 (Southend, Essex, 1986) 42–51

'Profile: at the edge of darkness: Brian Morton on Eric Mottram' *Times Higher Education Supplement* no. 855 (London, 24 Mar 1989)

[T. Wignesan] 'Curriculum vitae' and 'The complete Eric Mottram bibliography' *The Journal of Comparative Poïetics (Revue de Poïétique Comparée)* 1/1 (Paris, 1989–1990) 45–49, 56–63

Clive Bush 'From space to caves in the heart: recreating the collective world in Eric Mottram's poetry', *The Journal of Comparative Poïetics (Revue de Poïétique Comparée)* 1/2–3 (Paris, 1990–1991) 47–67

[T. Wignesan] 'Supplement to Eric Mottram's works list in vol. 1 no. 1 (1989-90)' in *The Journal of Comparative Poïetics (Revue de Poïétique Comparée)* 1/2–3 (Paris, 1990–1991) 68

William Sylvester: biographical note, selected list of publications and article on Mottram's *Selected Poems* (North & South, Twickenham, 1989), pp. 679–681 in *Contemporary poets* ed. Tracy Chevalier (St James Press, London, 5th edition, 1991)

Live all you can: interview and essay by Eric Mottram ed. Peterjon Skelt (Solaris, Twickenham, Middlesex, 1992)

Clive Bush '"This uncertain content of an obscure enterprise of form": Eric Mottram, America and Cultural Studies', pp. 145–168 in *A permanent etcetera: Cross-cultural perspectives on Post-War America* ed. A. Robert Lee (Pluto Press, London and Boulder, Colorado, 1993)

A. Robert Lee 'Introduction' pp. vi–viii in *A permanent etcetera: Cross-cultural perspectives on Post-War America* ed. A. Robert Lee (Pluto Press, London and Boulder, Colorado, 1993)

Clive Bush 'Eric Mottram and the poetics of protest' *The Poet's Voice* n.s.2/2 (Bath, 1995) 64–70 (an extract from *Out of dissent*, Talus, London, 1996)

Tribute by Jeff Nuttall in *First Offense* 10 (Stodmarsh, Kent, 1996) 52–53

Bill Griffiths 'Some evidence of Eric', *First Offense* 10 (Stodmarsh, Kent, 1996) 56–58

Lawrence Upton 'Not Uncle Eric', *First Offense* 10 (Stodmarsh, Kent, 1996) 59–62

Andrew Duncan 'Agitator blues: Eric Mottram (1924–95)', *Angel Exhaust* 12 (Cambridge, 1996)

Clive Bush 'A bird in Persepolis: Eric Mottram' pp. 417–532 in *Out of dissent: A study of five contemporary British poets* (Talus Editions, London, 1997)

Index

The Foreword and Preface are not indexed, nor are frequently occurring terms (such as 'Eric Mottram', 'Poetry Society', and *'Poetry Review'*). The index covers names, journal titles, presses, and institutions, but not book titles. The Sources and Bibliography sections are not indexed.

Lightning Source UK Ltd.
Milton Keynes UK
UKOW051404290512

193530UK00001B/37/A